Retrospecta 43

Yale School of Architecture
2019–2020

6–48   Discourse

Discourse houses the layers of discussion that ground, critique, and organize the production and analysis of architectural work at the Yale School of Architecture. These discursive and administrative links are visible in humble artifacts like the course listings as much as in the proceedings of a symposium. *Discourse* gathers together the activities that are both the foundation and the product of students' engagement with the curriculum, as well as illustrating connections between the School and the world beyond. This section includes dialogues, research, and events that generate a critical framework for the discipline of architecture as it repositions and evolves relative to foundational changes in society.

53–192   Design

Design presents student work produced in Core and Advanced Studios and in required and elective courses. This section's primary focus is the Yale School of Architecture design education. The diverse work generated at the School is represented through text and images from projects nominated by the faculty. These projects reflect a process of analysis, experimentation, and production, and are situated within a broader discourse by the studio prompts, course descriptions, and reflections included on the pages of *Design*.

Inserts   Fringe

Fringe gives space to the ephemera inherent in the design process, documenting everything that exists beyond the margins of the "final image." *Fringe* works to frame sketches, cast-offs, experiments, and collaborations. The collected material reveals students' exploration and development as they respond to their education.

Front Matter

Index

Publications

Exhibitions

Dialogues

Research

Building Project

As we started talking about *Retrospecta 43*, we realized that to represent the complexity of an architectural education, we needed to create a flexible structure for the book. Our conversations also revealed the importance of making space for what usually remains beyond the margins: conversations, perspectives, processes, and data. We sought to realize these aims through the book's organization which became clarified through our collaboration with an excellent graphic design team.

First, we divided *Retrospecta 43* into two sections—*Design* and *Discourse*—which offer parallel platforms for, on the one hand, the production and analysis of architecture, and, on the other hand, the mycelial conversations which organize, support, and give direction to that work. Second, we imagined a series of inserts, *Fringe*, which interrupts and stitches together the two sections, offering a look into students' chaotic flat file drawers and glimpses of paper scraps, fragments, and works in progress. Finally, we solicited written reflections from the studio faculty, program directors, coordinators of events, and the Dean. These work to frame the School's curriculum as something that is continuously designed, negotiated, and redesigned. We offer the format of reflection as a complement to critique.

After spring recess, when all courses moved online in response to a global viral pandemic, our interest in circumstance and process became more involved. These new and uncertain conditions both restricted and propelled students' efforts—either way demanding a re-evaluation. For some it was a dose of reality, while for others it spurred new speculations. Throughout this book the pandemic's effects are registered in reflections and student projects, and in our decision to print canceled and postponed courses and events in grey. We hope that *Retrospecta 43* not only represents the thoughtful work produced by students and faculty, but also reflects the unforeseen realities of education in 2019–2020.

Claire Hicks, Abraham Mora-Valle, Brian Orser, Rachael Tsai; Editors

- Editors' Reflections

Through the process of making *Retrospecta 43*, I've grown
to view the project not as a perfect and static book, but as
an archive—an unapologetic representation of the School
that is permitted to question itself in order to illustrate the
reality of what has truly been a complex year. I've been
surprised and excited by the outcome of this mentality and
of all of the musings, conversations, and reflections that
have coalesced to form this edition.
— Claire Hicks, Editor

This Retrospecta is the embodiment of debate, conflict,
and compromise. I hope that this edition pushes you, our
reader, to think critically about what makes work excep-
tional. YSoA has so much influence on the industry as a
whole and while these pages capture our collective reck-
oning, they also point towards a more egalitarian, just,
and inclusive future. Whether or not we get to that future
depends on how we engage with this material, and with
ideas not yet listened to.
— Abraham Mora-Valle, Editor

As we wrap up production of *Retrospecta 43* I wonder at
the role of the human voice, and its proxy the written
word, in shaping the built environment. This book was
itself the product of hundreds of thousands (really millions) of words spoken and written—and woven together—in conversations among editors, designers, students,
faculty, and administrators. Is architecture this process
by which words, and the voices that form them, translate
into images, buildings, landscapes, and more words?
— Brian Orser, Editor

Retrospecta was a remarkable and, at times, daunting
project. Organizing and reorganizing hierarchies of information and content to create a unique but legible reader
experience, coupled with the added pressure of somehow
representing the effects of COVID-19, was a challenge.
As the project comes to a close, I am struck by how much
faith the School puts into four first year students to produce a piece of archival work available for the rest of time.
I am proud of this year's edition of Retrospecta and might
add that it is almost, nearly perfect.
— Rachael Tsai, Editor

Letter from the Editors

This issue of Retrospecta covers the design studio and course work of the 2019–2020 academic year. After spring recess, the University closed its classrooms, lecture halls, and residential colleges in response to the spread of COVID-19. Students and professors dispersed around the world as classes went online, and the Yale School of Architecture tried to figure out how to teach design of the built environment.

Before—and even after—the pandemic ended campus life, it was an excellent academic year. This Retrospecta includes lectures, symposia, and student-run events; as well as data. This spring's crisis drove home the need to tackle global problems as they relate to architecture. Our students have always been passionate about design driving positive change; this attachment to tangible problems enhances their interest in form-making, technology, materiality, and beauty.

With the impact of COVID-19 forcing us to rethink our fundamental conception of community and urban life, the work of our students—architects, designers, and spatial and sustainable visionaries—has an urgency and an applicability that would have been unimaginable a year ago.

Whether teaching in Rudolph Hall or on our internet browsers, the YSoA faculty is committed to help our students enrich and expand their passions, broaden and enhance their knowledge, and become architects who will change the world. Our goal is that they have both an individual voice and a commitment to the common good; and a strong philosophical position in their creative work while respecting the creative motivations of others.

The present moment will be historically significant in a way that is already strangely palpable. But this volume of Retrospecta captures emerging views on architecture at a precise and unprecedented moment of multiple crises. This tragedy might be unprecedented for society, but our students' work displays strength, ingenuity, and the rigor necessary to meet daunting obstacles and plan for a better future.

Deborah Berke, Dean

- Dean's Reflection

With COVID-19 disproportionately affecting people of color, and our society's reaction to the murders of George Floyd, Breonna Taylor, Ahmaud Arbery, and too many others, designers, theorists, historians, and architects must learn to recognize the ways in which the built environment perpetuates oppression. This reaction is long overdue, but it is nonetheless right. Previous generations of designers used racialized zoning and urban renewal policies, designing segregated facilities and inadequate housing to damage Black communities in this country. Now, to stop perpetuating injustice, we need to examine how our inherited methodologies have been tools of oppression in urban spaces. By developing a practice of design justice, we stand to improve the discipline and practice of architecture, as well as the world we together build.

— Deborah Berke, Dean

Rudolph Hall

This graphic represents annual student enrollment over the last 20 years, analyzed in terms of race, ethnicity, gender, and citizenship. Academic year 1984–1985 is included for comparison.
*Deborah Berke became Dean of YSoA in July 2016.

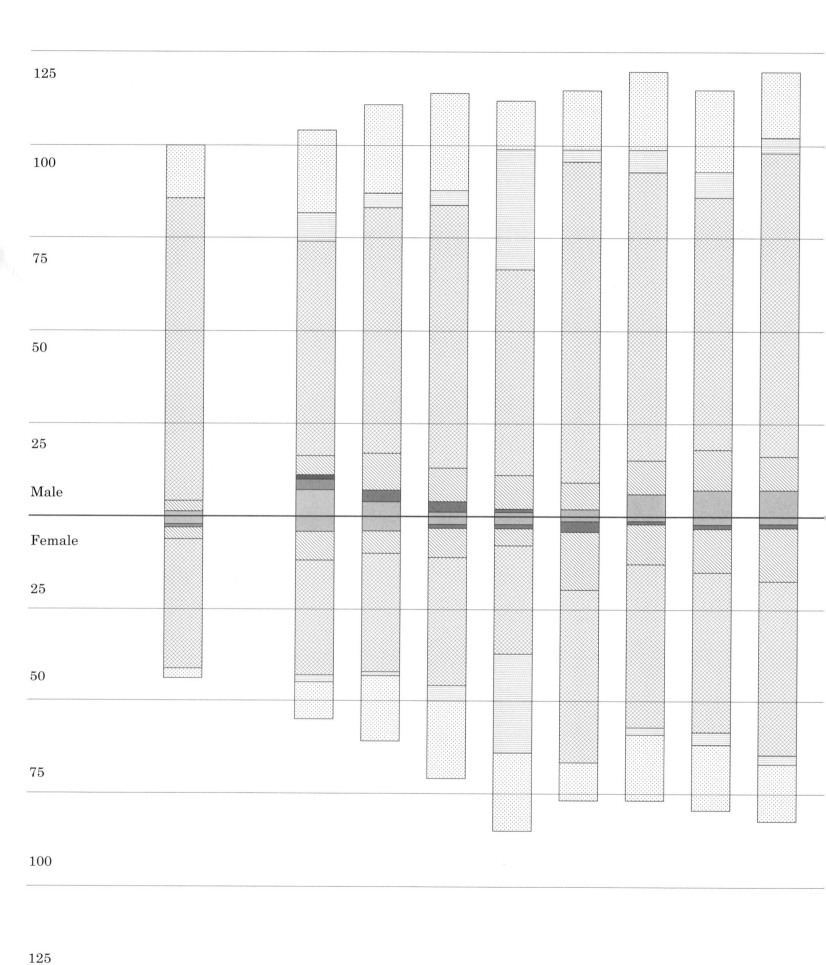

125

100

75

50

25

Male

Female

25

50

75

100

125

'84–'85   '00–'01   '01–'02   '02–'03   '03–'04   '04–'05   '05–'06   '06–'07   '07–'08

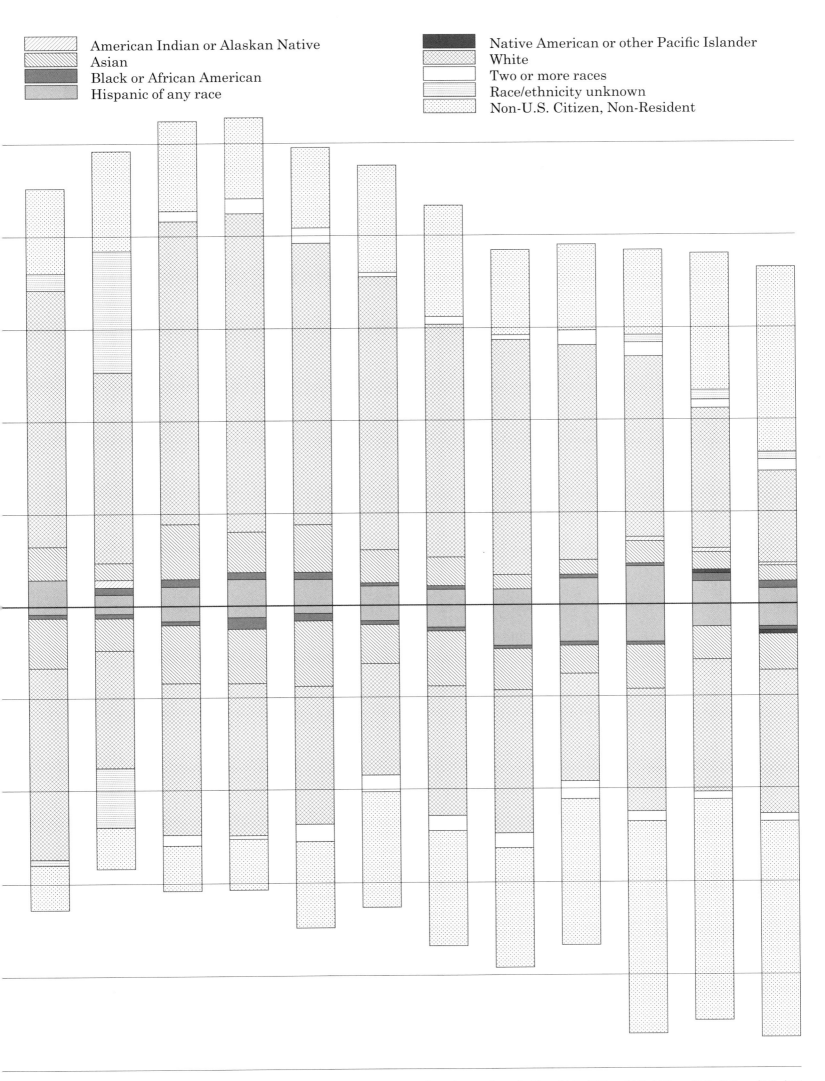

American Indian or Alaskan Native
Asian
Black or African American
Hispanic of any race

Native American or other Pacific Islander
White
Two or more races
Race/ethnicity unknown
Non-U.S. Citizen, Non-Resident

'08–'09   '09–'10   '10–'11   '11–'12   '12–'13   '13–'14   '14–'15   '15–'16*   '16–'17   '17–'18   '18–'19   '19–'20

11	Rachael Tsai
32	Left: Richard House Photography
	Right: Daniel Glick-Unterman
33	Left: Michael Vahrenwald
	Right: Richard House Photography
34	Left: Anjelica Gallegos
	Right: A.J. Artemel and Kay Yang
35	Left: Michelle Badr
	Right: David Schaengold
36	A.J. Artemel
37	Left: A.J. Artemel
	Right: Kate Altmann
38	A.J. Artemel
39	Max Wirsing
40	Holly Bushman
41	Holly Bushman
42	Open Access. HathiTrust Digital Library.
	Original Source: The Getty Research Institute.
45	Top: Nick Novelli
	Bottom: Mohamed Aly Etman
46	Zelig Fok and Iain Gomez
47	Zelig Fok and Iain Gomez
71	Deirdre Plaus
74	Page Comeaux
77	Daniel Whitcombe
80	Phoebe Harris
90	Michelle Badr
96	Seth Thompson
99	Leonardo Serrano Fuchs
120	Jingfei He, Jessica Kim, Caroline Kraska, Zishi Li, Paul Meuser, Jun Shi, Anjiang Xu
140	Alex Pineda
143	Michael Gasper, Gabriel Gutierrez Huerta, Rishab Jain, Kelley Johnson, Andrew Kim, Matthew Liu, Manasi Punde, Rukshan Vathupola, Darryl Weimer, Paul Wu
146	David Scurry
149	Yuhao Gordon Jiang
152	Michelle Badr
155	Mari Kroin
162	Liwei Wang
168	Phoebe Harris
177	Arno Hammacher
183	Raoul Hausmann

All images of design work were provided by students whose work was nominated.

Image Credits

Retrospecta 43
2019–2020
Published by the Yale School of Architecture
Edition of 5220

Editors
Claire Hicks
Abraham Mora-Valle
Brian Orser
Rachael Tsai

Graphic Designers
Luiza Dale
Nick Massarelli

Curator, *Fringe*
Adare Brown

Printer
Allied Printing Services
Manchester, CT

Paper
Endurance Silk 100lb Cover White
Accent Smooth Opaque 60lb Text White
Endurance Silk 70lb Text White
Mohawk Carnival Vellum 70lb Text New Black

Typeface
Akzidenz-Grotesk, Günter Gerhard Lange
Century Schoolbook, Morris Fuller Benton
LL Akkurat Mono, Laurenz Brunner

Distributor
Actar D
17th Floor
440 Park Avenue South
New York, NY 10016

For more information and copies of this book,
please write, call, or visit us at
Yale School of Architecture
3rd Floor
180 York Street
New Haven, CT 06511-11
+1-203-432-2288
www.architecture.yale.edu

For their advice and assistance in preparing
this book, we would like to give special thanks to
A.J. Artemel, Sunil Bald, Deborah Berke,
Michael Bierut, Richard DeFlumeri, Rich Kaplan,
Tanial Lowe, and Donna Wetmore

Thank you also to
Phillip Bernstein, Zelma Brunson, Luke Bulman,
Nina Rappaport, Kate Rozen, Rosemary Watts, and
Faculty and Students of YSoA

Colophon

Courses

Courses

Index

Faculty

Index

Awards

Professor King-lui Wu Teaching Award
Elihu Rubin

Students

Lillian Agutu, Kean University
Brandon Brooks, Maryland Institute College of Art
Adare Brown, Washington University in St. Louis
Claudia Carle, Hobart and William Smith Colleges
Lauren Carmona, Texas Tech University at El Paso
Katie Colford, Yale University
Lindsay Duddy, Case Western Reserve University
Audrey Fischer, University of Waterloo
Sam Golini, Dartmouth College
Sangji Han, Yonsei University
Jingfei He, University of Tokyo
Claire Hicks, Clemson University
Chocho Hu, South China University of Technology
Audrey Hughes, University of Virginia
Suhyun Jang, Hongik University
Yushan Jiang, Tongji University
Morgan Anna Kerber, Dalhousie University
Jessica Kim, University of Notre Dame
Sarah Kim, Northwestern University
Zhanna Kitbalyan, Columbia University
Caroline Kraska, University of Virginia
Zishi Li, Yale University
Calvin Liang, Columbia University
Perihan MacDonald, Columbia University
Hannah Mayer Baydoun, University of Minnesota
Paul Meuser, Rhode Island School of Design
Abraham Mora-Valle, Columbia University
Meghna Mudaliar, University of Toronto
Veronica Nicholson, Princeton University
Gustav Nielsen, Aarhus School of Architecture
Brian Orser, Pitzer College
Dominiq Oti, Leeds Metropolitan University
Yikai Qiao, Soochow University
Jingyuan Qiu, University of California, Los Angeles
Jack Rusk MEM**,** University of California, Santa Cruz
Taku Samejima, Keio University
Abby Sandler, Barnard College
Janelle Schmidt, Lawrence Tech University
Wenzhu Shentu, Zhejiang Normal University
Jun Shi MEM**,** College of William and Mary
Diana Smiljković, University of Bath
Andrew Spiller, Ohio State University, Columbus
Kevin Steffes, University of Chicago
Joshua Tan, Singapore University of Technology
    and Design
Hao Tang, College of Wooster
Yang Tian, University of Michigan, Ann Arbor
Rachael Tsai, University of Michigan, Ann Arbor
Tianyue Wang, University of the Arts London
Timothy Wong, University of Hong Kong
Anjiang Xu, South China University of Technology
Hao Xu, Ball State University
Tian Xu, University of Bath
Yuan Iris You, University of Pennsylvania
Calvin Yang Yue, University of Toronto
Christina Chi Zhang, Yale University
Alex Mingda Zhang, University of Illinois
    at Urbana-Champaign
Jessica Jie Zhou, University of Toronto

Ife Adepegba, University of Cambridge
Isa Akerfeldt-Howard, Kein University
Natalie Broton, Ball State University
Ives Brown, University of California, Los Angeles
Christopher Cambio, Hobart and William
    Smith Colleges
Martin Carrillo Bueno, Bennington College
Colin Chudyk, Dalhousie University
Rosa Congdon, Brown University
Jiachen Deng, Washington University in St. Louis
Janet Dong, University of Michigan, Ann Arbor
Xuefeng Du, Hunan University
Paul Freudenburg MEM**,** Yale University
Kate Fritz, James Madison University
Malcolm Rondell Galang, University of California,
    Los Angeles
Anjelica Gallegos, University of Colorado Denver
Yangwei Kevin Gao, University of Illinois at
    Urbana-Champaign
Jiaming Gu, Southeast University Nanjing
Ian Gu MBA**,** McGill University
Ashton Harrell, Ohio State University, Columbus
Liang Hu, University of Melbourne
Niema Jafari, University College London
Alicia Jones, University of California, Los Angeles
Hyun Jae Jung, University of Bath
Sze Wai Justin Kong, University of Hong Kong
Louis Koushouris, University of Colorado Boulder
Tyler Krebs, Ohio State University, Columbus
Hiuki Lam, University of Hong Kong
Pabi Lee, Parsons School of Design
Ming Xi Li, Washington University in St. Louis
Yidong Isabel Li, University College London
Dreama Simeng Lin, College of William and Mary
Qiyuan Liu, University of Hong Kong
April Liu, University of California, Berkeley
Araceli Lopez, University of Washington
Angela Lufkin, Arizona State University
Rachel Mulder, University of Michigan, Ann Arbor
Leanne Nagata, University of California, Berkeley
Naomi Ng, University of Melbourne
Louisa Nolte, New York University
Alex Olivier, University of Florida
Alix Pauchet MEM**,** Middlebury College
Michelle Qu, Renmin University of China
Nicole Ratajczak, University of Waterloo
Heather Schneider, Pennsylvania State University
Scott Simpson, Yale University
Christine Song, University of Toronto
Shikha Thakali, Mount Holyoke College
Ben Thompson, College for Creative Studies
Sarah Weiss, Brown University
Max Wirsing, Carleton College
Shelby Wright, Ohio State University, Columbus
Stella Xu, University of California, Los Angeles
Sean Yang, University of Waterloo
Peng Ye, Southeast University Nanjing
Leyi Zhang, University of Illinois at Urbana-Champaign
Yuhan Zhang, University of California, Berkeley
Kaiwen Zhao, Rhode Island School of Design
Sasha Zwiebel, Vassar College

Students

MArch 1, 2020

Cristina Anastase, Princeton University
Michelle Badr, University of California, Berkeley
Katharine Blackman, University of California, Berkeley
Samuel David Bruce [MEM], Bowdoin College
Emily Cass, Barnard College
Camille Chabrol, McGill University
Serena Ching, Judson University
Page Comeaux, University of Louisiana at Lafayette
Gioia Montana Connell [MEM], University of St. Andrews
Ruchi Dattani, New Jersey Institute of Technology
Deo Deiparine, Washington University in St. Louis
Clara Domange, École Spéciale d'Architecture
Miriam Dreiblatt, McGill University
Helen Farley, Haverford College
Adam Feldman, University at Buffalo SUNY
Nathan Garcia, Texas A&M University, College Station
Michael Gasper, Ball State University
Michael Glassman, Princeton University
Tianyu Guan, University of California, Berkeley
Phoebe Harris, University of Virginia
Will James, Washington University in St. Louis
Kelley Johnson, Northeastern University
Andrew Kim, Yale University
Katie Lau, Ohio State University, Columbus
Eunice Lee, University of California, Los Angeles
Rachel LeFevre, Washington University in St. Louis
Zack Lenza, Ball State University
Jackson Lindsay, University of British Columbia
Matthew Liu, RMIT University
Thomas Mahon, University of Waterloo
Andrew Economos Miller, Ohio State University, Columbus
Samantha Monge Kaser [MBA], Yale University
Layla Ni, Mount Holyoke College
Max Ouellette-Howitz, University of Minnesota
Jonathan Palomo, University of Kentucky, Lexington
Christine Pan, Cornell University
Jewel Pei, Washington University in St. Louis
Alex Pineda, Judson University
Deirdre Plaus, Colgate University
Manasi Punde, Parsons School of Design
Kelsey Rico, Swarthmore College
Jenna Ritz, Yale University
Limy Fabiana Rocha, University of Maryland, College Park
David Schaengold, Princeton University
Rhea Schmid, Barnard College
Armaan Shah, Washington University in St. Louis
Baolin Shen, University of Edinburgh
Maya Sorabjee, Brown University
Gus Steyer [MEM], Yale University
Megan Tan, University of Toronto
Brenna Thompson, University of Michigan, Ann Arbor
Seth Thompson, Yale University
Rukshan Vathupola, University of Hartford
Laélia Kim-Lan Vaulot, École des Ponts ParisTech

Alexander Velaise [MBA], Dartmouth College
Liwei Wang [MBA], University of Waterloo
Darryl Weimer, Amherst College
Xiaohui Wen, University of California, Berkeley
Daniel Whitcombe [MBA], Yale University
Paul Wu, Washington University in St. Louis
Kay Yang, University of California, Berkeley

MArch 2, 2021

Guillermo Acosta Navarrete, Tecnológico de Monterrey
Daniella Calma, Pratt Institute
Shuang Chen, Hefei University of Technology
Rebecca Commissaris, Rhode Island School of Design
Elaine ZiYi Cui, University of Southern California
Shuchen Dong, Tsinghua University
Yue Geng, Tianjin University
Gabriel Gutierrez Huerta, University of Tennessee, Knoxville
Rishab Jain, Southern California Institute of Architecture
Yuhao Gordon Jiang, Rhode Island School of Design
Srinivas Narayan Karthikeyan, Center for Environmental Planning and Technology
Mari Kroin, Pratt Institute
Shiqi Valerie Li, South China University of Technology
Ruike Liu, Wuhan University
Luka Pajovic, University of Cambridge
David Scurry, Virginia Polytechnic Institute and State University
Qizhen Tang, Tsinghua University
Alper Turan, Istanbul Technical University
Daoru Wang, North Carolina State University, Raleigh
Hongyu Wang, Harbin Institute of Technology
Hengyuan Yang, Tsinghua University

MArch 2, 2020

Hamzah Ahmed, University of Cambridge
Sara Alajmi, Kuwait University
Katherine Todd, Syracuse University
James Bradley, Rensselaer Polytechnic Institute
Taiming Chen, Syracuse University
Miguel Darcy de Oliveira Miranda, Pontifícia Universidade Católica do Rio de Janeiro
Gretchen Gao, Tongji University
Changming Huang, Tsinghua University
Ho Jae Lee, Hongik University
Smit Patel, Kamla Raheja Vidyanidhi Institute for Architecture and Environmental Studies
Leonardo Serrano Fuchs, Universidade Federal do Rio de Janeiro
Jen Shin [MEM], Drexel University
Arghavan Taheri, Tehran University of Art
Adam Thibodeaux, University of Texas at Austin
Jerome Tryon, University of Oregon
I-Ting Tsai, Chung Yuan Christian University
Justin Tsang, Architectural Association
Anna Borou Yu, Tsinghua University

Students

MED

Holly Bushman '20, Bates College
Cayce Davis '21, University of Tennessee, Knoxville
Alex Kim '21, Syracuse University
Mary Carole Overholt '21, Stanford University
Laura Pappalardo '21, Escola da Cidade

PhD

Katherine Ball, MFA, Portland State University
Christina Ciardullo, MArch, Columbia University
Iris Giannakopoulou Karamouzi, SMArchS-AD, Massachusetts Institute of Technology
Gary Huafan He, BArch, Cornell University
Theodossios Issaias, SMarchS-AU, Massachusetts Institute of Technology
Ishraq Khan, MA, Architectural Association
Phoebe Mankiewicz, MS-ArchSci, Rensselaer Polytechnic Institute
Zachariah Michielli, MArch, Southern California Institute of Architecture
Nicholas Pacula, SMArchS-AD, Massachusetts Institute of Technology
Mandi Pretorius, MS-Arch, Rensselaer Polytechnic Institute
Gabrielle Printz, MS-CCCP, Columbia University
Summer Sutton, MArch, Massachusetts Institute of Technology
Aaron Tobey, BS-Arch, University of Cincinnati
David Turturo, MPhil, Yale University
Jia Weng, MED, Yale University

Undergraduate Studies, 2021

Chelsea Chaug, Dustin Dunaway, Charles Hawkings, Noa Hines, Irene Kim, Nikita Klimenko, Ivy Li, Talia Morison-Allen, Kai Nip, Sam Oldshue, Jacob Payne, Robert Skoronski, Michelle Tong, Ava Vanech, Vicky Wu, Hannah Yi

Undergraduate Studies, 2020

Hafsa Abdi, Angel Adeoye, Trevor Chan, Hana Meihan Davis, Cole Fandrich, Sebastian Galvan, Julia Hedges, Jane Jacobs, Karin Nagano, Graceann Nicolosi, Ash Pales, Sophie Potter, Sam Rimm-Kaufman, Adam Thompson, Reanna Wauer

Fellowships

William Wirt Winchester Traveling Fellowship
Rhea Schmid, Jerome Tryon

Gertraud A. Wood Traveling Fellowship, awarded 2019
Rhea Schmid

George Nelson Scholarship, awarded 2019
Gioia Montana Connell [MEM]

David M. Schwarz / Architectural Services Good Times Award
Liwei Wang [MBA]

Medals and Prizes

American Institute of Architects Henry Adams Medal
Maya Sorabjee

Alpha Rho Chi Medal
Emily Cass

William Edward Parsons Memorial Medal
Serena Ching, Kay Yang

The H.I. Feldman Prize
Camille Chabrol, Thomas Mahon, Alex Pineda

The H.I. Feldam Nominees
Emily Cass, Camille Chabrol, Serena Ching, Page Comeaux, Rachel LeFevre, Matthew Liu, Thomas Mahon, Andrew Economos Miller, Alex Pineda, Deirdre Plaus, Rhea Schmid, Leonardo Serrano Fuchs, Jen Shin [MEM], Maya Sorabjee, Jerome Tryon, Justin Tsang, Liwei Wang [MBA], Kay Yang

Wendy Elizabeth Blanning Prize, awarded 2019
Maya Sorabjee

Sonia Albert Schimberg Prize
Rachel LeFevre

Janet Cain Sielaff Alumni Award
Jen Shin [MEM]

Moulton Andrus Award
Adam Thibodeaux

The Drawing Prize
Matthew Liu

Gene Lewis Book Prize
Hamzah Ahmed

David Taylor Memorial Prize B. Jack Hanly
Holly Bushman

Internships

Takenaka Corporation Summer Internship, awarded 2019
Matthew Liu

David M. Schwarz / Architectural Services Summer Internship and Traveling Fellowship, awarded 2019
Brenna Thompson

[MEM] Joint Degree Program, Master of Environmental Management, Yale School of the Environment
[MBA] Joint Degree Program, Master of Business Administration, Yale School of Management

Donors

The Yale School of Architecture is grateful to all those who provided financial support during the period July 1, 2019–June 30, 2020.

Friends

Kevin Dale Adkisson '12 BA
Nancy Alexander '79 BA, '84 MBA
David Bailey
Michael Corcoran Barry '09 BA
Mahnaz Ispahani and Adam Bartos
Dean Deborah L. Berke '16 MAH
Kent C. Bloomer '59 BFA, '61 MFA
Joan N. Borinstein
George R. Brunjes
Josephine Bush
John A. Carrafiell '87 BA
James C. Childress
Richard D. Cohen
Caswell Cooke, Jr.
Claire Creatore
Daniel Dawson
Thomas J. Deegan-Day '89 BA
Enid Storm Dwyer*
Sheryl and Jeffrey S. Flug
Warren Bryan Fuermann
Frank O. Gehry '00 DFAH
Marilyn M. and Raymond L. Gindroz
Elsbeth and Edward Haladay
Andrew Philip Heid '02 BA
Judith T. Hunt
James L. Iker
Adam Inselbuch
Elise Jaffe + Jeffrey Brown
Isaac Kalisvaart
Kathryn H. Kavanagh
San Lee
Elizabeth Lenahan
Dr. Keith G. Lurie '77 BA
Anne Kriken Mann
Kathryn Milano
William I. Miller '78 BA, '05 MAH
Michael A. D. Nock '19 MBA
Richard B. Peiser '70 BA
Karen L. Pritzker
William L. Rawn III '65 BA
William K. Reilly '62 BA, '94 MAH
Carolyn Greenspan and Marshall S. Ruben, Esq. '82 BA
Jeffrey J. Salzman '74 BA
Brenda Shapiro
Lynda Spence*
Billie Tsien '71 BA
James Von Klemperer
Mathew D. Wolf
Vivian Kuan and Pei-Tse Wu '89 BA
Arthur W. Zeckendorf

Corporations, Foundations, and Matching Gift Support

...a chance...fund, inc.
AIA Connecticut
American Endowment Foundation
Architecture & Town Planning LLC
Avangrid Foundation
Bank of America Corporation
The Barclays Bank PLC
Barry Family Foundation
The BPB & HBB Foundation
Canyon Wholesale Provisions
Centerbrook Architects & Planners
The David and Lucile Packard Foundation
David M. Schwarz Architects, Inc.
Deborah Berke Partners
Earl & Brenda Shapiro Foundation
Elisha-Bolton Foundation
Environetics Holdings NY, LLC
Erving and Joyce Wolf Foundation
Ethel & Philip Adelman Charitable Foundation, Inc.
The Fidelity Charitable Gift Fund
Genga Family Properties, LLC
Grace Farms Foundation, Inc.
The Jaffe Family Foundation
The Jewish Communal Fund
JP Morgan Charitable Giving Fund
Kohn Pedersen Fox Associates PC
Kraus Family Foundation
MAD Office Limited
MADE LLC
The National Philanthropic Trust
The Pannonia Foundation
Payette Associates
Robert A.M. Stern Family Foundation
    for Advancement of Architectural Culture
Schwab Fund for Charitable Giving
Seedlings Foundation
The Tang Fund
T.S. Kim Architectural Fellowship Foundation
TIAA Charitable
The U.S. Charitable Gift Trust
Vanguard Charitable
William Randolph Hearst Foundation
Yale Club of New Haven

Donors

Alumni

1949
Frank S. Alschuler*
Theodore F. Babbitt

1952
Donald C. Mallow

1953
Milton Klein
Dr. Julian E. Kulski

1954
Chester Bowles, Jr.
Boris S. Pushkarev
Thomas R. Vreeland, Jr.

1955
Sidney M. Sisk

1957
Ernest L. Ames
Edwin William de Cossy
Richard A. Nininger
William L. Porter

1958
James S. Dudley
Mark H. Hardenbergh
Allen Moore, Jr.
Malcolm Strachan II

1959
Bernard M. Boyle
Frank C. Chapman
Louis P. Inserra
Herbert S. Newman
Earl A. Quenneville
Bruce W. Sielaff
Robert M. Swedroe
Andrew C. Wheeler

1960
Larence Newman Argraves
Thomas L. Bosworth
Richard S. Chafee
Bryant L. Conant
John K. Copelin
Michael Gruenbaum
Robert A. Mitchell
Konrad J. Perlman

1961
Edward R. Baldwin II
Paul B. Brouard
Peter Cooke
Warren Jacob Cox
Francis W. Gencorelli
Lewis S. Roscoe
Yung G. Wang

1962
Richard A. Hansen
Tai Soo Kim
James Morganstern
Leonard P. Perfido
Renato Rossi-Loureiro
Meredith M. Seikel
Myles Weintraub

1963
Austin Church III
A. Robert Faesy, Jr.
Dr. Howard H. Foster, Jr.
F. Kempton Mooney
William A. Werner, Jr.

1964
Philip Allen
Theoharis L. David
Charles D. Hosford
M.J. Long*
Robert J. Mittelstadt
Joan F. Stogis

1965
Thomas Hall Beeby
H. Calvin Cook
Foster W. de Jesus
Norman E. Jackson, Jr.
Isidoro Korngold
Gary L. Michael
John I. Pearce, Jr.
Alexander Purves
Elliot A. Segal
Mason Smith
Robert A.M. Stern
Frederick C. Terzo
Leonard M. Todd, Jr.
Jeremy A. Walsh

1966
Anonymous
Andrew Andersons
Emily Nugent Carrier
Richard C. Carroll, Jr.
Loren Ghiglione
William F. Moore
William L. Riddle
Lester R. Walker

1967
William H. Albinson
Edward A. Arens
Charles M. Engberg
Alexander D. Garvin
Howard E. Goldstein
Glenn H. Gregg
Simon Lazarus III, Esq.
Chung Nung Lee
John W. Mullen III
Charles S. Rotenberg
Theodore Paul Streibert
Darius Toraby

1968
Frederick S. Andreae
Gail H. Cooke
Peter de Bretteville
John Fulop, Jr.
Christopher C. Glass
John Holbrook, Jr.
Louis Mackall
Peter C. Mayer
Yuji Noga
Franklin B. Satterthwaite Jr., PhD
Donald R. Spivack
Salvatore F. Vasi
John J. Vosmek, Jr.
James C. Whitney, Esq.

1969
Stephen Harris Adolphus
James E. Caldwell, Jr.
Samuel R. Callaway, Jr.
Robert J. Cassidy
David B. Decker
James M. Gage
Harvey R. Geiger
Jane L. Gilbert
Edward J. Gotgart
William H. Grover
Peter Hentschel
Roderick C. Johnson
Raymond J. Kaskey, Jr.
Jeffrey H. May
John H. Shoaff
Kermit D. Thompson

1970
Richard F. Barrett
Roland F. Bedford
Paul F. Bloom
F. Andrus Burr
Thomas Carey
Ronald C. Filson
Brin R. Ford
Lori Gladstone
Kathrin S. Moore
James V. Righter
Laurence A. Rosen
Merlin Jay Shelstad
Marilyn Swartz Lloyd
Walter C. Upton
Stuart H. Wrede
William L. Yuen, Esq.
F. Anthony Zunino

1971
John R. Benson
William A. Brenner
An-Chi H. Burow
Mazie Cox
Robert L. Miller
H. Rodriguez-Camilloni
Susan St. John

Donors

1972
Marc F. Appleton
Paul B. Bailey
Edward P. Bass
Frederick Bland
Phillip Mack Caldwell
Heather Willson Cass
William A. Davis, Jr., Esq.
John H. T. Dow, Jr.
Joseph A. Ford, III
Coleman A. Harwell II
William H. Maxfield
Barton Phelps
Jefferson B. Riley
Mark Simon
Henry B. Teague
Brinkley S. Thorne
Carl H. Wies
George Vincent Wright
Roger Hung Tuan Yee

1973
Judith Bing
J.P. Chadwick Floyd
Stephen R. Holt
Everardo A. Jefferson
Nancy Brooks Monroe
Karen Rheinlander-Gray
Steven C. Robinson
Michael J. Stanton
William A. Sterling
Stephen C. Thomson
R. Jerome Wagner
John W. Whipple
Robert J. Yudell

1974
Gordon M. Black
Jonathan G. Boyer
Sara E. Caples
Andres M. Duany
William E. Odell
Patrick L. Pinnell
Elizabeth M. Plater-Zyberk
Barbara W. Ratner
Barbara J. Resnicow
David M. Schwarz
George E. Turnbull

1975
Tullio A. Bertoli
Douglas J. Gardner
Karyn M. Gilvarg
Susan E. Godshall, Esq.
Margaret R. Goglia
Keith B. Gross
Edwin R. Kimsey, Jr.
Francis C. Klein
Larry W. Richards
J. David Waggonner III

1976
Anonymous
Benjamin M. Baker III
Shalom Baranes
Henry H. Benedict III
Anko Chen
Stefani Danes
Barbara R. Feibelman
Carl M. Geupel
James R. Kessler
Roy T. Lydon, Jr.
Eric Jay Oliner
Adrienne K. Paskind
Barbara Sundheimer-Extein
Scott Van Genderen

1977
James David Barnes
Louise M. Braverman
Bradley B. Cruickshank
W.J. Patrick Curley
Eric W. Epstein
Jonathan S. Kammel
James Hirsch Liberman
Kevin P. Lichten
Randall T. Mudge
Davidson Norris
Paul J. Pugliese
Stephen M. Tolkin
Alexander C. Twining

1978
Philip H. Babb
Frederic M. Ball, Jr.
Judith M. Capen
Shiao-Ling Chang
Kenneth H. Colburn
Cynthia N. Hamilton
Kaspar A. Kraemer
William S. Mead
William Hall Paxson
Daniel Arthur Rosenfeld
Julia Ruch

1979
Steven W. Ansel
Jack Alan Bialosky, Jr.
Richard H. Clarke
Jeffrey P. Feingold
Patti Lee Glazer
John Charles Hall
Michele Lewis
Richard L. McElhiney
Edward J. Miller
Thomas N. Patch

1980
Jacob D. Albert
J. Scott Finn
Stephen W. Harby
Ann K. McCallum
Julia H. Miner
William A. Paquette

1981
Brian E. Healy
Mitchell A. Hirsch
T. Whitcomb Iglehart
Michael G. Kostow
Jonathan Levi
Jane Murphy
Frances H. Roosevelt
Daniela Holt Voith
Spencer Warncke
Diane L. Wilk

1982
John A. Boecker
Domenic Carbone, Jr.
David P. Chen
Bruce H. Donnally
Eric J. Gering
Raymond R. Glover
Kay Bea Jones
John E. Kaliski
Charles F. Lowrey, Jr.
Theodore John Mahl
Paul W. Reiss
R. Anthony Terry

1983
Maynard M. Ball
Anthony Stephen Barnes
Phillip G. Bernstein
Carol J. Burns
Stuart E. Christenson
Ignacio Dahl-Rocha
Stefan Hastrup
Erica H. Ling
Elisabeth N. Martin
Elizabeth Ann Murrell
Nicholas J. Rehnberg
Jacques M. Richter
Gary Schilling
Brent Sherwood
Robert J. Taylor
Nell W. Twining
Michael R. Winstanley

1984
Bruce R. Becker
Paul F. Carr, Jr.
Marti M. Cowan
Teresa Ann Dwan
Douglas S. Dworsky
Ruth Slobin Harris
Blair D. Kamin
Elizabeth M. Mahon
Michael L. Marshall
David Chase Martin
Sharon Matthews
Timothy G. McKenna
Kenneth E. McKently
Scott Merrill
Jun Mitsui
Lawrence S. Ng
John R. Perkins

Kathryn L. Perkins
Ted Trussell Porter
Jennifer C. Sage
Kevin M. Smith
Mary E. Stockton
Marion G. Weiss

1985
Barbara A. Ball
William Robert Bingham
Robert L. Bostwick
Michael Coleman Duddy
Jonathan M. Fishman
Lucile S. Irwin
Charles H. Loomis
Peter B. MacKeith
Chariss McAfee
Joseph A. Pasquinelli
Roger O. Schickedantz
R. David Thompson

1986
Margaret J. Chambers
Tim Culvahouse
Carey Feierabend
David J. Levitt
Nicholas L. Petschek
Madeline Kay Schwartzman
J. Gilbert Strickler
John B. Tittmann

1987
John P. Blood
Mary Buttrick Burnham
William D. Egan
Elizabeth P. Gray
Andrew B. Knox
Douglas S. Marshall
Timothy Day Mohr
Lilla J. Smith
William L. Vandeventer

1988
Hans Baldauf
Andrew D. Berman
Cary Suzanne Bernstein
John David Butterworth
Allison Ewing
Stephen Clarke Fritzinger
Natalie C. Gray-Miniutti
Drew H. Kepley
Ann Lisa Krsul
Oscar E. Mertz III
David H. Must
Kathryn B. Nesbitt
Nicholas Alfred Noyes
Alan W. Organschi
Elaine M. Rene-Weissman
William Taggart Ruhl
Gilbert P. Schafer III
Matthew Viederman
Li Tze Wen
Robert Duncan Young

1989
Edward R. Burian
Larry G. Chang
Darin C. Cook
John DaSilva
Steve Dumez
Thomas J. Frechette
Kevin S. Killen
David J. Rush
Rossana H. Santos
Margaret Sherman Todd

1990
Lori B. Arrasmith Quill
Charles Bergen
Stephen Brockman
Kristen L. Hodess
Jeffrey E. Karer
David M. Levine
Marc D. L'Italien
Marie B. Wilkinson

1991
David M. Becker
Dominic L.C. LaPierre
Linda Stabler-Talty
Alexander M. Stuart
Lindsay S. Suter
Kevin Wilkes
Heather H. Young

1992
Andrew James Abraham
Kelly Jean Carlson-Reddig
Perla Jeanne Delson
Frederick Adams Farrar II
Bruce Marshall Horton
Maitland Jones III
Douglas Neal Kozel
Laura Auerbach Lapierre
Marc A. Turkel
Marion Converse Winkler

1993
Richard G. Grisaru
Louise J. Harpman
Michael A. Harshman
Jordan J. Levin
Laurence W. Odfjell
Gitta Robinson
Allen Douglas Ross
Evan Michael Supcoff
Katherine D. Winter

1994
Brendan Russell Coburn
Paul W. Jackson
Mark R. Johnson
William J. Massey
Tania K. Min
Jim Tinson
Mimi H. Tsai

1995
Carolyn Ann Foug
George Craig Knight
Johannes Marinus Knoops
Aaron Matthew Lamport
Michael Henry Levendusky
Dana Elizabeth Tang
John Christopher Woell

1996
Andrew C. Backer
Douglas C. Bothner
John B. Clancy
Ching-Hua Ho
Russell S. Katz
Michael V. Knopoff
Chung Yin J. Lau
Alexander Francis Levi
Thomas A. Lumikko
Nancy Nienberg
David A. Thurman
Mai-Tse Wu

1997
Victor E. Agran
Drew Lang
Peter Downing Mullan
David Jason Pascu
Linda Caroline Reeder
Ian Mark Smith
William James Voulgaris

1998
Thalassa Alexandra Curtis
Marjorie K. Dickstein
Clifton R. Fordham
Elizabeth P. Rutherfurd
Emily Sheya Kovner
Karl A. Krueger
Paul D. Stoller

1999
Kimberly Ann Brown
Celia Corkery Civello
Martha Jane Foss
Adrienne James
Bruce D. Kinlin
Raphael Sperry
Katherine E. Sutherland

2000
Benjamin Jon Bischoff
Bing Bu
Joseph Shek Yuen Fong
Oliver Edmund Freundlich
Donald Wayne Johnson
Ronald Michael Stelmarski

2001
Ghiora Aharoni
Jeff Allan Goldstein
Jaehee Kim
Christopher M. Pizzi

Donors

Adam Joseph Ruedig
Elizabeth Weeks Tilney
Can M.A. Tiryaki
Juliana Chittick Tiryaki
Zhonggui Zhao

2002
Noah K. Biklen
Rashid Jamal Saxton
Kayin Tse
Ma Yansong

2003
Andrew William Benner
Marcos Diaz Gonzalez
Li-Yu Hsu
Dongyeop Lee
William L. Tims

2004
Stephen Yuen-Hoo Chien
James C. Nelson III
Charles S.C. Sevin
Damian Delafield Zunino

2005
Ralph Colt Bagley IV
Brent Allen Buck
Jennifer N. Carruthers
Diala Salam Hanna
Derek James Hoeferlin
Brandon F. Pace
Brett Dalton Spearman
Nicholas Martin Stoutt

2006
Angel Paolo Campos
Michael Joseph Grogan
Sean A. Khorsandi
David Nam
Frederick C Scharmen

2007
Gabrielle Eve Brainard
Molly W. Steenson
Adrienne E. Swiatocha Turner

2008
Whitney M. Kraus
Jacob I. Reidel
Leo Rowling Stevens IV

2009
John Capen Brough III
Iben Andrea Falconer
Matthew A. Roman
Leah Rosa Weinberg
Rebecca B. Winik

2010
Helen B. Bechtel
Daniel David Colvard
Jacquelyn Page Wittkamp Hawkins

Scott Brandon O'Daniel
Tal Schori

2011
Marija Brdarski
Kipp Colby Edick
Alexandra Fox Tailer

2012
Kathryn L. Perez

2013
Antonia M. Devine
Altair L. Peterson
Ryan Salvatore
Paul C. Soper III

2014
Anonymous
Ali John Pierre Artemel
Mary F. Burr
Brittany L. Utting
Constance M. Vale

2015
Elena R. Baranes
Yifan Li
Hui Zhen Ng
Lauren E. Raab
Zachary A. Veach

2016
Jack J. Bian
Carl D. Cornilsen
Dante T.H. Furioso
Nicolas Thornton Kemper
John W. Kleinschmidt

2017
Anonymous
Ava Amirahmadi
Alexander O. Kruhly
Hannah L. Novack
Georgia M. Todd
Robert J. Yoos

2018
David Alston Langdon
Margaret F. Marsh
Tess K. McNamara

Tribute Gifts in Honor of

Everett M. Barber
Sasha C. and Edward P. Bass
Thomas H. Beeby
Deborah L. Berke
Kent C. Bloomer
Calvert S. Bowie
Charles H. Brewer
Peggy Deamer
Bryan Fuermann
Frank O. Gehry

Dylan Albert Grant
Phil Grausman
Steven Harris
Lee Yock Hua
Alberto C. Lau
Sophie Powell
Alexander Purves
Robert A.M. Stern
Ng Eng Teck

Tribute Gifts in Memory of

Constance M. Adams
Frank Alschuler
Diana Balmori
Everett M. Barber
George R. Brunjes
Frank Chang
Shu Chang
John E. Decell
Michael L. Glass
Dylan Albert Grant
Phil Grausman
Herbert M. Hodgman
Walter A. Hunt
Austin Kelly
Timothy Egan Lenahan
M.L. Long
Gerald A. Marshall
Carroll L. Meeks
Peter Millard
Charles J. Moore
Cesar Pelli
Sophie Powell
Drika Purves
Jean Sielaff
Stanley Tigerman
Benjamin Weintraub

*Deceased donors

Student Organizations

Equality in Design (EiD)

EiD is a coalition of committed students from the Yale School of Architecture seeking equity within the architectural profession and the built environment.

Paprika!

An independent, often-weekly broadsheet, produced by rotating teams of editors and designers. Covering an array of interdisciplinary topics, it is an "on-the-ground" student publication for the broader YSoA community.

National Organization of Minority Architecture Students (NOMAS)

NOMAS's mission is to champion diversity within the design professions by promoting the excellence, community engagement, and professional development of its members.

The Christian Fellowship

The Christian Fellowship is a community and discussion group of Yale architecture students that meets weekly to explore the overlap of ideas relating to the Christian tradition, our work, and architecture.

The Yale Architecture Forum

The Yale Architecture Forum serves as a place for discussion between PhD students from both the School of Architecture and the Department of the History of Art who share an interest in architectural history and theory.

OutLines

OutLines is a social and advocacy group for lesbian, gay, bisexual, transgender, queer, and allied students at YSoA. OutLines functions as a support system and social network focusing on LGBTQ issues within YSoA.

Green Action in Architecture (GAIA)

GAIA is a student group devoted to addressing sustainability and environmental health and wellbeing issues within the school, as well as promoting broader discussion of environmental considerations.

Indigenous Scholars of Architecture, Planning, and Design (ISAPD)

ISAPD is a collective student group focused on increasing the knowledge, consciousness, and appreciation of indigenous architecture and planning at the YSoA.

Rudolph Open

Rudolph Open is a biannual tournament for everyone to become ultimate badminton masters and add a little spice to studio life!

Index

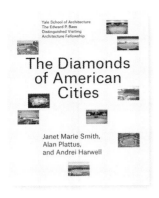

The Diamonds of American Cities
Yale School of Architecture, 2019

The Diamonds of American Cities presents the studio of Edward P. Bass Visiting Distinguished Architecture Fellow Janet Marie Smith, vice president of the Los Angeles Dodgers, Alan Plattus, and Andrei Harwell. The challenge was to analyze ballparks and their urban ramifications in a two-phased project, one each for a minor- and a major-league team.

Authors Janet Marie Smith, Alan Plattus, and
    Andrei Harwell
Editors Nina Rappaport and Ronald Ostezan
Designer MGMT.Design

Within or Without
Yale School of Architecture, 2019

Within or Without showcases how the work of three advanced studios at the Yale School of Architecture engages with conventions of architectural and cultural production and the boundaries of our discipline. It highlights methods of making and enclosing space developed by students of Scott Ruff, Jackilin Hah Bloom and Florencia Pita, and Omar Gandhi.

Editors Nina Rappaport and Benjamin Olsen
Designer MGMT.Design

Eyes That Saw: Architecture after Las Vegas
Yale School of Architecture, 2020

Eyes that Saw features a collection of scholarly essays based on the conference held at Yale celebrating the fortieth anniversary of the 1968 epochal Las Vegas Studio, led by Robert Venturi, Denise Scott Brown, and Steven Izenour. Three Yale studios brought students out into the world to both analyze and design projects and, in so doing, transformed architectural education.

Authors Scott Ruff, Florencia Pita, Jackilin Hah Bloom,
    Omar Gandhi
Editors Stanislaus von Moos, Martino Stierli, and
    Nina Rappaport
Designer Bruno Margreth

Kent Bloomer: Nature as Ornament
Yale School of Architecture, 2020

Nature as Ornament celebrates Kent Bloomer's indispensable intellectual and pedagogical contribution to the Yale School of Architecture and the profession of architecture over the last fifty years. Bloomer's dedication to the design and thinking of ornament in architecture has influenced collaborators and students in a broad range of fields, among them architects, historians, musicians, artists, philosophers, and biologists.

Editors Gary Huafan He and Sunil Bald
Designer Luke Bulman

Perspecta 52 Ensemble The Yale Architectural Journal

**Perspecta 52 Ensemble
The Yale Architectural Journal**
Yale School of Architecture, 2019

Editors Charlotte Algie and Alicia Pozniak
Designer Seokhoon Choi

Rural Functionalism in Vichy France
Jean-Louis Cohen

*Tides That Bind: Waterborne Trade and the
Infrastructure Networks of Jardine, Matheson & Co.*
Alex Bremner

Dublin, 1897: The Art of (Architectural) Street Fighting
Mark Crinson

Late to the After Party: Neo-Geo Architecture
Hans Tursack

*The Construction of Soviet Culture:
From Mass Spectacle to Synthetic Theater*
Anna Bokov

Christian Art in Kerala Between St. Thomas and St. Peter
Cristina Osswald

Building and Resistance in Barbados
Emily Mann

*Pavilions and Tents: Pietro della Valle's
Mobile Architecture*
Matteo Burioni

Lines of Infrastructural Control in Plantation Jamaica
Hayden Bassett

Reprise on the Villa Romana at Piazza Armerina
Extracts from a conversation with Kimberly D. Bowes

Other Methods
Yasmin Vobis and Aaron Forrest

Joseph Urban's Mar-a-Lago
John Loring

*The Epic of Gilgamesh and the Political Symbolism
of the Periphery*
Mark Jarzombek

Empire of the Senseless
Edward Mitchell

Observations
Heyward Hart, Rail Diwali, and Arko Datto

Abodes of the Goddess
Tapati Guha-Thakurta

*Fabricating Community and Public Space in Kolkata's
Durga Puja*
Swati Chattopadhyay

The American Architect on a Cosmic Stage
Bryan E. Norwood

War, Visuality and the Militarized City
Zahra Malkani and Shahana Rajani

"The only Hellenistic ruin of great interest in Jordan"
Miguel John Versluys

Colonial Prescriptions in Paris
Samia Henni

Notes on the Delphi Method: Toward a Definition
Curtis Roth

Northern/Cape: The Fibrils of an Asbestos History
Hannah Le Roux

*Empire, Networks and Systems: The International Insti-
tute of Tropical Agriculture, Nigeria, 1948 to 1980*
Itohan Osayimwese

Ten Love Letters
Jimenez Lai

*The Architecture of Communicating Vessels:
The Second World in the Age of Capitalist Realism*
Vladimir Kulić

Constructs
Fall 2019
Yale School of Architecture, 2019

<u>Editor</u> Nina Rappaport
<u>Designer</u> Hyo Kwon

Letter from the Dean
Deborah Berke

Conversations with Visiting Professors
Francis Kéré, Teddy Cruz, Fonna Forman,
Fernanda Canales, Henry Squire, David Gissen

Clouds, Bubbles, and Waves
Reviewed by Yoko Kawai

Japan: Archipelago of the House
Reviewed by Trattie Davies

Natures of Ornament
Reviewed by Richard Hayes

Stalking the Ganges Water Machine
Anthony Acciavatti

Cesar Pelli Remembered
Fred Clarke, Phil Bernstein, Aaron Betsky,
Marion Weiss, Aude Jomini

Heart of the City by Alexander Garvin
Reviewed by Daniel Rose

Swimming to Suburbia by Craig Hodgetts
Reviewed by Joe Day

*Designing Social Equity and Aesthetics Equals
Politics by Mark Foster Gage*
Reviewed by Matthew Allen

Jean Sielaff Remembered

Remembering Stanley Tigerman
Peter Eisenman, Emmanuel Petit, and Robert Somol

Constructs
Spring 2020
Yale School of Architecture, 2020

<u>Editor</u> Nina Rappaport
<u>Designers</u> Hyo Kwon and Goeun Park

Letter from the Dean
Deborah Berke

Conversations with Visiting Professors
Cazú Zegers, Ruth Mackenzie, Walter Hood,
Anupama Kundoo, Stella Betts

From Continuity to Infinity and Beyond
Reviewed by Paul Makovsky

Changing with the Seasons
Reviewed by Mary Carole Overholt

My Bauhaus: Transmedial Encounters
Reviewed by Romy Golan

Teaching Design and Culture: Core One Round Table
Nicholas McDermott, Brennan Buck, Joyce Hsiang,
Miroslava Brooks, Michael Szivos, Nikole Bouchard

Cesar Pelli Remembered
Fred Clarke, Phillip Bernstein, Aaron Betsky,
Marion Weiss, Aude Jomini

Bauhaus Futures
Reviewed by Tim Altenhof

Perspecta 52: Ensemble
Reviewed by Swamabh Ghosh

Space Settlements
Reviewed by Lydia Kallipoliti

*Graphic Assembly: Montage, Media, and Experimental
Architecture in the 1960s*
Reviewed by Lee Stickells

Eisenman Milanese: The Dialectics of Site
Alan Plattus

Still Facing Infinity:
The Tectonic Sculptures of Erwin Hauer
August 29 – November 16

Beginning in 1950, very early during my studies in sculpture, I developed a series of works that were modular in structure and featured surfaces that were continuous. They also showed the potential for continued progression toward infinity.

This is Erwin Hauer (1926–2017) describing the development of the first *Continua*, the modular planar sculptures that launched his career. The Austrian-born sculptor would go on to patent these designs, develop the technologies to manufacture them, and install several screen walls based on the designs for churches in Vienna. Based on the attention these screens generated, he was awarded a Fulbright Scholarship and came to the United States in 1955. Josef Albers invited him to join the faculty of Yale in 1957 where he taught until 1990. Hauer's patented designs for the *Continua* were licensed to the New York firm Murals Inc. and marketed throughout the United States and six other countries. The light-filtering screens were embraced and used as brise soleil and room dividers by modern architects including Edward Durell Stone, Gordon Bunshaft, and Florence Knoll. After about twelve successful years, the manufacture of the architectural screens ceased due to changing market conditions.

Organizer and Curator Enrique Rosado
Organization Team at Erwin Hauer Studios Bienvenido Hernandez, Clara Pysh, and Anthony Rosado
Installation Team Ryan Cyr, Jaime Kriksciun, Lauren McNulty, Matthew Shropshire, Charlie Taylor
Exhibition Graphics Erin Hyelin Kim
Support Knoll International, Spinneybeck, and Hyde Park Mouldings Inc.
Director of Exhibitions Andrew Benner
Exhibitions Coordinator Alison Walsh

garden – pleasure
December 2 – February 8

This project is an inhabitable scenography of seven "figures" sustaining a gathering space and a framework for engagement with the New Haven arts community. Over the course of two months, collaborating artists and community partners developed the space through a series of treatments in, of, and around this analogical garden. The cast of participants includes local art and educational organizations, students in the Yale Schools of Music, Drama, Art, and Architecture, graduates of these programs, and other independent contributors with connections to New Haven. Between events and performances, the scenography and seasonal treatments rest, inviting visitors to shed normative gallery behavior and explore, inhabit, rearrange, and play with the flexible elements of the garden.

Designers Daniel Glick-Unterman, Ian Donaldson, and Carr Chadwick
Contributors Aiv Rubino, Alteronce Gumby, Bek Andersen, Camille Altay, Carr Chadwick, Daniel Schlosberg, Derek G. Larson, DIS, Dwight Portocarrero, Dymin Ellis, Jesse Limbacher, Kate Hawkins, Kenneth Joseph, Max Menschen, Maria Romero, Martin Elliott, Melanie Moser (Mlle NOISE), Mooncha, Precious Musa, Sara Emsaki, Seth Thompson, Syd Bell, Sydney Lemmon, Toto Kisaku, Will Wheeler, Yo-E Ryou
Community Partners Artspace New Haven, Showmotion Inc., St. Luke's Steel Band, St. Martin de Porres Academy Orchestra
Director of Exhibitions Andrew Benner
Exhibitions Coordinator Alison Walsh

Swissness Applied
January 9 – February 15

Swissness Applied is a transcultural analysis of New Glarus that represents challenges in architecture and urban design as examples of current social transformations in global contexts. It is one of several towns in America founded by European immigrants that adapt the architecture to the image of their heritage. The exhibition questions the translation of the cultural image in architecture and illustrates through representational means the results and potential outcomes of the New Glarner Swiss-themed building codes.

Curation Nicole McIntosh
Exhibition Design Jonathan Louie and
    Nicole McIntosh, Architecture Office
Graphic Design Philipp Koller, Burrow
Yale Organizers Angela Lufkin and David Turturo
Supported by Consulate General of Switzerland
    in New York, Texas A&M University, Yale
    School of Architecture, YSoA PhD Dialogues, Yale
    MacMillan Center European Studies Council
Director of Exhibitions Andrew Benner
Exhibitions Coordinator Alison Walsh

Models, Media, and Methods:
Frei Otto's Architectural Research
February 20 – May 2

This exhibition, curated by Georg Vrachliotis, opens the archive of celebrated German architect Frei Otto (1925–2015), on the 60th anniversary of his guest professorship at the Yale School of Architecture. Frei Otto's way of thinking was distinguished by experimentation. His research manifested an "operative aesthetics" oscillating between the precision of scientific tools and artistic imagination, material culture, and media technology. His techniques of modeling, drawing, measuring, and evaluation formed the basis of a creative experimental culture embodied in the Institute for Lightweight Structure and its publications, which furthered architecture research as interdisciplinary and innovative knowledge production as well as served as the starting point for a collective discourse on the future of society.

Curator Georg Vrachliotis
Project Assistance Senay Memet
Exhibition Design Lukas Bessai, Florian Bengert,
    and Marcel Schaaf
Project Management Claudia Iordache
Restoration of Archival Material Isa Strunk
Reproduction of Archival Material Christoph Engel
    and Bernd Seeland
Graphic Design Floyd E. Schulz, WTHM-Buro Fur
    Gestaltung Berlin
Video Editor Iden Sungyoung Kim
Lending Institutions Sudwestdeutches Archiv fur
    Architektur and Karlsruhe Institute of Technology
Director of Exhibitions Andrew Benner
Exhibitions Coordinator Alison Walsh
Fabrication Eric Sparks, True Line Productions
YSoA Exhibition Graphics Erin Kim
Catalog Nina Rappaport, David Reinfurt, and
    Bryce Wilner
Installation Team Ryan Cyr, Alyse Guild,
    Jaime Kriksciun, Lauren McNulty,
    Matthew Shopshire, Charlie Taylor

**Making Space for Resistance:
Past, Present, Future**
August 29 – October 5

2019 marks the 50th Anniversary of the Alcatraz Island Occupation, an act of Indigenous resistance compelling justice and recognition of tribal self-determination and sovereignty. American Indians from across the nation seized the former federal prison for 19 months to recharge American Indian rights and spotlight the broken promises made by the United States to Indian Tribes.

Various political movements were burgeoning nationwide to advance Indian rights through forms of spatial resistance. The act of occupying Alcatraz highlighted a demand for the federal government to honor unfulfilled treaties that guaranteed lands, waters, resources, education, housing, and health care to American Indian peoples in exchange for the cession of millions of acres that formed the United States.

Making Space for Resistance highlights past, present, and future visions of Indigenous space connected to objectives expressed during the Occupation of Alcatraz Island in 1969.

Exhibition Design and Creative Direction
    Indigenous Scholars of Architecture, Planning, and
    Design (ISAPD) at Yale
Curators Charelle Brown, Anjelica Gallegos, and
    Summer Sutton
Exhibited Architects and Designers Chris Cornelius,
    Kenny Glass, Douglas Miles, Joe Big Mountain,
    Adrian Standing Elk Pinnecoose, Mariah Quincy,
    Charlene and Frank Reano, Charlotte and
    Percy Reano, Santiago X

In Search of Space-Time
October 10 – November 15

In Search of Space-Time is an immersive installation that presents viewers with an ode to the Bauhaus, a spin of the *Vorkurs* wheel inflected with the bush-hammered walls of Rudolph Hall and the hyperbole of digital media. It seeks to present the process and products of a Bauhaus pedagogy applied in the twenty-first century. It is intended not as a display of student works, but an archive of attempts to capture space-time, the synthetic apotheosis of the *Bauhausler*.

In a world where type and image have become our lingua franca, we turn to the Bauhaus on its centennial to celebrate and reinterpret its design lessons. We look back as we look forward, forever revolving in space-time suspension.

Exhibition Credits Fall 2018 seminar Bauhaus @ 100
    taught by Trattie Davies and Eeva-Liisa Pelkonen
Student Curators and Participants Diego Arango,
    Lani Barry, Samuel David Bruce, Emily Cass,
    Sunny Cui, Kerry Garikes, Tianyu Guan,
    Orli Hakanoglu, Kelley Johnson, Louis Kourshouris,
    Jen Lai, Mengi Li, Rachel Mulder, Iven Peh,
    Maya Sorabjee, Luke Studebaker, Jingqiu Zhang

reVEIL
December 2 – January 2

According to the U.S. Census Bureau, more than half of the service industry's workforce is foreign-born. Under the veil of cook, cashier, sales rep, dishwasher, cleaning lady, delivery guy, janitor, or valet, the service industry initiates this workforce into the hidden realm of work— the backdrop for survival.* Surroundings are subverted by the need and desire to conduct daily rituals, creating an internal network of covert spaces. *reVEIL* celebrates this collective identity and the act of sustaining it within a foreign territory.

*survival: n. The continuance of a custom after the conditions in which it originated or which gave it significance have passed away

Curation Michelle Badr, Alex Pineda, Limy Fabiana
    Rocha, Brenna Thomson
Installation Assistance Andrew Benner, Allison Walsh,
    and the Yale School of Architecture Gallery Team
Supported by Tsai Center for Innovative Learning at
    Yale, La Casa Latino Cultural Center, the Council on
    Latin American and Iberian Studies (CLAIS) at
    the MacMillan Center, Yale School of Architecture

In Memoriam
February 20 – March 28

Along with poets and gravediggers, architects belong to a very small group of people who might be expected to take a professional interest in how they are memorialized after death. And many architects have indeed designed their own tombs, from Mimar Sinan to Le Corbusier.

In Memoriam presents tombs that architects design for themselves, in the past and the present, as a starting point in a conversation about memory and death in architecture. What do we as architects choose to remember and honor—and how?

Curators Luka Pajovic, David Schaengold, and
    Jerome Tryon
Participants Barozzi Veiga, Adolf Loos (as drawn by
    David Schaengold), Deborah Berke, Samantha Mink,
    Fala, Erin and Ian Besler, Miles Gertler, Lina Malfona,
    Mark Foster Gage, Enric Miralles (as drawn by
    Jerome Tryon), Cazu Zegers, Sam Jacob, John Soane
    (as drawn by Jerome Tryon), Clark Thenhaus,
    Alan Maskin and Juan Ferreira of Olson Kundig,
    Igor Bragado, Christopher Wren (as drawn by
    Luka Pajovic), OMMX, Aniket Shahane, Barclay and
    Crousse, Ariane Lourie Harrison, Young & Ayata,
    Joze Plecnik (as drawn by Luka Pajovic), Peter Baldwin,
    Margaret McCurry and Stanley Tigerman, Brian
    Delford Andrews, Bryan Cantley, Mimar Sinan
    (as drawn by David Schaengold), Níall McLaughlin,
    Flores and Prats, Stephen Slaughter and Aaron Tkac,
    Neri&Hu
Acknowledgements Kurt Forster, Mark Foster Gage,
    Mary McLeod, Margaret McCurry, Bryan Fuermann,
    Kyle Dugdale, Andrew Benner, Alison Walsh, the Yale
    Architecture Gallery Staff

Lectures

Atmospheres for Enjoyment: Sports, Resorts, and Weather of All Sorts
Janet Marie Smith, John Spence[1], and Ann Marie Gardner[2]

ROTOR: Messages from the Field
Renaud Haerlingen[3]

Unwalling Citizenship
Teddy Cruz[4] and Fonna Forman[5]

Architecture & Cinema: Studio MK27 in Motion
Marcio Kogan and Gabriel Kogan

Private Spaces, Shared Structures
Fernanda Canales[6]

A Time of Heroics: Paul Rudolph and Yale, 1958–1965
Robert A.M. Stern[7]

Looking for Role Models in All the Wrong Places
Alexandra Lange[8]

The Bauhaus: Complexities and Contradictions at Modernism's Foremost Art School
Dietrich Neumann[9]

Anni and the Feline: Performative Investigations into Selected Bauhaus Fabrics and Their Design Context
Judith Raum

Indigeneity in Contemporary Architecture
Tammy Eagle Bull

Work Report
Francis Kéré[10]

***Mondo Nostro*: The 21st Century Urgency**
Cazú Zegers[11]

LANDSCAPE/ARCHITECTURE: Bridging the Divide Between Nature and Culture
Margie Ruddick[12]

Building Knowledge
Anupama Kundoo

Saving America's Cities in the Suburban Age: Taking Another Look at Urban Renewal
Lizabeth Cohen

Authenticating Figures: Algorithms and the New Politics of Recognition
Wendy Chun

The Social and Ecological Aspects of the Psychology of Place (postponed)
Mindy Thompson Fullilove

Recent Work (canceled)
Walter Hood

Thirteen Ways (canceled)
Stella Betts

Models, Media, and Methods: Frei Otto's Architectural Research (canceled)
Georg Vrachliotis

DS+R: Recent Work (canceled)
Liz Diller

My Bauhaus: Transmedial Encounters
J. Irwin Miller Symposium
October 31 – November 02

The two-day event brings together art and architecture historians, artists, and curators to investigate the history and legacy of the legendary institution and its key protagonists through various transdisciplinary perspectives and presentation formats. The title hints at the focus of their respective inquiries and the symposium at large: mining the Bauhaus as a site of transmedial experimentation.

Keynote Address Dietrich Neumann, Brown University; and Judith Raum, artist
Organized by Henry Balme and Shira Miron
Introductions Bryson Tedford, Columbia University; Sandra Neugärtner, University of Erfurt; Jungmin Lee, Harvard University; Julia Medina, Princeton University; Eeva-Liisa Pelkonen, Yale University
Pedagogy Brenda Danilowitz, Albers Foundation; Zeynep Çelik Alexander, Columbia University; and Craig Buckley, Yale University
Medium Wallis Miller, University of Kentucky; Oliver Botar, University of Manitoba; and Jeffrey Saletnik, Indiana University
Drawing Demonstration Alec Purves, Yale University
Technic Sarah Meister, Museum of Modern Art; Spyros Papapetros, Princeton University; and Nicola Suthor, Yale University
My Bauhaus Anoka Faruqee, Yale University; Katie Dixon, Powerhouse Arts; Enrique Ramirez and Blake Marques Carrington, Yale University and Pratt Institute
Closing Remarks Fatima Naqvi, Yale University

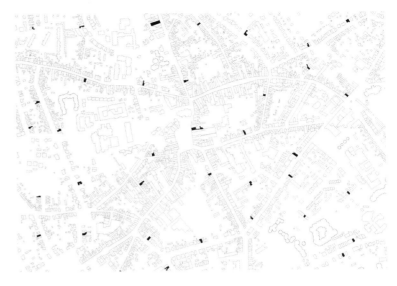

Beyond the Visible: Space, Place, and Power in Mental Health (postponed until Fall 2020)
J. Irwin Miller Symposium
March 26 – March 28

This symposium seeks to make designers and architects aware of their capacity to improve access to and perceptions of mental health. One-quarter of the global population will suffer from mental illness at some stage of life. The built environment—the setting where we live and work—therefore becomes an urgent site for addressing mental health. The rise of urban inequality has huge impacts on access to mental health services. This symposium will explore issues of mental health at three scales: the hospital, the home, and the city. This inaugural symposium is part of a long-term initiative at Yale, building on the work of the Yale Mental Health Colloquium which took place in 2019. In engaging an interdisciplinary team to explore these themes, we can begin to understand how practitioners influence design methods for mental health in the built environment.

Keynote Address Mindy Thompson Fullilove, The New School
Introduction Christopher Payne, artist
The Hospital Christian Karlsson, Karlsson Arkitekter; Kelechi Ubozoh, mental health advocate; Martin Voss, PSYCH.RAUM; Jason Danziger, PSYCH.RAUM
The Home Alison Cunningham, Yale University; Earle Chambers, Albert Einstein College of Medicine; Sam Tsemberis, Pathways Housing First; Hannah Hull, artist
The City Nupur Chaudhury, New York State Health Foundation; Bryan Lee, Colloquate; Molly Kaufman, University of Orange; Phillip Corlett, Yale University
Collaborations Joel Sanders, Yale University; Antonia Caba, Yale University; and Judith Lichtman, Yale University

PhD Dialogues

PhD Dialogues is a series of events organized by the second-year students of the PhD in Architecture program. Ranging from lectures by invited guests to presentations of student research and panel discussions, these events are the public voice of the YSoA PhD cohort.

Coordinators Nicholas Pacula and Jia Weng

- Coordinators' Reflection
During the past academic year, the PhD Dialogues series put on six events intended to give members of the PhD cohort an opportunity to share their research programs and the voices involved with the YSoA community. In all, we heard from four members of the PhD cohort, one member of the History of Art PhD cohort, three Yale faculty members, and three guests from other universities.
— Nicholas Pacula and Jia Weng

Caryatids, Cults, and Chorai
Soffia Gunnarsdottir, PhD Candidate in the History of Art, and David Turturo, PhD Candidate in Architecture, in conversation with Anthony Vidler, Visiting Professor, Yale School of Architecture

Killing Time
Zach Michielli, PhD Student in Architecture, in conversation with Caleb Smith, Professor of English and American Studies, Yale University

Marking Place
Summer Sutton (Lumbee), PhD Student in Architecture, in conversation with Tammy Eagle Bull (Oglala Lakota), FAIA, NCARB, AICAE

Rethinking Reproduction: Copying after Print
Michael J. Waters, Assistant Professor of Art History and Archaeology, Columbia University

Wendy Chun, Professor of New Media, Simon Fraser University, in conversation with Amy Kapczynski, Professor of Law, Yale Law School

Ornaments of the Third Republic: Antonin Raguenet and the *Matériaux et documents d'architecture et de sculpture*
Gary Huafan He, PhD Candidate in Architecture

Brown Bag Lunch Series

Equality in Design's Brown Bag Lunch Series is a platform that invites a diverse body of voices and perspectives to expand design-related discussion beyond our curriculum. Typically small gatherings around coffee and packed lunches in Rudolph Hall's 4th-floor pit, Brown Bag events allow for informal conversation between students and guests.

Coordinators Lillian Agutu, Katie Lau, Araceli Lopez,
    Rhea Schmid, Max Wirsing
Contributors Emily Cass and Maya Sorabjee

● Coordinators' Reflection
Several of our Brown Bag events this year focused on practice: on striking balances between work life and home life, on shaping a workplace where your values are reflected in the culture, and on the journeys that our mentors went through to find those work environments. In a moment when the job market is suddenly much more precarious and previously held notions of our next steps are shifting, it feels timely to reflect on our guests' advice. What changes do we want to see in architectural practice and what tools do we have or need to create to make those changes?
    — Lillian Agutu, Katie Lau, Araceli Lopez,
      Rhea Schmid, Max Wirsing

Fall 2019

f-architecture's latest
Gabrielle Printz, Co-founder of Feminist f-architecture, co-editor of *Beyond Patronage: Reconsidering Models of Practice*

EiD Debate
"Is providing architectural services to underserved communities more likely to benefit local residents, or lead to gentrification and displacement?" Moderated by Elisa Iturbe, Critic, Yale School of Architecture

Spring 2020

Hong Kong Protests: The Art of Hubbing and Mobile Political Space
Helen Siu, Professor of Anthropology and former chair of the Council on East Asian Studies, Yale University

Charting a Path: Launching a Next Generation Design Firm
Ming Thompson, Co-founder of Atelier Cho Thompson

Henning Larsen: Practice and Culture
Amalia Gonzales Dahl and Sara Rubenstein, Associate Partners at Henning Larsen

MED Program

Started in 1967, the Master of Environmental Design (MED) program remains one of the first and most relevant and intensive of its kind. The program has long addressed the environment as the aggregate of objects, conditions, and influences that constitute the constructed surroundings. Today that environmental scope informs many crucial contemporary issues from climate change and global inequality to digital ubiquity and the influence of large sociotechnical organizations.

Director Keller Easterling

Enrolled Students Holly Bushman '20, Cayce Davis '21, Alex Kim '21, Mary Carole Overholt '21, Laura Pappalardo '21

- Director's Reflection
A return to the origins of the Master of Environmental Design program, started in 1967, energizes an activist conception of design. This year's graduating student completed a thesis combining architectural evidence and literary texts to uncover some obscured stories about an East German city. The four students in the first-year cohort have worked on post-WWII Polish architecture and urbanism, activist feminist spaces at multiple scales from the 1960s to the present, spatial consequences of social media, and territorial claims of an indigenous tribe in the city of São Paulo.
— Keller Easterling, Professor

Kurt Leucht's master plan for Stalinstadt included four Wohnkomplexe or "living complexes," collections of apartments interspersed with civic buildings. The façade above belongs to Wohnkomplex II, photographed July 2019.

Interview with Holly Bushman

<u>Retrospecta 43</u> Could you explain a bit about the process of developing a research proposal and carrying it out through the duration of the program?

<u>Holly Bushman</u> I was really struck by the duality of Eisenhüttenstadt—a place that's been described as "Socialist Disneyland" and promoted through a strange type of post-socialist tourism—and the experiences of people who live there while in the precarious position of waiting for an asylum decision. Something about that tension put the kernel of an idea for a research project in my mind, and in my application to the MED program I proposed studying Eisenhüttenstadt as a sort of contemporary metaphor for post-socialist Germany and more thoroughly investigating social and political dynamics in such communities.

<u>R43</u> Could you elaborate a bit more on your decision to pursue ideas of urban cultural identity within Eastern Germany in particular?

<u>HB</u> "Urban cultural identity" is an interesting way to consider the content of the project! I think my approach has always been to isolate each aspect and understand where they talk to each other, but not seek out one cohesive urban cultural identity in Eisenhüttenstadt. Put another way, the planning of model cities in the GDR provides a rare opportunity to scrutinize nearly all decisions, bureaucratic, architectural and otherwise, that went into the development of a community.

The building in the background is an *Ankunftszentrum* or "arrival center," a facility for those who have filed for political asylum.

<u>R43</u> What does the city of Eisenhüttenstadt look like today in terms of its economy and the built environment?

<u>HB</u> Many of the heavy industry projects of eastern Brandenburg were closed or considerably downsized following the Reunification. The EKO steel plant has seen its workforce dip significantly, though it is still in operation. Many of its former employees have taken jobs in other parts of Germany, and many young people have left for cities like Berlin or Leipzig with no plans to return. Currently Eisenhüttenstadt's population is about 25,000, less than half of what it was in 1989. As a result, unused housing, particularly that constructed in the 1980s, is being razed as the cost of maintenance far exceeds the cost of demolition.

<u>R43</u> What can architects and urban planners learn from the history of cultural and economic transformation at Eisenhüttenstadt?

<u>HB</u> Certainly we can learn from Eisenhüttenstadt that the idea of neoliberalism as "triumphant"—vis a vis Fukuyama or any of the scholars of the 90s so quick to declare the West the "winners" of the Cold War—was a total fallacy; we can observe that the purported benevolence of West German capitalism did not ultimately serve many citizens of the former GDR. What I argue in the conclusion of my thesis, however, is that what we should be paying attention to is not the lessons of the past but the present and immediate future of Eisenhüttenstadt. We can see in this community the intersection of some of the most pressing challenges facing Europe today: the emergence of a base for a far-right political party, the fallout of those reunification policies, the legacy of a major migration crisis. Architects and planners talk a lot about how architecture can address those challenges. They seem very interested in designing new spaces and less interested in understanding the existing built environment as complicit in the political and social conditions that make the position of the asylum seeker so precarious in the first place.

Steel remains central to Eisenhüttenstadt's economy. "This steel was made here. It will stay that way!"

The PhD program offers two tracks of study: History and Theory of Architecture and Ecosystems in the Architectural Sciences. Both aim to educate teachers capable of effectively instructing future architects and to contribute new knowledge to their fields of inquiry and to culture at large. Students develop outstanding research skills and a deep grasp of critical issues facing the built environment past, present, and future.

Director of Doctoral Studies Joan Ockman
Program Assistant M. Surry Schlabs

Ecosystems in the Architectural Sciences

The environmental and societal challenges faced today require a deeper understanding of the interrelationships between humans and non-human living systems. In the Ecosystems track, students develop experimental frameworks to design and test novel material and/or informational approaches to urban and architectural interventions. Research related to living systems behavior and socio-cognitive processes is prioritized.

Coordinator Anna Dyson
Students Christina Ciardullo, Katherine Ball, Phoebe Mankiewicz, Mandi Pretorius

- Coordinator's Reflection

Arch 2236b Design/Data/Biology: Theories of Ecosystemic Intelligence examines frontiers opening up across design disciplines as a result of the revolution in biotechnology and bioinformatics. This spring we explored historical relationships and critical ways in which architecture, agriculture, and urbanism have shaped our genetics, as well those of other species, while questioning identities that separate built environments from extended ecosystems. We read Boden, Latour, Guattari, Nagel, Haraway, and others.
— Anna Dyson, Hines Professor of Sustainable Architectural Design and Professor of Forestry and Environmental Studies

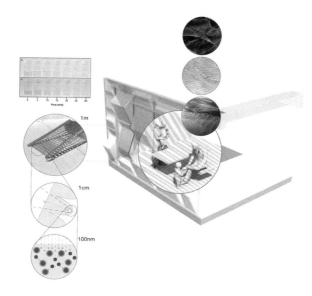

Reimagining Built Ecologies through the Medium of Water. Mandi Pretorius (PhD). An interdisciplinary collaboration integrating water-energy processes into the design of transparent building enclosures.

History and Theory of Architecture

The History and Theory track provides sound training in architectural history and historiography, preparing candidates for careers in university teaching, cultural advocacy and administration, museum curatorship, and publishing. Students work on research topics related to diverse cultural and geographic contexts, benefiting from a wide array of disciplinary perspectives within YSoA and the wider university. Alongside their dissertation work, they acquire solid teaching experience and take part in an engaged and supportive scholarly community.

Coordinator Joan Ockman
Students Gary Huafan He, Theodossios Issaias, Iris Giannakopoulou Karamouzi, Ishraq Khan, Zachariah Michielli, Nicholas Pacula, Gabrielle Printz, Summer Sutton, Aaron Tobey, David Turturo, Jia Weng

- Coordinator's Reflection

Arch 552/554/3300b is a spring-semester seminar required of first- and second-year PhD students in History and Theory and open to MED and other advanced students. This spring's course, The Idea of an Avant-Garde in Architecture: Reading Manfredo Tafuri's *The Sphere and the Labyrinth,* addressed the role and function of avant-gardes in architecture. We asked whether the concept of avant-gardism is still relevant today or should be consigned to the dustbin of 20th-century ideas. A close reading of Tafuri's book provoked debates about both architectural ideology and writing history. Despite library closures, students carried out impressive independent research on their chosen topics.
— Joan Ockman, Vincent Scully Visiting Professor of Architectural History

Arch 552/554/3300b Student Papers

The Ruin in Postwar Poland: Former Avant-Gardes, Posters, and a New Whole
Cayce Davis (MED)

Raoul Hausmann, the 'Architect': Architecture without Architects, the Adventures of the Avant-Garde, and the Politics of the Senses
Iris Giannakopoulou Karamouzi (PhD 1)

This Historiographic Image: Manfredo Tafuri's Use of the Diagram in The Sphere and the Labyrinth
Nicholas Pacula (PhD 2)

Techniker Vor! *The Origins of Martin Wagner's Realpolitik*
Gabrielle Printz (PhD 1)

Manhattan, the Abstraction of the Ground, and the Contradictions of Avant-Garde Practice in the Quintessential Commercial City
David Scurry (MArch 2)

Into the Laboratory of New Relations
László Moholy-Nagy and His Biotechnique
Jia Weng (PhD 2)

Interview with Gary Huafan He

<u>Retrospecta 43</u> How did you decide to leave professional practice and take on a deeper study of architecture in the PhD program?

<u>Gary Huafan He</u> I was always writing pieces for myself, not as a part of a discourse. Eventually I realized that it would benefit—not my practice—but my own thinking about architecture, if I just had some time to develop something that interested me and allowed me to engage the scholastic community at a deeper level.

<u>R43</u> You've studied Antonin Raguenet's work—would you outline its significance?

<u>GH</u> His main project, *Matériaux et documents d'architecture et de sculpture*, is a documentation of Parisian, European, and world architecture from 1872–1914. During this time Raguenet catalogs—by etching in eight-page monthly pamphlets—over 14,000 ornaments that he's found, almost as if specimens in a natural science museum, dissecting architecture into over 150 categories. I would say its primary significance is its "empirical method" of curating the ornaments in a progressive chronology. You can still go visit them in Paris, and you'll see that he's drawn them quite accurately, either on-site or from photographs. He also includes project information, like client and street address.

Matériaux et documents d'architecture et de sculpture. Vase with Symbolic Figures, from the Museum of Luxembourg, Paris. A. Injalbert, Sculptor. Issue 455, page 7. Vase.

<u>R43</u> How do you relate 19th-century ornament to an organicist conception of history?

<u>GH</u> This is sensitive because organicism and romanticism are often tied to totalitarian politics, but we cannot study 19th-century ornament without getting into these ideas. In 1868 [César Daly] writes that the word "style" in architecture is equivalent to the word "species" in natural history and should be used with as much rigor, so there's a direct and heavy-handed appeal to this organicist metaphor, which has real

consequences for what we believe to be a more normative idea of progress. For example, when you speak in organicist metaphors, you immediately denote distinctions like normal and healthy growth against unhealthy, grotesque, or mutated.

Matériaux et documents d'architecture et de sculpture. Antique capital from the Palatine Hill in Rome. Issue 349, page 2. Chapiteau.

<u>R43</u> Why does an empirical approach to ornament and modernity feel important to you?

<u>GH</u> The discourse on ornament today remains trapped in theoretical maneuvers, so that we always return to abstract dichotomies like honesty versus illusion, or highly charged terms like criminality, degeneracy, and mutation. These concepts have become a common way to talk about ornament, but they are also very moralistic terms. The conceptual cost of that is quite great. It's preventing us from looking at this period (which I think is quite rich), but also it's causing unnecessary angst and political bickering over things that actually require more understanding. Often we don't even know how we got these emotions regarding ornament. And so Raguenet is important precisely because he doesn't write. His project is wholly visual, but also offers the idea that the visual is political in its own right—that it can speak for itself in a way that I think hasn't been allowed to happen in this discourse in the last 100 years.

<u>R43</u> For designers today, what is the significance of 19th-century ornament and Raguenet's work?

<u>GH</u> What he made was a mirror of his time, and so I hope that architects who read my thesis will come to see their own work as also being a mirror of what's around them, refracting everything. And maybe there's a creative way to think about refraction that isn't about controlling it. That would be interesting to me—that's new, and frees you from the idea of a critical project that either fails or succeeds, and on which your whole value and integrity is based. I think it's about going beyond the myth that one can somehow change incrementally the whole structure of society through aesthetic production—that is something that needs to be challenged.

Yale Urban Design Workshop

The Yale Urban Design Workshop (YUDW) provides a forum for faculty and students from the School of Architecture and other professional schools at Yale to engage in the study of issues, ideas, and practical problems in the field of urban design. Since its founding in 1992, the YUDW has worked with communities across the state of Connecticut, providing planning and design assistance on projects ranging from comprehensive plans, economic development strategies, and community visions to the design of public spaces, streetscapes, and individual community facilities. The YUDW's clients include small towns, city neighborhoods, planning departments, Chambers of Commerce, community development corporations, citizen groups, and private developers.

Founding Director Alan Plattus
Director of Research Marta Caldeira
Director of Design Andrei Harwell
Postgraduate Associate Martin Man
Student Fellows Cristina Anastase, Gioia Montana
    Connell, Jincy George Kunnatharayil, David Scurry,
    Alex Mingda Zhang

- Director's Reflection
The YUDW was established in the early nineties, at a time when Yale and the School were engaged in initiatives to better connect with New Haven and its local communities. It was conceived as a vehicle for mobilizing the faculty and students of the School, along with other professional schools at Yale, to collaborate with underserved communities in the region in work and research on real world issues of community development, public space, mobility, housing, and sustainability. Since that time, the core mission of the YUDW has expanded to include both local and global projects where design is deployed as a form of community organizing to create local identity, opportunity, capacity, and shared community spaces.
— Alan Plattus, Professor

DesignCase Lindholmen, an initiative in Gothenburg, undertaken by Fusion Point in collaboration with YUDW.
Project Team: Daphne Agosin, Gioia Montana Connell, Jincy George, Martin Man, David Scurry.

Center for Ecosystems in Architecture

The Center for Ecosystems in Architecture (CEA) is a joint academic initiative between the Yale School of Architecture and the Yale School of the Environment. CEA unites researchers across multiple fields in the development of transformative systems for the built environment. The Center's research purposefully prioritizes the requirements of living ecosystems towards the development of innovative methods for buildings and cities that support bio-diversity with clean energy, water, and materials. CEA takes a unique approach in leveraging the ongoing explosion of knowledge in life sciences and information technology to fundamentally re-inform the built environment process, which is currently the sector responsible for the largest consumption of toxic, non-renewable resources and greenhouse gas emissions globally.

<u>Founding Director</u> Anna Dyson
<u>Director of Engineering Research</u> Nick Novelli
<u>Director of Communications</u> Hind Wildman
<u>Research Scientists</u> Naomi Keena and
    Mohamed Aly Etman
<u>Student Fellows</u> Christina Ciardullo,
    Phoebe Mankiewicz, Mandi Pretorius,
    I-Ting Tsai

- Director's Reflection

Yale CEA supports interdisciplinary research teams that aim to radically rethink our relationships to each other and to other living systems. Taking a post-anthropocentric approach towards the innovation of methods for metabolizing energy, water, airflow and material life cycles, in the last year we have solidified international and local partnerships. In line with our research into new ways of seeing and communicating, we became a core partner with the United Nations World Environment Situation Room (WESR) Project, which will deploy our BEEM Lab and SEVA (Socio-Ecological Visual Analytics) technologies for a series of immersive rooms in Africa, Europe and Asia.

    — Anna Dyson, Hines Professor of Sustainable Architectural Design and Professor of Forestry and Environmental Studies

UNEA-4 Exposition
Ecological Pavilion for the United Nations Environment Program (UNEP) International Assembly, Nairobi, Kenya

CEA collaborated with international partners to install an experimental exposition featuring solar, water, and material innovations being co-developed by collaborators in the U.S. and across multiple African countries. The pavilion itself was constructed from the largest 3d-printed structure in the world made from post-agricultural bamboo, and the systems being exhibited featured products and environmental systems cultured from multiple waste streams, such as mycelia, rice, coconut, and soya.

<u>Exhibition Partners</u> Yale School of Engineering and
    Applied Science, University of Rwanda, Strawtec
    Building Solutions Ltd., Willow Technologies, Ecova-
    tive Design, SHoP Architects, Branch Technologies
    and Oak Ridge National Lab, Kenyatta University,
    University of Nairobi

UNEP Ecological Pavilion, Nairobi, Kenya, demonstrates novel biomaterials and on-site, solar-driven construction methods from post-agricultural waste bio-products.

A collaboration with the University of Nairobi, Kenyatta University, Willow Technologies, Oak Ridge National Labs, SHoP Architects, Ecovative, and NEWT at the Yale School of Chemical and Environmental Engineering

Triple Decker

Jim Vlock First Year Building Project
Completed Fall 2019

Since 1967, the Yale School of Architecture has offered its first-year students the opportunity to design and build a structure as part of their graduate education. Unique among architecture schools, this program is mandatory for all members of the cohort. The Building Project typically results in a dwelling for people experiencing homelesness in an underprivileged neighborhood.

Director of Building Project 1: Research, Analysis, Design Alan Organschi
Director of Building Project 2: Construction Adam Hopfner
Faculty Kyle Bradley, Amy Lelyveld, and Joeb Moore
Selected Proposal Designers Malcolm Rondell Galang, Louis Koushouris, April Liu, Louisa Nolte, Leyi Zhang

This year's project takes inspiration from New Haven's traditional housing stock. In particular, the triple-decker—a type of house divided into three stacked units—provides the DNA of the design and allows it to fit in harmoniously with its neighbors by matching their silhouette and setback from the street.

The apartments each have the same floor plan, but are rotated to allow entrance from a common entry staircase. The rotation of the stacked units also provides acoustic separation between the apartments.

The large porch spaces provide generous views out over the backyard and street but are screened with wooden slats to protect residents from being overly visible, a primary concern discovered during student interviews with New Haveners experiencing homelessness.

A photovoltaic array is installed on a roof specially designed with the optimum slope and solar orientation, generating low-cost and sustainable power.

Entry seen from Plymouth Street

Stair as it reaches the third-floor unit

The overall massing and arrangement of the house fits in well with the neighborhood context.

Design Contents

micro climate
pear region
water + urban
shade of tree

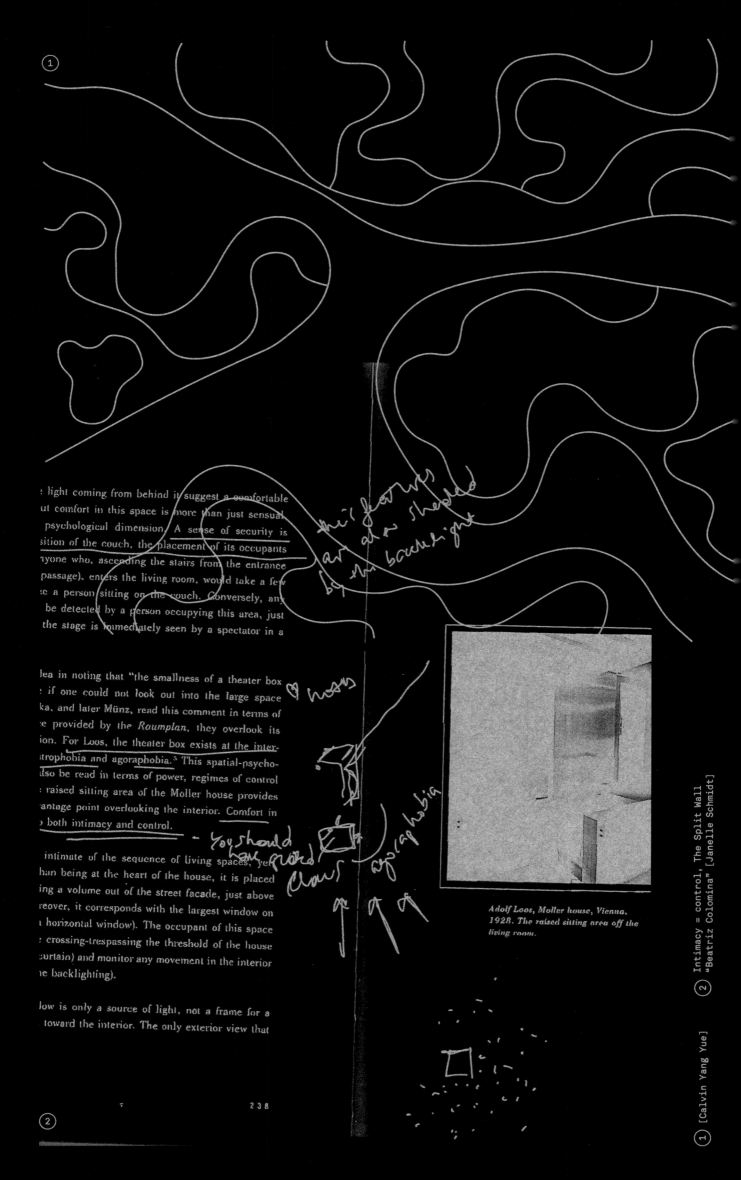

: light coming from behind it suggest a ~~comfortable~~
ut comfort in this space is more than just sensual
psychological dimension. A sense of security is
sition of the couch, the placement of its occupants
nyone who, ascending the stairs from the entrance
passage), enters the living room, would take a few
e a person sitting on the couch. Conversely, any
be detected by a person occupying this area, just
the stage is immediately seen by a spectator in a

lea in noting that "the smallness of a theater box
: if one could not look out into the large space
ka, and later Münz, read this comment in terms of
e provided by the *Raumplan*, they overlook its
ion. For Loos, the theater box exists at the inter-
trophobia and agoraphobia.[5] This spatial-psycho-
lso be read in terms of power, regimes of control
: raised sitting area of the Moller house provides
antage point overlooking the interior. Comfort in
both intimacy and control.

intimate of the sequence of living spaces, yet
han being at the heart of the house, it is placed
ing a volume out of the street facade, just above
reover, it corresponds with the largest window on
horizontal window). The occupant of this space
: crossing-trespassing the threshold of the house
curtain) and monitor any movement in the interior
e backlighting).

low is only a source of light, not a frame for a
toward the interior. The only exterior view that

Adolf Loos, Moller house, Vienna,
1928. The raised sitting area off the
living room.

① [Calvin Yang Yue] ② Intimacy = control, The Split Wall "Beatriz Colomina" [Janelle Schmidt]

③ Image Object: Plaster + Tension [Janelle Schmidt]

④ A simple diagrid reveals opportunities in plan

③

④

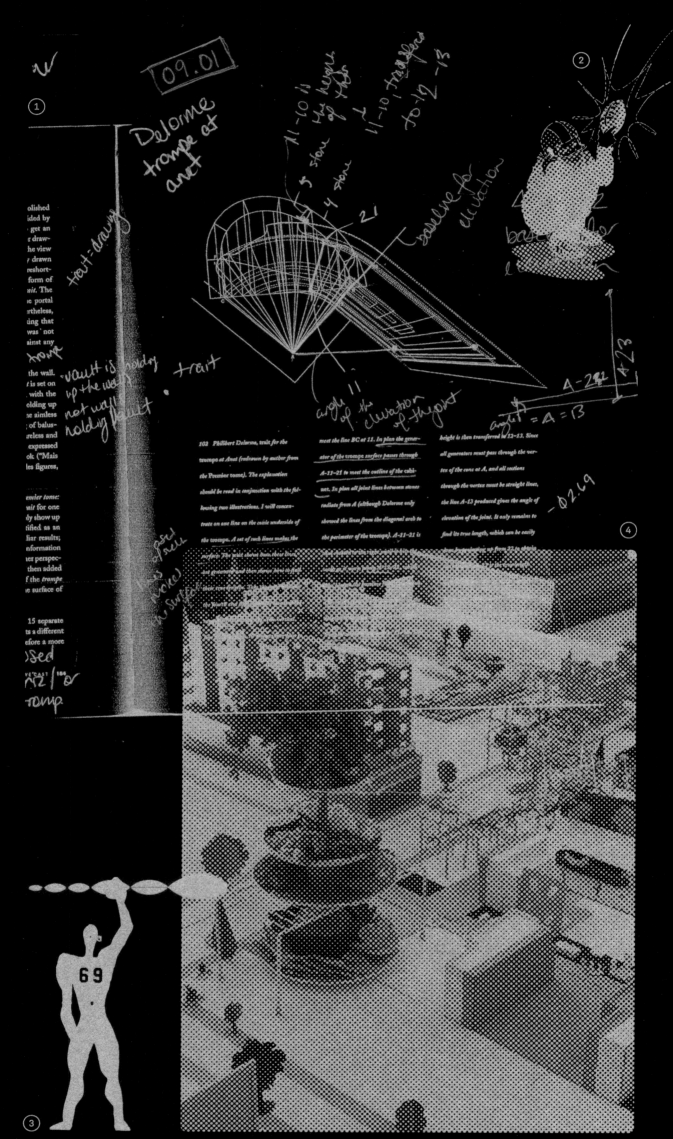

① A = ?!?, The Projective Cast "Robin Evans" [Janelle Schmidt]

② @ysoa.flagfootball [Paul + Abby]

③ The Modulor was made to play

④ Mid Review model of Cocina de Tanda smelling bad from sunlight [Hojae Lee]

Summer 2020

COURSEWORK

This course is an immersion into architectural representation, visualization, history, and theory. Students are introduced to techniques and conventions for describing the space and substance of buildings and environments.

FACULTY
Miroslava Brooks, John Blood, and Kyle Dugdale

MANIFESTO
Lillian Agutu

SPACE POSITIVE
Students examine the volumetric, tangible, and plastic qualities of interior space.

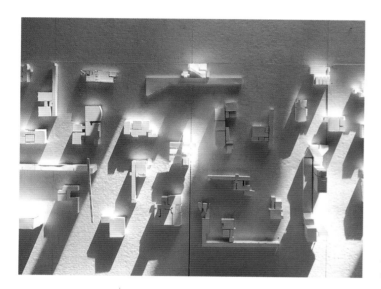

Architecture exists in a bubble / It starts at Architecture school / Where we'll read about/by/from / Staffed with working architects / Critiqued by more (other) architects / A fair enough amalgamation / Sometimes the bubble will expand / And one will find themselves somewhere abroad / A different culture, a different speed / Maybe mostly looking up, / Or down at dead stones / A world view of shapes / Then comes the architecture office / Where one will know a lot / but nothing at the same time / Meetings will be had / Hours long, necessary evils / Yet there is a lot to be said / And done / If Architecture stopped being so insular / Find an interdisciplinary approach / With socio-political contemporary life / And carve out a presence, not just as a luxury / But as a vital proponent / So that instances when real impactful positions, / for architects, and urbanists, and planners / Such as the / Secretary / Of / Housing / Development / Goes to a complete oxymoron / A dimwitted brain surgeon / There would be more of an outcry / By an elephant trying to fly / But that can only happen / If Architecture entangles with the world at large / Ensuring even in the tangled mess / It is a constant presence

1262c   Computation Analysis Fabrication

This course investigates and applies computational theories and technologies through design and fabrication of full-scale building components, implementing static, parametric, and scripted modeling paradigms, structural and sustainability analysis, and fabrication technologies.

FACULTY
Amir Karimpour

THE CASCADE
Rebecca Commissaris and
Yuhao Gordon Jiang

Two trapezoidal modules are cast in concrete multiple times and stacked to form this outdoor staircase. The initial idea: to encourage the body to move. The subsequent idea: to create a path for rainwater to flow continuously from top to bottom.

This studio is the first of four core design studios where students bring a wide range of experiences and backgrounds to the School. Exercises introduce the complexity of architectural design by engaging problems that are limited in scale but not in the issues they provoke. Experiential, social, and material concerns are introduced together with formal and conceptual issues.

The projects in this studio ask students to develop their work primarily through spatial and formal exploration. Typically this development follows the analysis of a building site, the enumeration of a building program, and/or the constraints of construction. Instead, this studio begins with the experiential, organizational, and social capacity of built form and volume. Site, program, and construction are considered after and defined in response to each student's initial approach to space and form. As each project develops, students examine the implications of a given formal strategy and how it reveals a building's many effects on the world around it.

JURY
Emanuel Admassu, Daisy Ames, Annie Barrett, Andrew Benner, Marta Caldeira, Sean Canty, Debbie Chen, Angie Co, Trattie Davies, Peggy Deamer, Ivi Diamantopoulou, David Gissen, Sophie Debiasi Hochhäusl, Abigail Coover Hume, Mariana Ibanez, Elisa Iturbe, Jaffer Kolb, Max Kuo, Ane Gonzalez Lara, Jason Lee, Sergio Lopez-Pineiro, Jennifer Newsom, Nate Hume, Alessandro Orsini, Megan Panzano, Miriam Peterson, Bryony Roberts, Violette de la Selle, Aniket Shahane, Rosalyne Shieh, John Szot, Ryan Thomas, Ming Thompson, Aaron Tobey, Lexi Tsien-Shiang, Hans Tursack, Ife Vanable, Yasmin Vobis, Andrew Witt, Emmett Zeifmann, Peter Zuspan

FACULTY
Brennan Buck (coordinator), Nikole Bouchard, Miroslava Brooks, Joyce Hsiang, Nicholas McDermott, Michael Szivos

■ COORDINATOR'S REFLECTION
The studio is tasked with covering the fundamentals of representation while also providing an expansive, imaginative and even destabilizing start to the MArch program; we start with a completely open strategy of appropriation and interpretation and end up with large, detailed plan and section drawings. For the most part, students were able to take speculative ideas about space and organization and manifest them as concrete forms described clearly through drawing. My biggest hesitation in retrospect is the isolated way that each format of representation is dealt with—the mediums we work in inevitably overlap and the conventions of representation are open for redesign as well.
— Brennan Buck, Senior Critic

Brennan Buck
Lillian Agutu
Claire Hicks
Jessica Kim
Sarah Kim
Calvin Liang
Brian Orser
Jingyuan Qiu
Joshua Tan
Christina Chi Zhang

Nikole Bouchard
Brandon Brooks
Katie Colford
Audrey Fischer
Sangji Han
Suhyun Jang
Caroline Kraska
Abraham Mora-Valle
Dominiq Oti
Andrew Spiller
Tian Xu

Miroslava Brooks
Claudia Carle
Lauren Carmona
Jingfei He
Yushan Jiang
Morgan Anna Kerber
Veronica Nicholson
Kevin Steffes
Yang Tian
Calvin Yang Yue

Joyce Hsiang
Lindsay Duddy
Chocho Hu
Zhanna Kitbalyan
Paul Meuser
Gustav Nielson
Wenzhu Shentu
Diana Smiljkovic
Yuan Iris You
Hao Xu

Nicholas McDermott
Audrey Hughes
Zishi Li
Perihan MacDonald
Yikai Qiao
Jack Rusk
Abby Sandler
Janelle Schmidt
Jun Shi
Timothy Wong
Jessica Jie Zhou

Michael Szivos
Adare Brown
Sam Golini
Hannah Mayer Baydoun
Meghna Mudaliar
Taku Samejima
Hao Tang
Rachael Tsai
Tian Wang
Anjiang Xu
Alex Mingda Zhang

Core Studio

The first project addresses the studio's first architectural medium: the image. Images are often considered peripheral to a discipline with drawing at its core, but image-making is an increasingly crucial mode of production given the proliferation of images in contemporary culture. Beginning with images allows us to consider and engage cultures and contexts outside of the traditional bounds of architecture. Representation is commonly understood to follow from and signify an object or objects, but this assignment reverses that hierarchy, conceiving an object that originates in representation.

Students are asked to construct a three-dimensional image—an image-object—that is both representational and physical. Creating form from image requires reconsideration of the qualities one normally associates with digital images, particularly their flatness and immateriality. The specific spatial and material qualities of the image are then analyzed and used to create three-dimensional, physical objects. This analysis can be perspectival, scenographic, or filmic.

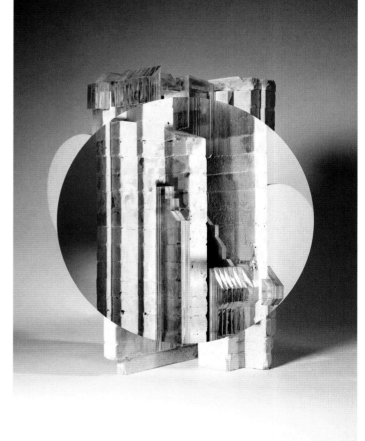

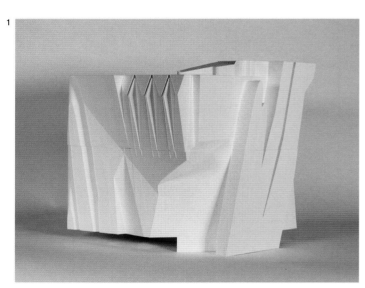

1. Gustav Nielsen; 2. Timothy Wong; 3. Diana Smiljković

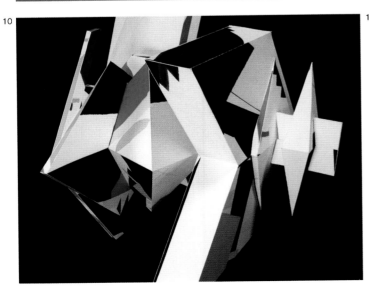

Core Studio

Fall 2019

4. Tianyue Wang; 5. Jessica Jie Zhou; 6. Tian Xu; 7. Veronica Nicholson; 8. Janelle Schmidt; 9. Audrey Fischer; 10. Lindsay Duddy; 11. Lillian Agutu

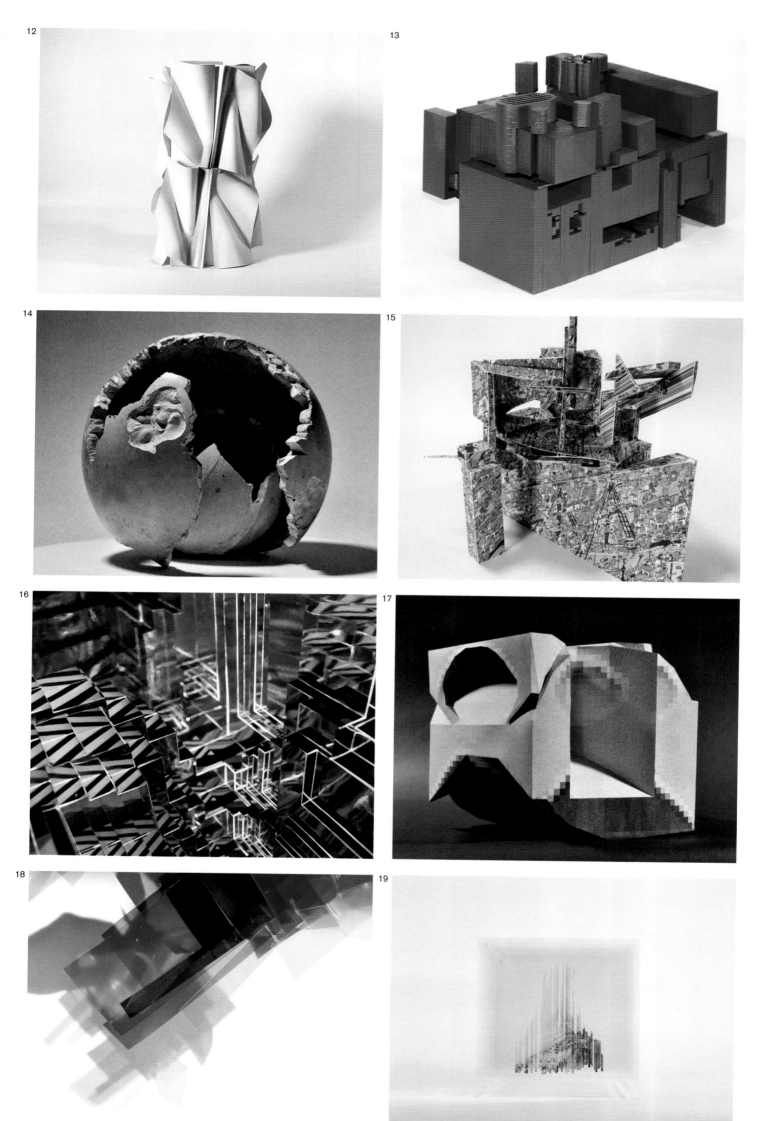

12. Audrey Hughes; 13. Zhanna Kitbalyan; 14. Abraham Mora-Valle; 15. Taku Samejima;
16. Sangji Han; 17. Jack Rusk; 18. Andrew Spiller; 19. Claire Hicks

The second project addresses the studio's second architectural medium: plan. Plans organize space and activity and configure the social relationships in a building. They are typically constrained by site context, distance to daylight and predefined programs, but in this project, plan begins instead with an unconstrained search for organizational possibility through patterns of lines, curves, and figures.

Students are asked to begin by selecting non-architectural drawings or patterns and reading them organizationally, as configurations of volumes and objects and potential activities and relationships. Appropriating material from outside the discipline allows us to engage with a broad array of cultural contexts, audiences, and ideologies. Reading these patterns through a disciplinary lens, as a variation, hybridization, or disruption of conventional plan typologies, allows us to speculate on and discuss their architectural potential.

In keeping with the overall focus on form and space this semester, this project asks students to speculate on the spatial and organizational potential of plan first, allowing those potentials to guide other factors such as tectonic and material development, relation to context, and how the plan is occupied and programmed.

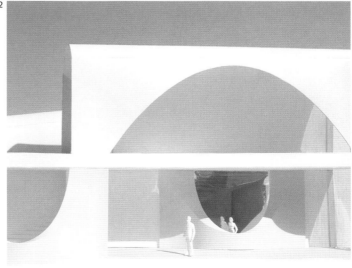

Core Studio

Fall 2019

1. Paul Meuser; 2. Calvin Yang Yue

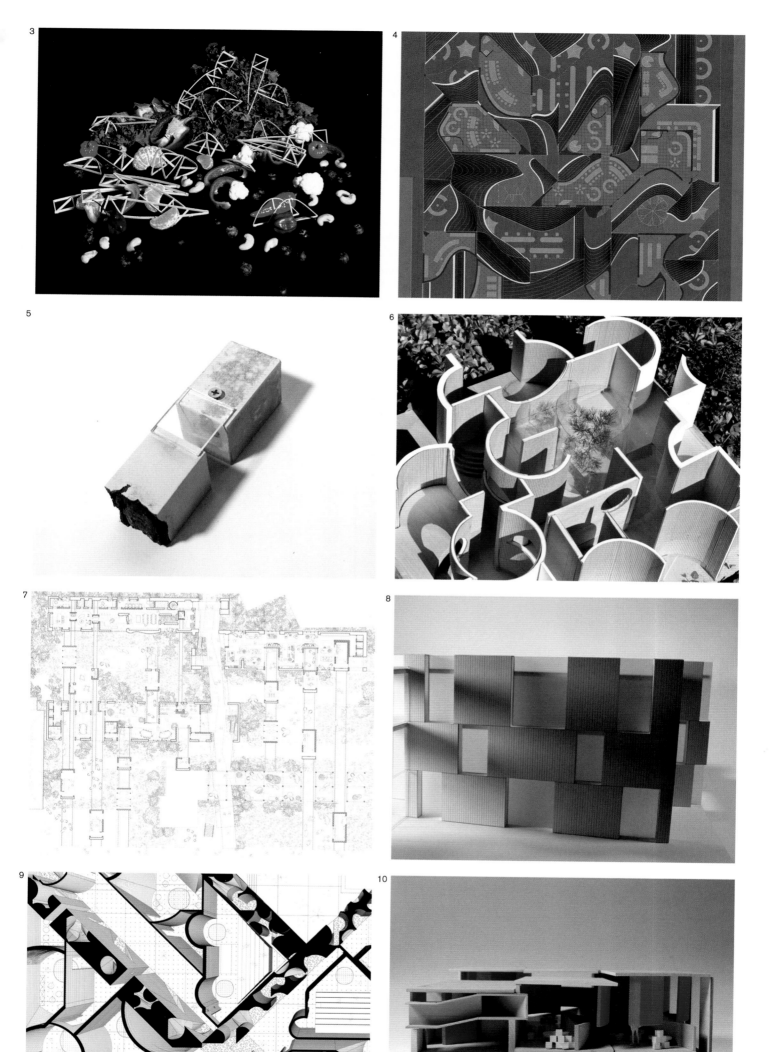

3. Katie Colford; 4. Jingfei He; 5. Caroline Kraska; 6. Abby Sandler;
7. Morgan Anna Kerber; 8. Perihan MacDonald; 9. Yikai Qiao; 10. Joshua Tan

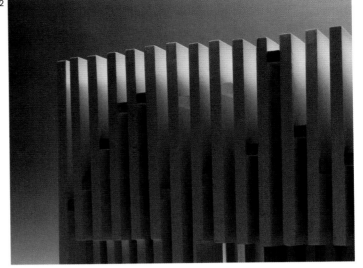

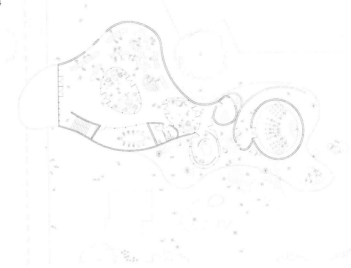

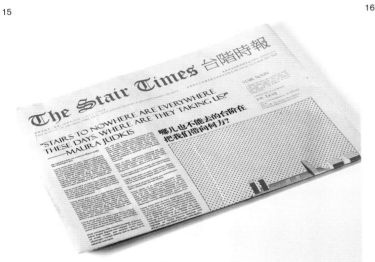

Core Studio

Fall 2019

The final project addresses the studio's third architectural medium: section. The section negotiates two key relationships: building-to-ground and floor-to-floor. Students are asked to expand those possibilities by taking their own work, specifically their plans from Project 2, as found artifacts to be reinterpreted and transformed. Appropriation, by definition, would seem to exclude one's own work as source material, but the things one makes collect over time to form a body of work that can be drawn from and reimagined to produce new work. Employing past ideas, knowledge, or even random artifacts from previous work is one way to give greater depth and substance to a project and reinforce the collective strength of the arguments and artifacts produced.

Sections, like plans, are typically developed in response to site, program, and structure. As with the previous two, this project inverts that sequence, experimenting with the form and relationship of spaces in section first and then speculating on the implications of those strategies through the siting, programing, and construction of the building. A site is selected by each student, program is maintained and adapted from Project 2, and the materiality and structure of the building is designed as students develop the project.

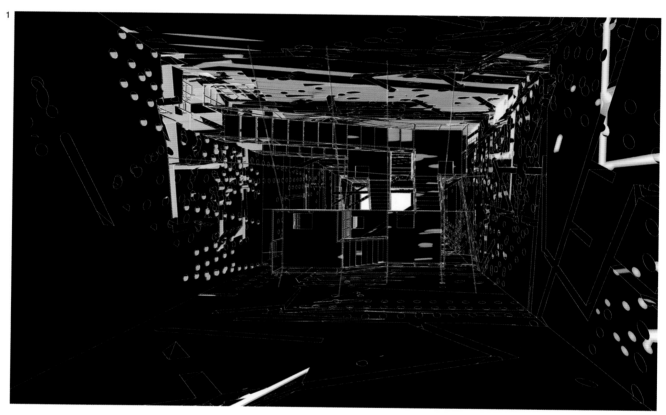

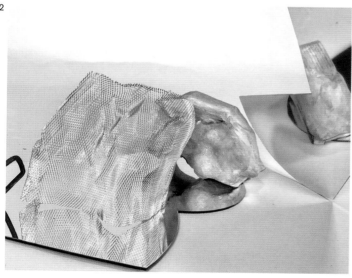

1. Adare Brown; 2. Meghna Mudaliar; 3. Dominiq Oti

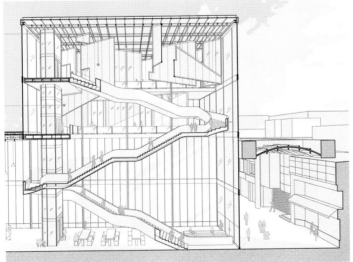

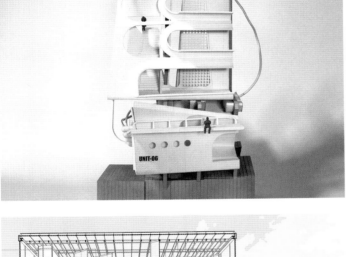

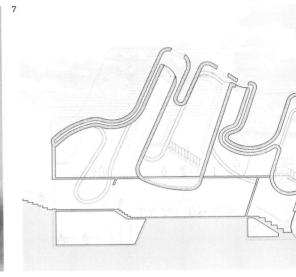

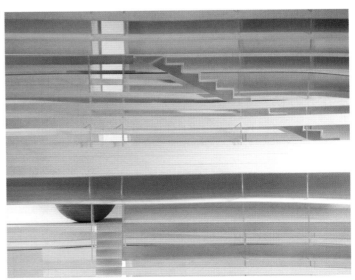

Fall 2019

4. Suhyun Jang; 5. Chocho Hu; 6. Yang Tian; 7. Jun Shi; 8. Zishi Li; 9. Hannah Mayer Baydoun; 10. Kevin Steffes; 11. Anjiang Xu

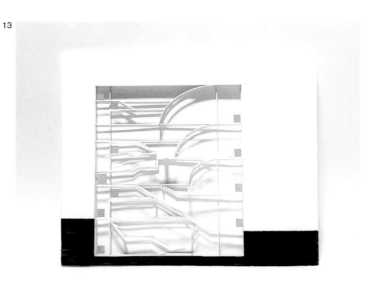

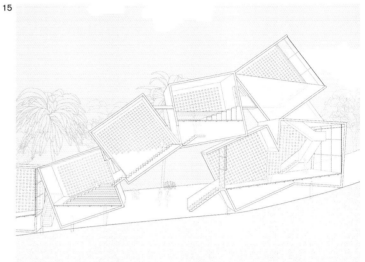

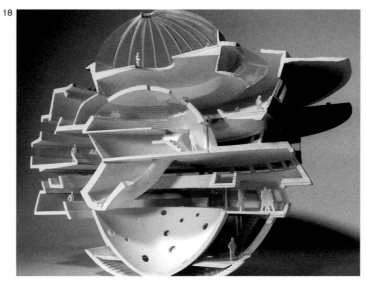

12. Claudia Carle; 13. Hao Xu; 14. Yuan Iris You; 15. Jessica Kim; 16. Sarah Kim;
17. Calvin Liang; 18. Lauren Carmona; 19. Yushan Jiang

As part of the integrated design studio sequence, this studio—the third core studio in the MArch 1 program—concentrates on a medium-scale public building, focusing on the integration of composition, site, program, mass, and form in relation to structure and methods of construction. These issues are addressed through the lens of program during the development of a single project over the course of the whole semester. Interior spaces are studied in detail, and large-scale models and drawings, as well as perspective views, are developed to explore design issues. This studio is intended both as an introduction into the design of civic spaces as well as a larger look into who (and what) forms our local communities and how architects may work to serve their neighbors. Students are asked to develop three Centers for Immigrant Services in three Connecticut towns: Stamford, Hartford, and New Haven.

JURY
Tamar Zinguer, Summer Sutton, Anthony Acciavatti, Marie Law Adams, Benjamin Cadena, Anka Badurina, Andrew Berman, James Bhandary-Alexander, Ceren Bingol, Gerald Bodziak, Anna Dyson, Lisa Gray, Ming Hu, Alicia Imperiale, Theodossios Issaias, Jane Lea, Mae-ling Lokko, Kyle May, Chris McVoy, Jennifer Newsom, Miriam Olivares, Julio Palacios, Mark Rukamathu, Lexi Tsien-Shiang, Constance Vale

FACULTY
Emily Abruzzo (coordinator), Annie Barrett, Iñaqui Carnicero, Peter de Bretteville, Gavin Hogben

■ COORDINATOR'S REFLECTION
This studio asks students to design a public building over the course of an entire semester, and over the last few years we've been looking at civic programs. Most recently, we've been teaming up with local Connecticut organizations working towards specific social justice goals. This year we worked with organizations who provide legal, social, educational, and other services to the many immigrants that make up Connecticut's global community. The results were buildings that demonstrated the complexity of engendering belonging while providing security, creating a landmark while allowing for discretion. Complex questions revolving around welcomeness, transparency, and threshold drove the work.
— Emily Abruzzo, Critic

Emily Abruzzo
Ife Adepegba
Natalie Broton
Jiachen Deng
Paul Freudenburg
Sze Wai Justin Kong
Pabi Lee
Qiyuan Liu
Rachel Mulder
Leanne Nagata
Sean Yang
Sasha Zwiebel

Annie Barrett
Colin Chudyk
Janet Dong
Ian Gu
Niema Jafari
Alicia Jones
Mingxi Li
Dreama Simeng Lin
Naomi Ng
Louisa Nolte
Scott Simpson
Sarah Weiss
Peng Ye

Iñaqui Carnicero
Martin Carrillo Bueno
Xuefeng Du
Kate Fritz
Malcolm Rondell Galang
Anjelica Gallegos
Jiaming Gu
Hiuki Lam
Alex Olivier
Michelle Qu
Ben Thompson
Yuhan Zhang

Peter de Bretteville
Christopher Cambio
Rosa Congdon
Liang Hu
Hyun Jae Jung
Tyler Krebs
Yidong Isabel Li
April Liu
Araceli Lopez
Nicole Ratajczak
Max Wirsing
Leyi Zhang

Gavin Hogben
Isa Akerfeldt-Howard
Ives Brown
Yangwei Kevin Gao
Ashton Harrell
Louis Koushouris
Angela Lufkin
Heather Schneider
Christine Song
Shikha Thakali
Shelby Wright
Stella Xu
Kaiwen Zhao

Core Studio

Fall 2019

THE NEIGHBORHOOD CENTER
Sean Yang

As we approached we could make out the organs of steel, wood, and fabric under a skin of concrete columns and glass. The Center was designed for its own demise, anticipating and awaiting the day its services are no longer needed. Interior rooms are separated from the structure, envelope, and core, simplifying renovation processes needed for its repurposing.

DYNAMIC–PNEUMATIC
Rachel Mulder

This Center is filled with bubble-like inflatable objects that respond to changing programmatic needs and allow occupants a means of escape. The exterior lattice structure provides flexible space and visual connections. Using lightweight, inexpensive inflatables, multiple configurations and arrangements are possible, offering the institution a new visual identity.

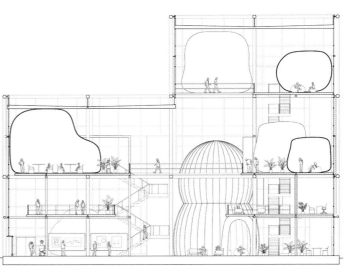

■ FACULTY REFLECTION
This studio provided an opportunity for students to think freely about space—with the challenge that they had to both conceive of a building that made its openness to the public known, while putting themselves in the position of someone who might be apprehensive about the services they are seeking. The results demonstrate this complexity architecturally, as well as in terms of programmatic interpretation.
— Emily Abruzzo, Critic

VILLAGE
Naomi Ng

This project is about a village and its walls. Although pulled apart into three programs (legal, recreational, and educational), each space negotiates with one another by sharing a second skin. A wall is simultaneously the entrance of a building and the façade of another. As the wall's identity becomes blurry, the spaces it defines become hazy too, encouraging navigation and discovery.

CENTER FOR IMMIGRATION SERVICES
Scott Simpson

The Center critiques the neo-classical tropes of American public architecture by removing ornament that 'others' foreign-born constituents and exploring non-hierarchical spaces amidst circular forms. A hypostyle grid of columns suggests distinct rooms across open space. Public programs are centralized while private programs are atomized to provide anonymity and comfort.

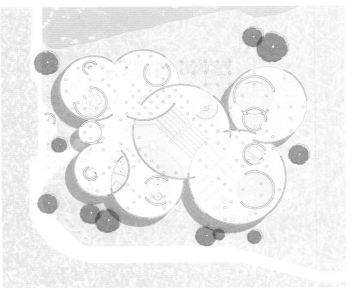

■ FACULTY REFLECTION
This year's studio provoked students to contend with interlaced political, programmatic, and formal questions. An open-ended brief challenged students to consider the social and legal meaning of "immigrant" alongside other dimensions of otherness in the United States, and to take a stance on how architecture—the organization of people, program, and materials in space—facilitates safety, community, and collectivity within a politically tenuous time for its primary audiences.
— Annie Barrett, Critic

This project evokes a sense of belonging, familiarity, and freedom that allows for the expression of one's individuality and heritage. The center provides a framework for learning and mixing of different cultures. Fragments of familiar urban spaces, extracted from around the world, are used to domesticate the site, dismantle cultural hierarchy, and produce unique spaces.

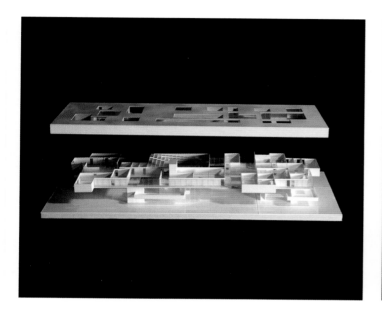

COMMUNITY COURTYARDS
Alex Olivier

Woven between existing buildings in New Haven, the proposed immigration center extends the lines of its context by creating a series of courtyards and pedestrian paths which provide safe outdoor space for the community. Rotating panels allow the building to be open or closed to the courtyards and adjacent sidewalks, blurring the boundaries between inside and outside.

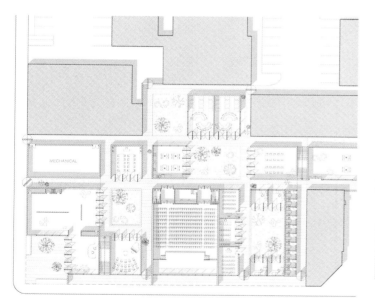

■ FACULTY REFLECTION
I have enjoyed so much the variety of responses and the creativity shown by the students while negotiating with the constraints of a difficult site, transformed in most of the cases into a public space which, besides responding to the given requirements, fosters community engagement. The typologies tested and implemented by the students have been elaborated in a process that challenges conventions and clichés in order to experiment with unfamiliar solutions.
— Iñaqui Carnicero, Critic

WALLS AS SPACES—AN IMMIGRATION CENTER
Araceli Lopez

The center grasps the site boundaries, creating a conceptual stitching between two distinct districts. Program is allocated, penetrating the interior conditions of the walls, creating contracted and compressed spaces. The exterior remains an aggressive force, only penetrated at a vestibule. The project allows users to have a protected yet open area to find escape within.

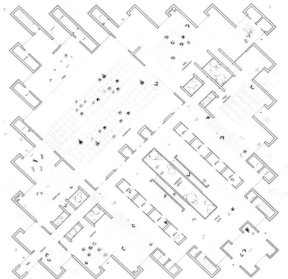

FROSTED ARCHITECTURE
Yidong Isabel Li

Architecturally, frost is defined as the blurring of thresholds and merging of atmospheric qualities. Inspired by Colin Rowe's phenomenal transparency, frost is defined as *literal*—when blurring is achieved through material—and as *phenomenal*—when spaces are implied behind façades. These two concepts are applied to two different axes of the immigration center proposal.

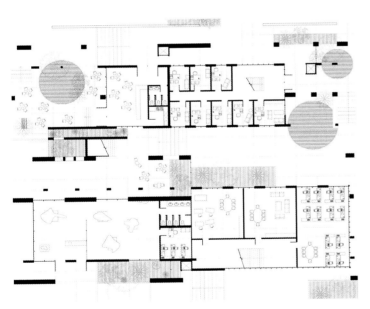
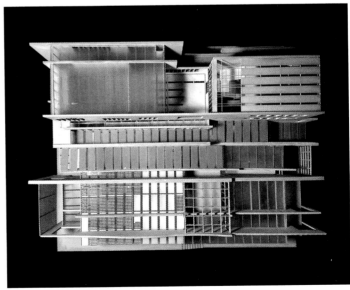

■ FACULTY REFLECTION
As is usual in this studio, and most certainly in my group, the variety of proposals was extraordinary in formal terms, in the understanding of the program, and in each student's unique intentions. This studio, characterized by a social justice program, has been engaging and stimulating for both students and faculty. In this moment of unrest and rising awareness of the history of racial injustice, this theme and these projects resonate.
— Peter de Bretteville, Critic

GARDEN STREET REVIVAL
Louis Koushouris

Harbor Point in Connecticut is a diverse community. This project aims to restore public life at the scale of the city block in reaction to the displacement of vibrant communities built in the early 20th century. The focus is the urban threshold which mediates between building and street, a fundamental condition in growing a neighborhood and establishing a community.

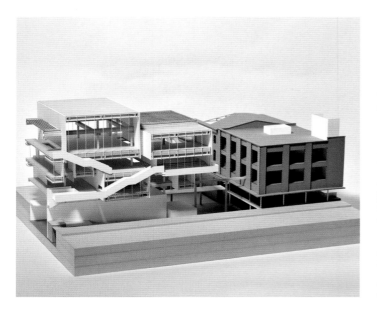
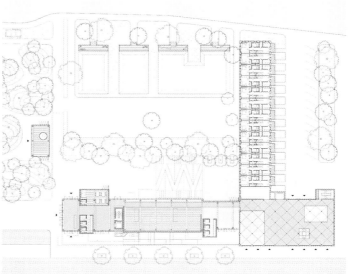

IMMIGRATION CENTER AS AN ACTIVE SHARED SPACE
Shikha Thakali

Identifying the importance of social life and community identity to immigrants, the project proposes an open theater that overlooks a rich garden. Below the theater lies the formal programs that can be discreetly accessed from the street. The project emphasizes multiplicity by creating two distinct realms that can be independently entered and used, but which remain connected.

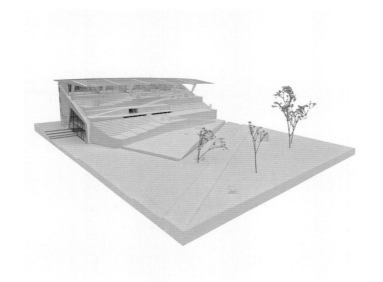
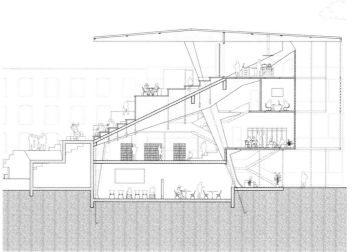

■ FACULTY REFLECTION

The studio tests how architects engage with a pressing social concern—support and justice for immigrant groups. The work was impressive at two levels: first, how students listened to and learned from those directly working in the field; and second, how they situated the particulars of the program in a larger social and cultural horizon—designing schemes that also addressed adaptive re-use, urban agriculture, paths to entrepreneurship, and celebrations of food and health.
— Gavin Hogben, Critic

This studio challenges familiar design strategies and architectural tropes, aiming to expand students' understanding of who architecture can be for—dismantling any architectural norms governing user, location, materials, and processes. This challenge opens up space for the development of new paths of design thinking and a "new" kind of architecture.

The studio considers informal settlements in Burkina Faso—a country in the Sahel region of Africa—as places of inquiry and inspiration. Students learn to approach a space which is unfamiliar to most contemporary architectural practices, and to understand that space and associated building practices as having inherent design ingenuity. In order to understand and experience building materials and community structures available in the neighborhoods and towns of Burkina Faso, the studio visits settlements in Ouagadougou, the capital city, as well as outlying villages. Students are challenged to develop architectural concepts that respond to substandard living conditions, socio-spatial exclusion, and overall lack of infrastructure.

Advanced Design Studio

Fall 2019

JURY
Anna Dyson, Keller Easterling, Yasaman Esmaili, Mimi Hoang, Elisa Iturbe, Lesley Lokko, John Paul Rysavye, Billie Tsien, Tod Williams

FACULTY
Francis Kéré and Martin Finio

PARTICIPANTS
Guillermo Acosta Navarrete, Katharine Blackman, Gioia Montana Connell, Helen Farley, Tianyu Guan, Kelley Johnson, Ho Jae Lee, Deirdre Plaus, Manasi Punde, David Schaengold, Hengyuan Yang

■ FACULTY REFLECTION
Visiting a world that contemporary architecture has largely ignored can't help but affect one's priorities as an architect. Every day we ask ourselves "What does it mean to be human, living on the surface of the earth?" but it's a different question in Ghana than it is in New Haven. Whether we can answer it from where we sit, or from where we stand, is an open question.
— Francis Kéré, William B. and Charlotte Shepherd Davenport Visiting Professor of Architectural Design, and Martin Finio, Senior Critic

This studio traveled to Ouagadougou, Burkina Faso.

STRUCTURE OF EXCHANGE:
AGBOGBLOSHIE *TROTRO* STATION AND MARKET
Deirdre Plaus

Sited in the Old Fadama settlement in Accra, this project explores systems of movement and exchange between the existing market and *trotro* station. The boundary between programs is blurred through their mutual support and use of space, though this symbiotic relationship lacks an infrastructural connection. By investigating the spatial behaviors of street vendors and the larger *trotro* network, the design organizes space through a system of shade and programming to extend the capacity of the market while facilitating flexible movement and exchange.

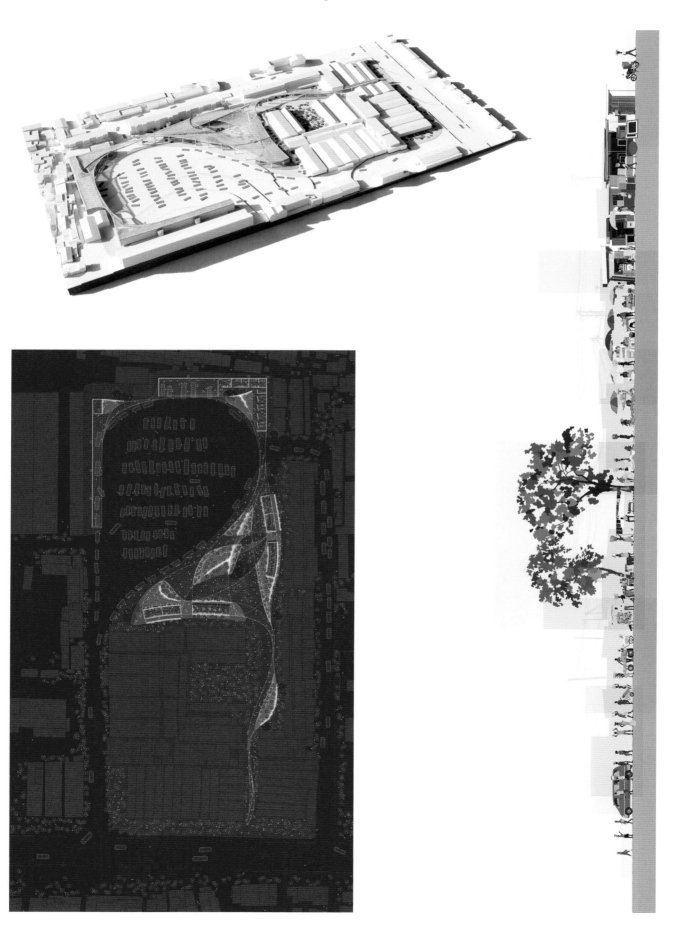

URBAN OASIS
Hengyuan Yang

In reaction to the abandoned structures and food contamination problems in Accra City, the design redefines the exposed structure with a new "productive" enclosure: a new roof for collecting clean rainwater and a planting façade made out of local bamboos with hydroponics techniques. The new building transforms from a blighted ruin into an urban oasis, as a new tool for the community.

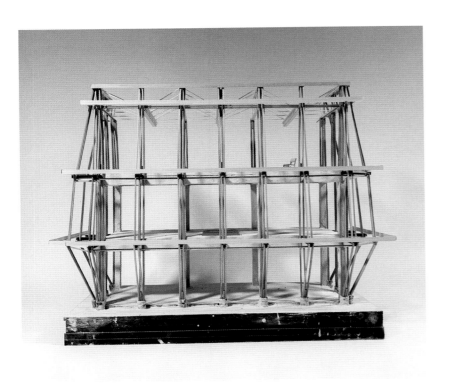

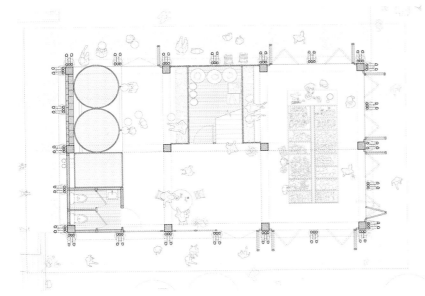

Advanced Design Studio

Fall 2019

The Tijuana-San Diego border region is a global laboratory for engaging the central challenges of urbanization today: ever deeper social and economic inequality, dramatic migratory shifts, urban informality, climate change, the thickening of border walls, and the decline of public thinking. This studio intervenes at this site of localized geopolitical conflict, recognizing that the environmental ravages of border wall securitization are a problem that is shared by both Mexico and the United States. In the current geopolitical moment, how can these two border cities tackle this condition collaboratively, in order to protect their shared water and environmental resources? Students engage this urgent challenge of designing binational environmental cooperation and strategies of coexistence at the border at a time of unprecedented polarization and division. Studio projects are sited in Tijuana, inside the informal settlement of Laureles Canyon. Students design hybrid infrastructural/landscape/architectural interventions for a proposed cross-border commons, with collaborative programmatic activity that transforms these sites into inclusive public spaces and civic/pedagogic nodes.

JURY
Patrick Bellew, Andy Bow, Jordan Carver, Keller Easterling, Rania Ghosn, Alan Plattus, Joel Sanders, Mabel Wilson

FACULTY
Teddy Cruz, Fonna Forman, and Marta Caldeira

PARTICIPANTS
Sara Alajmi, Page Comeaux, Deo Deiparine, Adam Feldman, Rachel LeFevre, Thomas Mahon, Rhea Schmid, Maya Sorabjee, Katherine Todd, Alexander Velaise

■ FACULTY REFLECTION
Our studio was embedded in a site of dramatic inequality and ecological crisis at the international border between San Diego and Tijuana. Committed to designing both physical things and protocols, our interventions included visualizing conflicts, opportunities, and strategies for reorganizing institutional culture. We were excited by the extraordinary quality of student research and design production, critical thinking and narrative, evocative diagrammatics and visualizations, all wrapped around a robust social commitment.
— Teddy Cruz, William Henry Bishop Visiting Professor of Architectural Design, and Fonna Forman, William Henry Bishop Visiting Professor of Architectural Design

This studio traveled to Tijuana, Mexico, and San Diego, United States.

WASTE TO RESOURCES:
LAS FLORES COMMUNITY WASTE BROKERS
Page Comeaux and Rachel LeFevre

A series of open-air bridges placed throughout the site increase pedestrian accessibility and formalize waste management practices, while providing additional space for classrooms, workshops, and businesses. A network of performative structures managed by Community Waste Brokers, community members focused on materially and economically productive waste exchange at material depots, serve the dual function of sorting multiple streams of waste and recouping their values for the benefit of the neighborhoods that they serve.

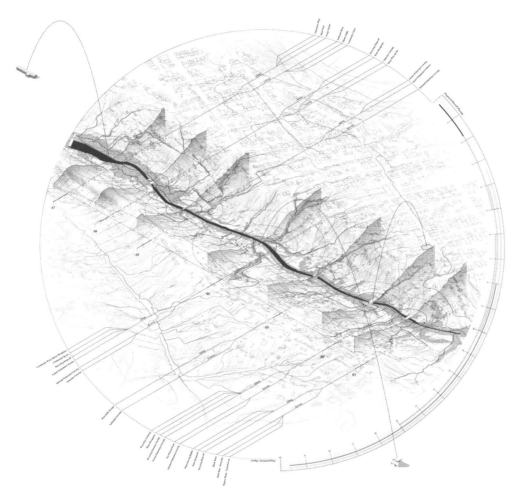

GROWING TOGETHER
Rhea Schmid and Maya Sorabjee

Our project critiques existing manufacturing practices along the United States-Mexico border and prevailing models of land conservation, while proposing an alternative system centered on human-plant coevolution. The architecture that emerges from this process uses strategies of planting and elements of bio-construction to create a productive buffer zone, between developed and undeveloped land, of reconfigurable spaces. Both preventative and remedial, these strategies begin to address local needs, create a sustainable form of development, and protect the watershed.

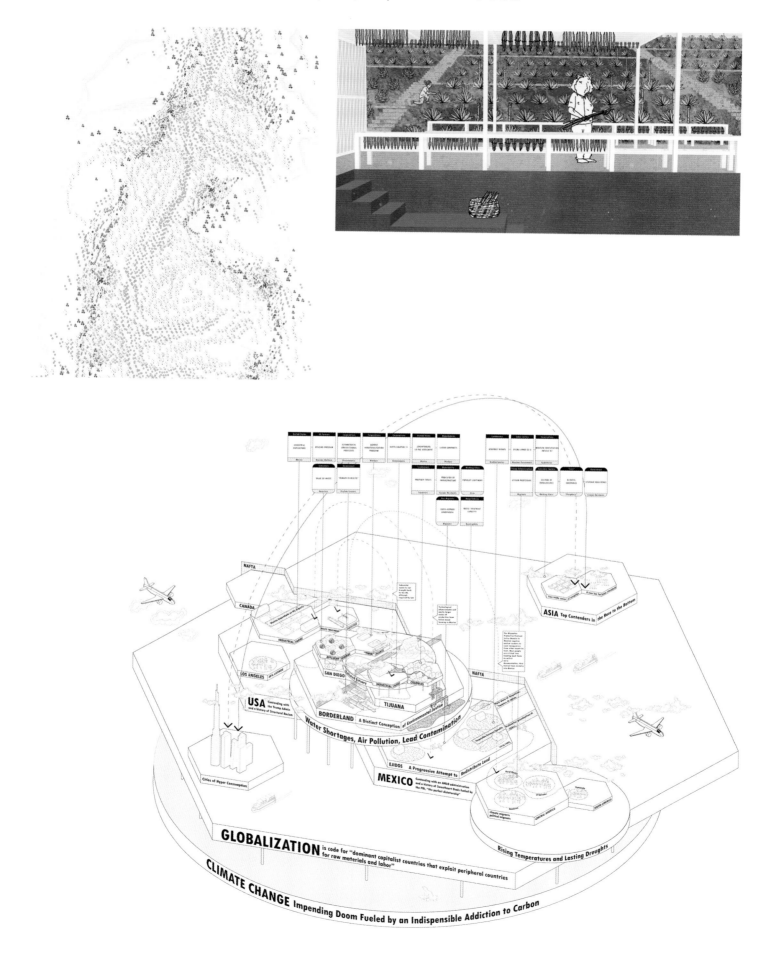

This studio contributes to studies sponsored by Vienna's Academy of Fine Arts and the city's municipal government to reduce the experience of physically debilitating solar heat within Vienna's urban core. The increasing sunshine and heat in Vienna due to a changing climate has inspired a series of landscape proposals to increase vegetation and shade tree-lined areas in the city. Students examine how architecture, in dialogue with urban environmental history, can complement and contribute to this effort to redesign the geography of brightness, darkness, heat, and cooling in Vienna. This architectural, environmental historical method acknowledges how urban reformers and architects once railed against the shadowy streets and courts and dim, dank interiors of this and other cities. Modernist architects attempted to eliminate these subnatural conditions by "solarizing" urban spaces—increasing a populace's exposure to sunlight with terraced, pyramidical, and crystalline architectural forms. Instead, this studio explores how a future Viennese architecture might "gain darkness" as a positive vision of a late-modern city.

Advanced Design Studio

Fall 2019

JURY
Ariane Lourie Harrison, Daniel A. Barber, Enrique Ramirez, Elisa Iturbe, David Turturo, Marta Caldeira, Eva Blau, Rania Ghosn, Graham Harman, El Hadi Jazairy, Eeva-Liisa Pelkonen, George Ranalli, Violette de la Selle, Anthony Vidler, Charles Waldheim, Jia Weng, Elia Zenghelis

FACULTY
David Gissen and M. Surry Schlabs

PARTICIPANTS
Andrew Economos Miller, Yue Geng, Gabriel Gutierrez Huerta, Srinivas Narayan Karthikeyan, Shiqi Valerie Li, Kelsey Rico, Qizhen Tang, Adam Thibodeaux, Alper Turan, Hongyu Wang, Daniel Whitcombe

■ FACULTY REFLECTION
Sun-filled, glazed, and sparkling crystalline aesthetics remain key qualities of a modernized architectural and urban environment. Climate change and increasing urban heat forces us to imagine another modernity—one more cautious about its physical engagements with sunlight and the aesthetics of "radiance." Our studio explored a counter-architecture that cultivates daytime darkness in Vienna, Austria—a city where the municipal government has recently committed to developing an alternative form of environmental modernism.
— David Gissen, Eero Saarinen Visiting Professor of Architectural Design, and M. Surry Schlabs, Critic

This studio traveled to Vienna, Austria.

APARTMENT BLOCK IN VIENNA
Andrew Economos Miller

The singular, solarized aesthetic of the modernist project was enabled through a ruthless program of demolition. This project responds to that demolition by reappropriating modernism's lost materials. By opposing the singularized solar aesthetic with a layered bottom-up material historicity, this architecture counters the power exerted through the modern project; instead proposing an anti-solar aesthetic that allows complex narratives of temporal change to affect the building, controlled by its inhabitants.

1

1. Material method study applied to the New York UN building

URBAN FRAMEWORK IN VIENNA
Shiqi Valerie Li

This project started from the analysis and inversion of Bruno Taut's *The City Crown*, which serves as a compelling monument that offers a sense of orientation at a distance. By editing the existing context and inserting an arcade system, this project proposes an urban framework to support diverse urban development. Ultimately, the framework creates a playful and open-ended labyrinth where wanderers meet, and collective experiences of darkness can take place.

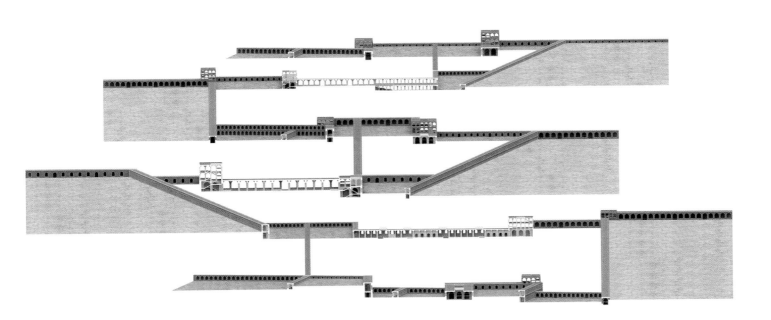

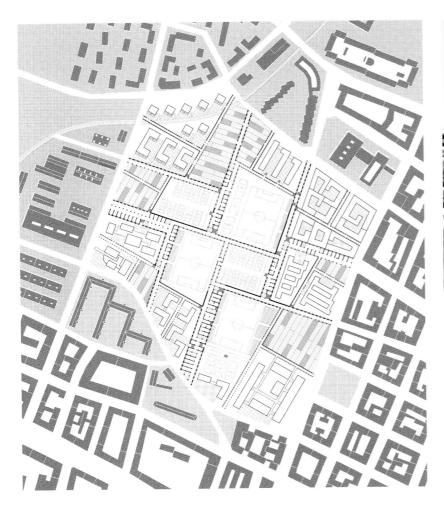

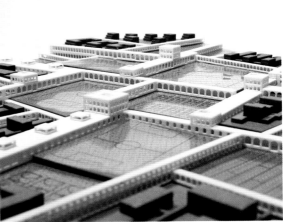

This studio aims to create a place in San Antonio, Texas for the continued cultivation of the musical tradition known as *conjunto*. Literally meaning "ensemble,"
conjunto is tied to a unique hybrid form of Mexican-American folk music that
arose in South Texas in the 19th century. During this era, farm workers of Mexican,
German, and Czech heritage mingled in the fields and shared their musical traditions; *ranchera* songs melded with polka beats, driven by the interplay of the
Spanish twelve-string guitar *(bajo sexto)* and the accordion. However, having lost
the infrastructure of radio stations, record labels, and a Grammy category that
might help maintain its influence, this musical tradition is in crisis.

   Beginning in the 1950s, Lerma's Nite Club in San Antonio was a key
venue for conjunto as it was one of the few clubs at the time that would employ
Hispanic musicians to play to integrated audiences. This studio takes these
developments as a starting point to reimagine Lerma's as the anchor in a new
cultural complex focused on conjunto music.

JURY
Norma Barbacci, Marlon Blackwell, Martin Finio,
Wendy Evans Joseph, Francis Kéré, Miriam Peterson,
Rosalyne Shieh

FACULTY
Billie Tsien, Tod Williams, and Andrew Benner

PARTICIPANTS
Samuel David Bruce, Taiming Chen, Rebecca Commissaris,
Phoebe Harris, Changming Huang, Will James,
Andrew Kim, Jackson Lindsay, Jonathan Palomo,
Christine Pan, Darryl Weimer

■ FACULTY REFLECTION
Conjunto music provided us a bridge across cultures
and a path to encounter the West Side of San Antonio and
its residents. It was challenging and unsettling trying to
connect to this community without setting in motion forces
that could erase what had drawn us there. The students'
responses eventually found forms and programs that effectively counterpointed or even harmonized with the local
narratives and envisioned vibrant and inclusive futures.
   — Andrew Benner, Critic

This studio traveled to San Antonio, United States.

BETWEEN GARDEN WALLS
Samuel David Bruce

San Antonio's West Side bears the divisive impacts of Texas highway development and auto-centric urbanism. This proposal for the preservation of Lerma's nightclub co-opts a piece of abundant Texas infrastructure—the pre-stressed concrete highway beam—to brace the Lerma's façade and infuse classrooms, a recording studio, and a concert venue between three garden walls.

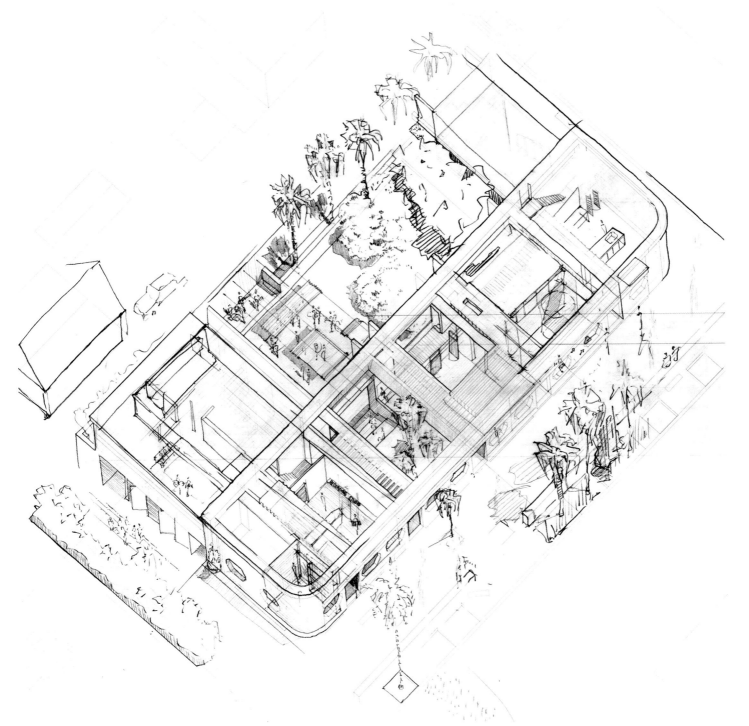

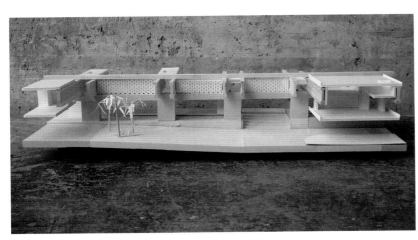

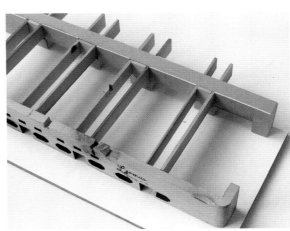

PATHWAY TO CONJUNTO!
Rebecca Commissaris

Anticipating the development of San Antonio waterways as an interconnected park, the project links Alazan Creek to the heritage of Lerma's nightclub. Distinctive structures project into the new pedestrian-only laneway providing specific spaces for activities around conjunto music. A heavy adobe building, set into the earth provides both thermal coolness and a safe, internalized space for lessons. Across a native garden, a lightweight timber dance hall opens up to the warm climate, allowing music to propagate.

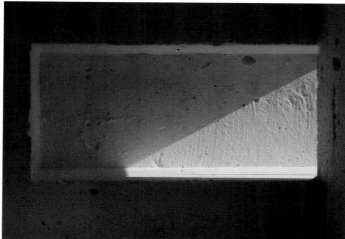

The site of this studio is Greece's Argosaronic Gulf and its varied coastlines. The Saronic Gulf—the body of water with its five islands lying in front of and protecting modern Athens/Piraeus—lies at the heart of the most intense cultural and archaeological tourism in Greece. Every day thousands of visitors are moved through this landscape by bus or boat, only to disappear again. Despite its historical significance, its beauty, and its intensive local use, the Argosaronic gulf is not a favored leisure destination. Thus, there is an intensive urban use of the coastline, which bypasses and ignores not only the archaeological sites, but also the rich landscape. There is little to no opportunity to inhabit the place. This studio proposes an archipelago of interventions whose purpose is to extend the possibilities of tourism for leisure, business, scholarship, the arts, and sport. The projects seek to develop prototypes for a new form of high-value tourism. These prototype designs are for long-term but temporary inhabitation by various special interest groups.

JURY
Emily Abruzzo, Andrew Benner, Fernanda Canales, Peter Eisenman, Kurt Forster, Theodossios Issaias, Eeva-Liisa Pelkonen, Radhika Singh, Henry Squire, Alice Tai, Billie Tsien

FACULTY
Elia Zenghelis and Violette de la Selle

PARTICIPANTS
Daniella Calma, Miguel Darcy de Oliveira Miranda, Gretchen Gao, Michael Gasper, Michael Glassman, Eunice Lee, Matthew Liu, Luka Pajovic, Jewel Pei, Liwei Wang, Paul Wu

■ FACULTY REFLECTION
The semester's pursuit was to coalesce an archipelago of interventions on the archipelago of the Argosaronic Gulf. The studio addressed the tourist industry, reaching into the region's mythological past, confronting its political present, its historiography, and its geographical context. The students accomplished a consolidated, whilst varied, response to the tourist operations in place, with individual projects to refocus and reform them, in a collective undertaking that transcended the sum of its parts.
— Elia Zenghelis, Norman R. Foster Visiting Professor, and Violette de la Selle, Critic

This studio traveled to Athens, Greece.

FLOATING MONUMENT
Jewel Pei

The *Floating Monument* is a traveling museum of facsimiles that brings seasonal exhibitions around the Saronic Gulf. The museum of facsimiles challenges the narrative of a continuous and homogenous Greek culture, resists the package tour experience that prescribes a schedule and narrative, and offers multiple narratives through architectural fragments. The museum invites seasonal tourists to see the multiplicity of these architectural fragments in the context of their sublime landscape.

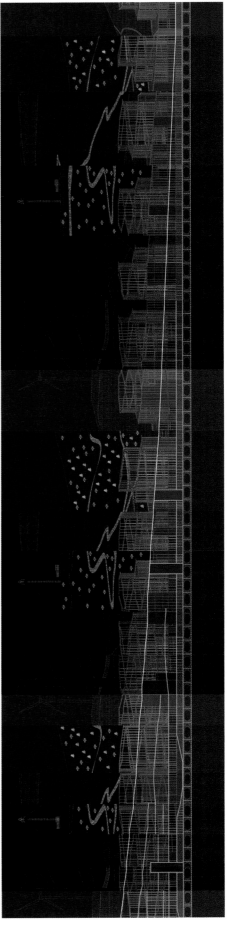

Mapping blue water supply
and usage in Metropolitana
Region, Chile.

④ Plaster + Tension + Compression [Janelle Schmidt]

⑤ An ideal ant [Anjiang]

⑥ Notional study for the Baltimore Harbor [Jen Shin]

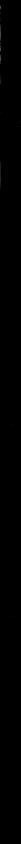

CALENDAR
Liwei Wang

Calendar began with the idea to place a spotlight above the island of Aegina programmed to turn 360 degrees in a year. The light grazes an area of Aegina's terrain, and its movement illustrates the time and date like the hands on a massive clock. The project is a meditation on the abstract concepts of time and place, and designs phenomenological experiences to celebrate the cycle of seasons.

While the housing shortage in the world grows by the millions, so does the amount of empty homes. From Detroit to Ciudad Juarez, urban expansion no longer follows population growth, but rather, market-driven decisions that benefit only a few: grow more to sell more. This studio investigates new housing alternatives in abandoned neighborhoods in Mexico, along the most frequently crossed border in the world. Addressing issues of migration, identity, privacy, housing, and production, students design new possibilities of collective living without the boundaries that characterize our contemporary life: imagine cities with no walls. The studio looks back to the *vecindades,* a traditional Mexican urban typology for multi-family tenement mixed-used housing arranged around a central courtyard with shared services. These are historical examples of flexible design and a shared sense of belonging—a space between the public and the private spheres. Students engage in new ways of understanding the concept of collective dwelling, producing proposals that turn the typical forms of housing into more flexible, collaborative ways of living.

JURY

Emily Abruzzo, Paola Aguirre, Tatiana Bilbao, Ruth Díaz Gurria, Alan Plattus, Kenneth Frampton, Michael Marshall, Nina Rappoport, Lorena del Río, M. Surry Schlabs, Clara Solà-Morales, Jia Weng, Carlos Zedillo, Elia Zenghelis

FACULTY

Fernanda Canales and David Turturo

PARTICIPANTS

Emily Cass, Michelle Badr, Camille Chabrol, Clara Domange, Shuchen Dong, Miriam Dreiblatt, Layla Ni, Alex Pineda, Limy Fabiana Rocha, Armaan Shah, Xiaohui Wen

■ FACULTY REFLECTION

Thinking about the meaning of "home" and of "wall" meant broadening oppositions between public and private space. The studio caused us to rethink the space between a bed and a sidewalk, between "my home" and "our city," the space that belongs to one but affects everyone. The dialogues we had with our jurors encouraged thinking through new models for collective dwelling. Now, more than ever, we need to build those new possibilities.

— Fernanda Canales, Louis I. Kahn Visiting Assistant Professor

This studio traveled to Mexico City, Mexico, Zumpango, Mexico, and Tijuana, Mexico.

BUILDING BLOCKS: AN INCREMENTAL HOUSING STRATEGY
Emily Cass

Paseos del Vergel is a housing development in Tijuana composed of 3,000 identical homes scattered across steep topography. The intense terrain impedes community as well as circulation between home and school, housing project and city. An incremental housing strategy distributes investment across the site through a series of discrete improvements that current and future homeowners can make to their dwellings. These critical interventions create a catalogue of possibilities that allow plug-and-play based on residents' needs and desires.

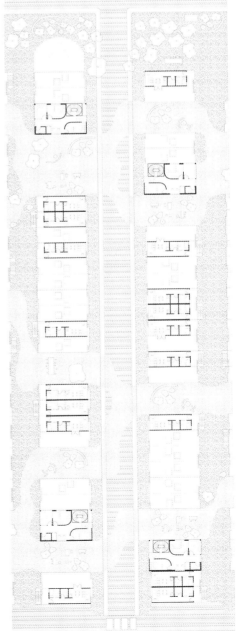

The project is located on a long slope in a suburban community named El Laurel, in Tijuana, Mexico. Considering the common problem that undeveloped long slopes reduce accessibility and increase risks in that area, this project explores the concept of a boundary-house that works as both a connection and a protection, and also provides systematic stages of daily life with a hierarchy of private and public space.

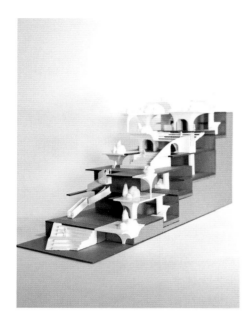

As the world comes to recognize climate change morphing into a full-fledged climate disaster, it increasingly falls to architects and designers to find ways to mitigate and minimize the impacts of the developments and buildings that they design. Every question and decision that architects make, including perhaps whether to build at all, can be studied through the lens of environmental impact. This project seeks to go beyond mere ambitions of sustainability, producing instead a proposition of community and endeavor that is "sustaining" and restorative, not just less bad. This studio travels to the remote island of Gili Meno, located off the coast of Lombok, Indonesia. Here students develop proposals for a new type of beach-based resort, built around the principles of sustainable development, designed to minimize environmental impact in construction and operation, and to be restorative to the ecosystem and the local community. The studio focuses on the impact of global tourism on these fragile environments and works to develop propositions for a particular site on this tropical island.

Advanced Design Studio

Fall 2019

JURY
Michel Bordier, Andy Bow, Judy Chapman, Mark Foster Gage, Ann Marie Gardner, Dana Getman, Abby Hamlin, Thomas Heyne, Nico Kienzl, Eeva-Liisa Pelkonen, Barbara Römer, Shanta Tucker

FACULTY
Patrick Bellew, John Spence, Henry Squire, Timothy Newton

PARTICIPANTS
Cristina Anastase, Elaine ZiYi Cui, Samantha Monge Kaser, Smit Patel, Jenna Ritz, Baolin Shen, I-Ting Tsai, Justin Tsang, Rukshan Vathupola, Laélia Kim-Lan Vaulot, Anna Borou Yu

■ FACULTY REFLECTION
The Bass Studio focused on the remote island of Gili Meno, one of the Gili Island group located off the coast of Lombok in Indonesia. The students developed proposals for a new type of beach-based resort, built around the principles of sustainable development, designed to minimize environmental impact in construction and operation and to be restorative to the ecosystem and the local community.
　— Timothy Newton, Critic

This studio traveled to Gili Meno, Indonesia.

SOLAR SONGKET
Justin Tsang

Solar Songket is an environmentally- and socially-woven, play–work–blended Lifestyle resort inspired by *songket*, an important fabric produced communally in the Indonesian culture. The relationships between vacationers and local neighborhoods are reinforced through crafting workshops and culinary exchanges that contribute to their daily necessities. Harnessing solar energy and recycling water are enabled by the environmentally integrated architecture and landscape. These circular systems compose the intricate engineering which resembles the motif of the *Solar Songket*.

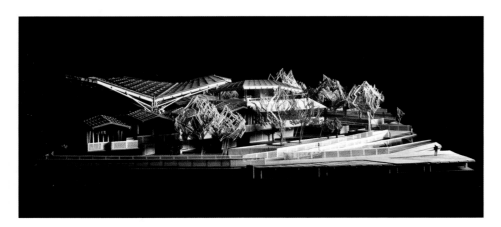

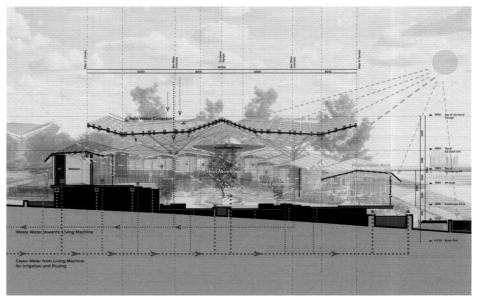

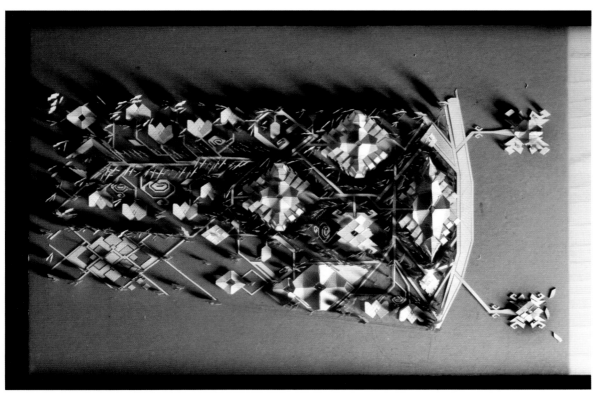

ALAM—A 21ST CENTURY CO-LIVING RETREAT
Samantha Monge Kaser

Alam: world, realm, natural, native. Alam Gili Meno is a co-living resort with community and experiences at its core. Through its carefully crafted programming and corresponding amenities, *Alam* emphasizes interpersonal exchanges and keeps private space to the essentials, expanding opportunities for socialization and time in the outdoors. From local construction materials and passive and modular design, to programmed booking packages and cultural traditions, *Alam* proposes a holistically sustainable approach to tourism.

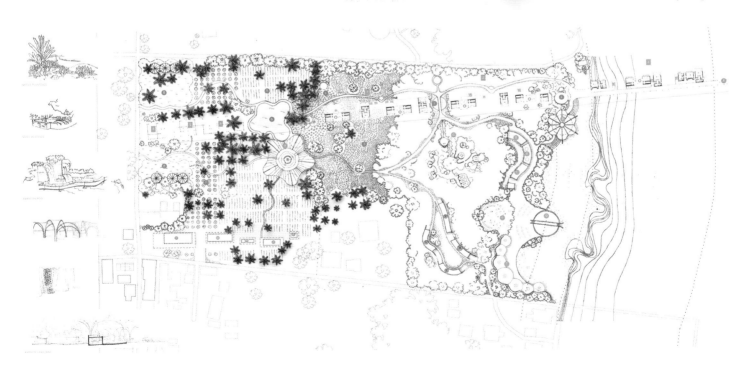

Gothenburg, Sweden's second largest city and a major port and technology center on the western (North Sea) coast of the country, has had a particularly vivid experience of the economic and social transformations that are reshaping cities in the late twentieth and early twenty-first centuries. In addition, as a coastal city shaped by shipping and industry, it faces the challenges of sustainability, resilience, and adaptation in relation to climate change, human migration, and increasingly uneven distribution of income and opportunity. This studio explores the role, both performative and representational, of architecture and urban design in identifying and implementing innovative responses to these challenges.

    The spatial epicenter of these explorations is a riverfront area, known as Lindholmen, across from the historic city center and until the 1970s, the site of some of the world's biggest ship building companies. Lindholmen has become a focus and symbol of Gothenburg's transition from an older economy of Fordist production to the characteristic new economy fueled by research, knowledge and innovation.

JURY

Faranas Bengtsson, Marta Caldeira, Fernanda Canales, Teddy Cruz, Fonna Forman, Paul van der Grient, Gavin Hogben, Ishraq Khan, Chris Marcinkowski, Carl Mossfeldt, Daniel Pittman, Âsa Swan, Annette Vejen Tellevi

FACULTY

Alan Plattus and Andrei Harwell

PARTICIPANTS

Shuang Chen, Serena Ching, Rishab Jain, Yuhao Gordon Jiang, Zack Lenza, Max Ouellette-Howitz, David Scurry, Seth Thompson, Daoru Wang, Kay Yang

■ FACULTY REFLECTION

With a focus on the waterfront of Gothenburg, Sweden, we considered the challenges and opportunities facing a riverine urban landscape responding to the transformations of a globalizing city. Issues like the shift from industry to knowledge production and the threat of climate change provided the provocation for student work. Going beyond the conventional framework of site-specific urban design "projects" to articulate regional strategies that produce local interventions led to diverse and innovative proposals.
— Alan Plattus, Professor

This studio traveled to Gothenburg, Sweden.

GRÖN KANT
Rishab Jain and Zack Lenza

The project, located on the Frihamnen docks, addresses issues of infrastructural and cultural disconnect between Gothenburg's north and south shores. Creating a soft edge condition, this acts as a hinge between the historic center and innovation/research hub. A new Transportation Hub and an Ecology Center, connected by a pedestrian bridge, unite the two shores while providing a new urban experience of the city, the river, and natural landscape in geological time.

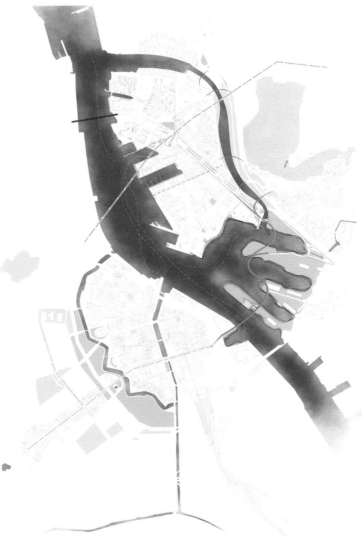

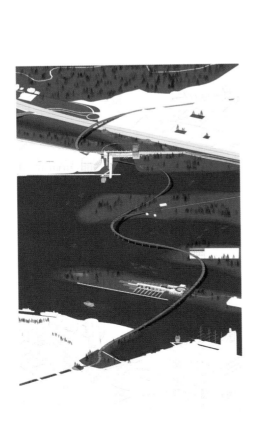

Serena Ching and Kay Yang

As an alternative to Gothenburg's top-down, large-scale development model, the project proposes incremental, infill, informal interventions to create a network of river-centric social amenities specific to the needs of each community. The goal is to decentralize the methods of production, delivery, and use of spaces within an urban neighborhood to support diverse people, groups, and lifestyles. This proposal brings together the industrial, recreational, and educational assets of Gothenburg, through interventions within Ringon, Frihammen, and South Lindholmen.

1. Prefabricated modules help introduce new use on the existing parking lot
2. The repair facility is subdivided to promote visual access across the river
3. Common living spaces overlook the courtyard while maintaining a sense of privacy

The title, *The Architecture of Thought*, has many possible meanings, all of which are explored in this studio to better inform the act of architectural design. This slippery title can simultaneously refer to the design of physical buildings that themselves are locations for, or encourage, reflection and thought—or it can refer to developments within architectural theory that have acted as prompts to change the course of architecture throughout its history. Lastly it can call one's attention to the very structures of the human mind itself where thoughts are developed, thereby encouraging larger questions regarding the nature of being, existence, and the status of reality. This design studio is unique in that it considers all of these readings through the medium of a single architectural design problem—an actual building or small complex of buildings. So while the intellectual context of the course is broad, the design agenda is focused in particular on a new and singular building typology: a think-tank policy retreat for the Brookings Institution, creating space specifically to address issues of Trans-Himalayan international policy.

Advanced Design Studio

Fall 2019

JURY
Kutan Ayata, Jefferson Ellinger, Catherine Ingraham, Ariane Lourie Harrison, Lydia Kallipoliti, Karel Klein, Monique Roelofs

FACULTY
Mark Foster Gage and Graham Harman

PARTICIPANTS
Hamzah Ahmed, James Bradley, Nathan Garcia, Mari Kroin, Katie Lau, Ruike Liu, Alix Pauchet, Leonardo Serrano Fuchs, Megan Tan, Brenna Thompson, Jerome Tryon

■ FACULTY REFLECTION
The studio that Graham and I taught was, literally, about reflection—being titled *The Architecture of Thought*. One surprise for me was the nearly studio-wide emergence of a strong relationship between reflection and what one might call a form of architectural gravitas. Many projects aspired to prompt human thought through the built presence of something much larger, in effects rather than actual size, than the actual human. A type of monolithic-ness.
— Mark Foster Gage, Associate Professor

This studio traveled to Lhasa, Tibet.

INDEXING WATER: LHASA'S RESOURCE POLICY RETREAT CENTER
Katie Lau and Brenna Thompson

Applying philosophies of Object-Oriented Ontology and Hyperobjects, this design investigates how architectural form can shape thought on the future distribution of Himalayan freshwater resources. Throughout the complex, water is active, breaking conventional functions of water and becoming "present at hand," rather than a component of a scenic backdrop. The building's machine-like aesthetic confronts false dichotomies of man and nature and positions human actions and systems as inseparable from surrounding ecosystems.

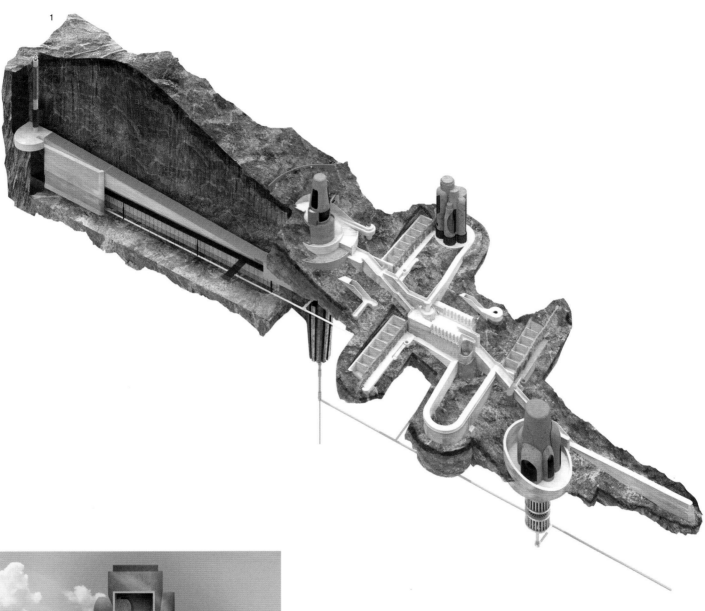

1. Site and building axonometric
2. Entry under water cistern
3. Section through hydroponic greenhouse cistern

INEFFABLE FORM
Leonardo Serrano Fuchs and Jerome Tryon

In the foothills of the Himalayas, pressed against the Tibetan skies, the building is conceived of as ineffable form. Formally incomplete, it depends upon the hillside, the site, the lake, and the distant mountains to become whole. Slightly in and out of phase with its environment, it achieves a gentle dissonance through an uncanny resemblance of geology. The building continually recedes into itself. A pattern of high and low, bright and dark, open and closed spaces continually draw the beholder through the building which is never resolved in itself.

With the increasing sophistication of digital technologies, architecture is undergoing its most comprehensive transformation in centuries. This course examines the development of perspective through rigorously constructed drawings.

FACULTY
Victor Agran

TRANSLATING COMPUTATION
Zack Lenza

This drawing explores the interaction between machine and designer. A composition was developed via scripting, then translated through the Mimaki. At intervals of roughly eight minutes, the machine was stopped, the drawn lines were erased digitally, and the paper moved a few inches to restart the drawing. The density of lines meant not all were erased, so the drawing captures errors in the process as it moves across the page.

1217a   Architectural Product Design

This course attempts to broaden the design experience through designing architectural objects not usually found in architectural building commissions. Issues of detail, scale, proportion, aesthetics, manufacturing, and commercial viability are explored.

FACULTY
John D. Jacobson

TAPE DISPENSER
Daniel Whitcombe

This horizontally-oriented tape dispenser indexes the functions essential to a conventional tape dispenser, providing each function with an individual formal expression while also being fully adjustable to accommodate its placement on a desk. A heavy blackened-steel base ensures the necessary weight to keep the dispenser stationary while the painted wood posts float playfully above.

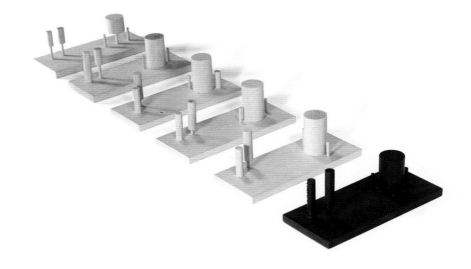

Students learn to see and read as an architect through architectural analyses of late-medieval theocentrism, Renaissance humanism, and 18th-century Enlightenment thought. Unlike the average user, an architect must see beyond the facts of perception.

FACULTY
Peter Eisenman

BRAMANTE'S CORNER: PALAZZO DUCALE, URBINO, AND SANTA MARIA DELLA PACE, ROME
Diana Smiljković

The central entrance and corners of Palazzo Ducale compartmentalize each interior elevation. This enclosure of the cortile is contrasted with the circulation of Santa Maria Della Pace's colonnade. Here the corner creates continuity rather than enclosure. The entrance from the corner promotes multiple views through movement as opposed to singular frontal views.

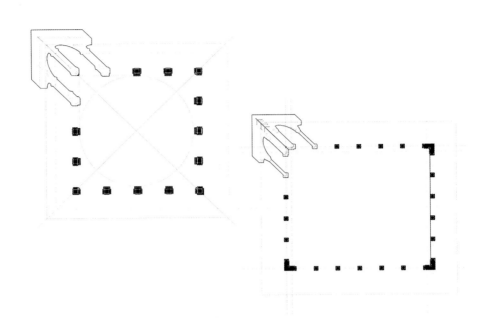

Design and Visualization

Coursework

1233a   Composition and Form

This seminar addresses composition and form in sequential exercises titled Form, Structure, Section, and Elevation. Leaving aside program and site, these exercises develop techniques by which words, briefs, descriptions, intentions, and requirements are translated into three dimensions.

Fall 2019

FACULTY
Peter de Bretteville

ELEVATION STUDIES
Kelsey Rico

These schemes are explorations in building assemblies using three different circulation structures as the driver: L-shape, 3 axis bracket, and wishbone shape.

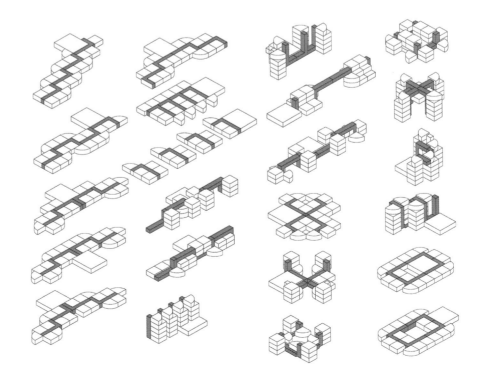

This seminar engages the expectation that architecture more directly address the social and political problems of today. Students speculate about other ways to discuss these issues rather than relying on critical-theory tropes that have governed architecture's ambitions for decades.

FACULTY
Mark Foster Gage

HANDS IN A POST-
MANUAL WORLD
Andrew Kim

This object comes from a world in which manual labor, manual operation, hand-working, even handling, are obsolete—a post-manual economy, driven by automation. With xenofeminist thinking, this projection predicts that vestigial hand-bound alterations and encrustations enhance and disengage expressions of identity from sex and gender.

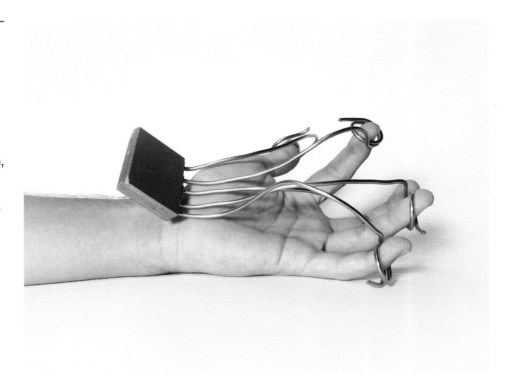

1289a   Space–Time–Form

The course explores key concepts, techniques, and media that have affected the design, discussion, and representation of architecture beginning in the 20th century. Students work through a series of experiments based on the *Vorkurs* offered at the Bauhaus.

FACULTY
Trattie Davies and
Eeva-Liisa Pelkonen

TYPOGRAPHY EXPERIMENT:
MOVEMENT TO FORM
Max Wirsing

"Movement gives birth to form, form gives birth to movement. If I want to experience a line, I must either move my hand in accordance with the line or I must follow the line with my senses: hence, I have to be physically moved."

Johannes Itten
Utopia: Documents of Reality

EVEN THE SLIGHTEST SENSATION IS A FORM THAT RADIATES MOVEMENT.

This course introduces the analysis and design of building structural systems (and the evolution and impact of these systems on architectural form), covering structural classifications, fundamental principles of mechanics, and computational methods.

FACULTY
Kyoung Sun Moon

ORDERS IN ORDER
Yushan Jiang

The project takes columns (orders) as the generator of space. The hovering roof, supported by steel beams, is tectonically detached from the concrete columns—in between are steel rods which work as joints between the columns and the roof. Structurally, the rods reduce resonance from the roof garden. The little gap created by the joint allows subtle sunlight to pass through to cast the structure's shadow on the ground.

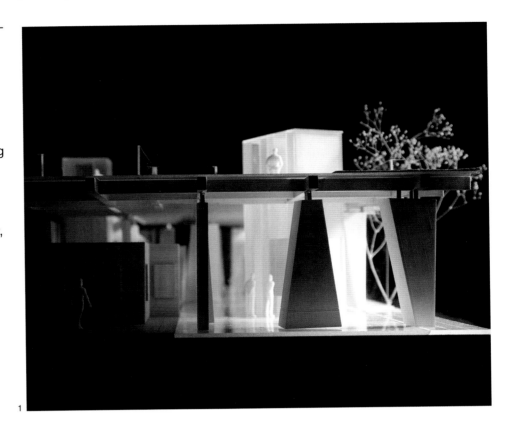

1

Technology and Practice

Coursework

2018a   Advanced Building Envelopes

Studying emerging theory and technology, and developing a design research project, students reconsider novel ways of redirecting energy and water flows, fulfilling social mandates to transform relationships between the built environment and ecosystems.

Fall 2019

FACULTY
Anna Dyson and Mohamed Aly Etman

MOZAMBIQUE PRESCHOOL
Naomi Ng and Liang Hu

Mozambique Preschool is for children with disabilities, affected by social exclusion. Passive sun shading strategies are implemented, including dense existing vegetation in courtyards as natural shading, operable screens along each conditioned room for interior shading, and brise soleil screens along each corridor. The roof is folded to maximize cool and humid air flows. To assist with downdraft, roofs are overhung and the deck is elevated above the ground.

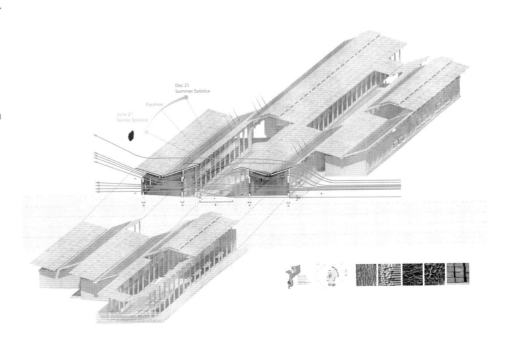

1. This project was designed for Arch 1011a Architectural Design 1. The structural systems were further developed in this course.

This course examines the fundamental scientific principles governing the thermal, luminous, and acoustic environments of buildings, and introduces students to the methods and technologies for creating and controlling the interior environment.

FACULTY
Anna Dyson and Naomi Keena

CAFÉ ELEMENTARY
Yangwei Kevin Gao

Designed with precision, the two levels present different environmental qualities while sharing a similar character of having outdoor playgrounds. Sand pits and the ground level floor function as thermal masses to store and release heat when needed. On the second level, the operable shading screens work with the "foot windows" to secure a consistent indoor temperature of 18–23 °C for the exhibition of artwork.

2031a   Architectural Practice and Management

This course investigates the fundamental structure and organization of the profession, the mechanisms and systems within which architects work, and the organization, management, and execution of architectural projects.

FACULTY
Phillip Bernstein and John Apicella

Proposal for Energist Headquarters
Samuel David Bruce, Gioia Montana Connell, Zack Lenza, Samantha Monge Kaser, Armaan Shah, Laeila Kim-Lan Vaulot

In this simulation, the members of our team, Studio X, crafted a business proposal based on project drivers, as we responded to an RFP for 67,000 gross square feet of office, research, and interpretive space housed on 55 acres of former brownfield in Redding, Connecticut. Streamlined schedule and budget planning, environmental revitalization and long-term sustainability, and delivery of cutting-edge design as a showcase of our client's mission and vision drove the decisions behind project schedule, delivery, and scope.

As proud winners of the Dreamers Award, Studio X members proposed an ambitious plan for tech-startup Energist's New England headquarters. We centered our project in a unique value proposition based on the studio's experience with optimizing complex projects through dynamic collaboration and speedy delivery for adaptive reuse, environmental design, and prefabrication.

The Studio X project bid featured an Integrated Project Delivery structure to incentivize and facilitate team integration; phased masterplanning and module design and construction using cradle-to-cradle prefabrication methods; and office research into the latest live/work spaces and passive design to craft an effective and inspiring pitch.

From form-making structures to surface-defining enclosures, physical components of architecture are nothing but cold steel members, massive concrete, and glass. Yet when these products are combined in architecture, they become both functional and aesthetic.

FACULTY
Kyoung Sun Moon

EXPANDABLE HABITAT: MULTI-CORE AND MILE-HIGH
Qiyuan Liu and Stella Xu

As buildings grow taller the proportionally enlarged floor plans gradually become less habitable. Using a multiple-core system, the project studies how to balance the expansion through restoring habitable space and urban life at a mega-scale.

Coursework

2222a   The Mechanical Eye

Mechanical eyes can open new ways of inscribing information into our material world and also reveal our own biases and habits. This course examines the human relationship to mechanized perception in art and architecture.

Fall 2019

FACULTY
Dana Karwas

LOG: A COLLABORATION OF THE DIGITAL, THE MECHANICAL, THE NATURAL, AND THE HUMAN
Max Wirsing

Centering around a piece of a newly felled oak tree, this game of 'telephone' ratcheted between modes of human and mechanical seeing. The project manifested as a process—an exquisite corpse of physical observation, 3d scanning, environmental rendering, the virtual inhabitation of the rendered landscape, and 'dancing my log'—a physical interpretation of the log through movement, subsequently motion captured, extracted as data, and turned into three-dimensional form, which was then carved…out of the log.

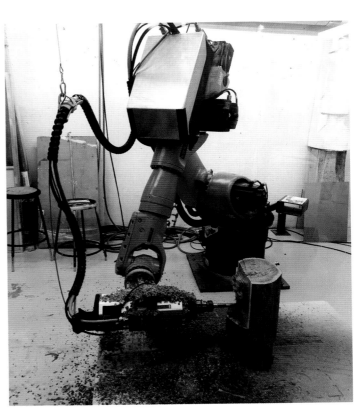

The course is an intensive investigation into the relationship between a material's substance and its performance metrics and qualities. Students explore the role of materials in the formation and execution of a spatial concept.

FACULTY
Emily Abruzzo

REFLECTING RUDOLPH
Daniella Calma, Mari Kroin,
and Alper Turan

This is a material study on plastics and the potentials of reflection, color, and transparency. Sited at the Loria entrance lobby, the installation mimics the texture of Rudolph Hall's characteristic wall, which remained unchiseled due to the removal of an adjoining building during the renovation. The intervention creates a new interaction of light in the space as well as increased human interaction with the iconic wallscape of Rudolph Hall through reflection.

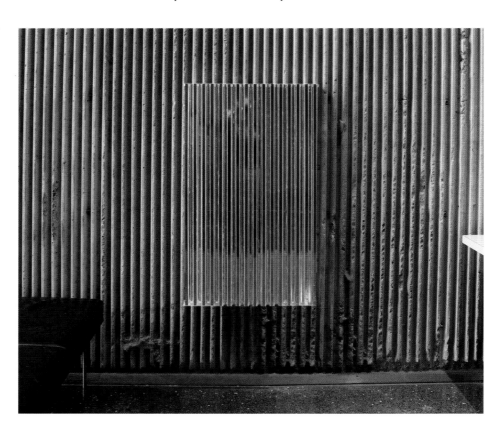

2237a   Computational Composite Form

This seminar researches the use of carbon fiber, computation, and robotics for architectural design; documents relationships between geometries and material behavior; and rigorously tests their structural, aesthetic, and architectural properties.

FACULTY
Ezio Blasetti

COMPOSITE COMPONENT
Gabriel Gutierrez Huerta, Ruike Liu,
and Hongyu Wang

The design aims to create a flexible structural system based on carbon fiber's inherent material properties and digital fabrication techniques. The basic module is a 4-axis prong, woven on a structural MDF frame with carbon fiber tow. Once cured, the frame can be disassembled, and multiple modules combined into a variety of self-supported composite structures.

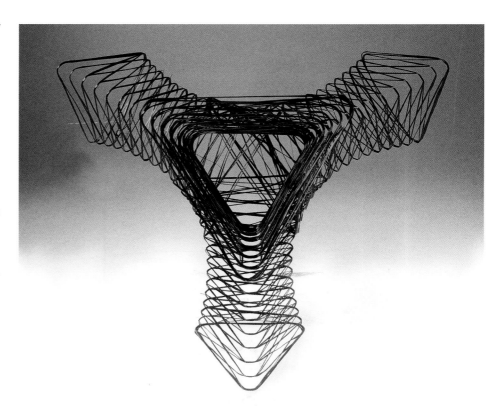

As traditional fables began to yield to more scientifically conceived ideas of architecture's role in civilization, architecture gained importance in advancing social and industrial agendas and built a basis for theoretical reflection and visionary aesthetics.

FACULTY
Anthony Vidler

Student Paper Topics

Intent and Extent: The Limits of Architecture for Gunnar Asplund
Katie Colford

A parallel reading of Gunnar Asplund and Bernard Tschumi reveals a connection between one architect displaced from the narrative of Modernism and the other from that of Postmodernism: both were concerned with the limits of architecture as a spatial experience. Tschumi interrogates this question in his *Architecture and Limits* (1980–1) essay series and again in his writings on "disjunction" in the 1990s. He frames the destabilization of architecture as a way of reinvigorating ideas of program and "event," a suggestion that finds a parallel in Asplund's own writing on the "dissolution" of space. An analysis of Asplund's Gothenburg Law Courts Extension (1913–36) and Woodland Chapel (1918–20) reveals a spatial response to the question of limits: the two projects imply a continuous feedback loop between the scale of the detail and the scale of the landscape. Analyzed through the lens of Tschumi's writing, Asplund's project is fifty years ahead of its time, challenging both the in-tent and ex-tent (from the Latin tendere, to stretch) of architecture. Stretching inward to intimate scales of use, program, and Tschumian "event" and stretching outward to infinite scales of landscape and movement, Asplund's work invites a reconsideration of not only the limits of architecture but also the limits of Modernism and Postmodernism.

Wittgenstein's Handles, Wittgenstein's Thoughts
Brian Orser

This paper begins to reinterpret one branch of early modern architecture through a close look at the *Palais Stonborough* (1926), a house designed in Vienna by philosopher Ludwig Wittgenstein, in collaboration with Adolf Loo's student Paul Engelmann. The architecture of the *Palais* has commonly been interpreted to be symbolic of Wittgenstein's philosophy of logic. Instead I argue that seeking a one-to-one correspondence between his ideas and his architecture (in particular its custom door handles) oversimplifies Wittgenstein's definition of logic, ignores his aesthetic theories, and reduces his architecture.

Rather than illustrating his thought with architectural forms, Wittgenstein was working to synthesize complex aesthetic, conceptual, and functional forces within his cultural context. A careful reading of Wittgenstein's theory of aesthetic judgment supports this interpretation. He points to a common error resulting from the object-predicate structure of aesthetic expressions: "'Beautiful'… is an adjective, so you are inclined to say: 'This has a certain quality, that of being beautiful.'"[1] Against this belief that objects have aesthetic value, he maintains that aesthetic judgment takes place within a language game which is part of both the cultural context and the specific context in which the judgment and its expression occur. To describe the meaning of this judgment, "we would have to describe the whole environment."[2] The mechanisms and tectonics of the *Palai's* door handles are often read as signs of Wittgenstein's logic (as in 'The door handles are logical.'). I test the contrary theory that the design and execution of the door handles reveal Wittgenstein working both with logic and with that which escapes logic, which he calls the "whole environment," or "primordial life."

History and Theory

Coursework

Fall 2019

1. Ludwig Wittgenstein, *Lectures and Conversations on Aesthetics, Psychology and Religious Belief*, ed. Cyril Barrett (Berkeley: University of California Press, 2007), 1.
2. Ibid., 7.

Investigating a broad range of projects and practitioners, this course is designed as a forum for post-professional students to discuss and explore their unique interests and backgrounds as they define their own practice.

FACULTY
Aniket Shahane

DECONSTRUCTING FABRICATED MEMORIES
Jerome Tryon

This drawing is part of a series consisting of 18 drawings that explore visual memory and spatial perception. Successive drawings were developed to test the fidelity of a remembered object and explore the outcomes of media interference, spatial simultaneity, and perceptual decomposition and reassembly.

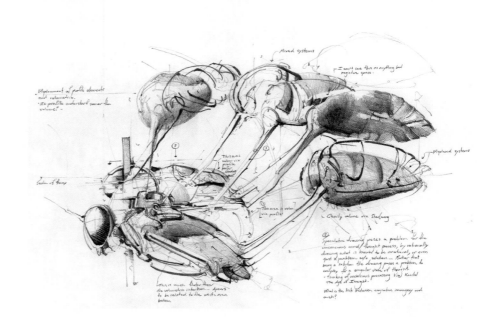

3072a   Design Research 1: Cross-Disciplinary Perspectives

This course explores how to conduct applied design research through multiple lenses. Students gain a general background in some key humanitarian challenges where designers can make a difference in the next century.

FACULTY
Joel Sanders

LOCKIVE
Elaine ZiYi Cui and Hengyuan Yang

Locker space at Yale University Art Gallery is hidden around the corner, causing discomfort and congestion for different bodies in space. Our proposal, *Lockive*, relocates the locker space to the museum lobby, with adjustable units for ergonomic comfort and transparent materials for aesthetic and environmental values. Overall, the concept engages a variety of different ages and abilities to see and be seen.

Tradition and innovation, often accepted to be mutually exclusive discourses in the "New Tradition" of the first half of the twentieth century, in fact share common genealogy and are integral to an understanding of modern architecture.

FACULTY
Robert A.M. Stern

GIO PONTI FAÇADE
FOR STRADA NOVISSIMA
Kay Yang

This façade was designed in the manner of Gio Ponti for a fictional exhibition in 1940, highlighting the *Strada Novissima* as a return to the street and a formative element of the city. Using elements from Ponti's early houses as a starting point, such as the Laporte House in Via Benedetto Brin (1935–36), the façade uses screens, layering, and color to anticipate his future work, particularly the Taranto Cathedral.

3232a   Politics of Space

This seminar explores the relationship between space, power, and politics in the urban environment from the Enlightenment period to the present. Students investigate how power is produced and embodied in the physical environment.

FACULTY
Mary McLeod and Summer Sutton

False Promises: The Transnational Spectacle of the American Dream
Emily Cass

Border Space
Page Comeaux

Towards a New Monumentality: How the People of Hong Kong Make Monuments Out of Everyday Space
Hana Davis

Redefining Space with Xenofeminism
Michael Gasper

Architecture of the Silent Majority
Eunice Lee

Politics of Skin: From the Post-modern to the Contemporary Façade
Mary Carole Overholt

Systems of Surveillance
Deirdre Plaus

The Death and Life of Great Urban Opacity
Adam Thibodeaux

Two Coffee-Drinking Publics
David Schaengold

Bigness, Junkspace and Urban Acupuncture in Singapore
Joshua Tan

Transactions of Circulation
Rachael Tsai

The Image of Representation
Rukshan Vathupola

Hong Kong's Lady Liberty Statue: The Reproducible Grassroots Monument
Timothy Wong

This seminar confronts historical knowledge with speculation about the intentions and realization of architectural designs. The challenge is in the effort to understand the beginnings of new ideas during the Renaissance, to grow aware of their evolution and consequences, without distorting their historical nature.

FACULTY
Peter Eisenman and Kurt Forster

RE-COMPOSING
SAN GIORGIO MAGGIORE
Luka Pajovic

Re-composing San Giorgio Maggiore began as an attempt to reconstruct the original polychromy of Palladio's Venetian masterwork, known since its partial re-emergence in the 1990s, but rarely probed for the new insights it offers into the architect's mind and creative process. By restoring color to the majestic interior of San Giorgio, a different Palladio emerges—one as interested in the ruinous present as he was in the monumental past of classical architecture.

1

3240a   Spatial Concepts of Japan: Their Origins and Development in Architecture and Urbanism

This seminar explores the origins and development of Japanese spatial concepts, and surveys how they help form the contemporary architecture, ways of life, and cities of the country.

FACULTY
Yoko Kawai

Japanese Architecture Is like a Haiku
Leyi Zhang

Inspired by the charming resonance of poetry and architecture throughout history, this paper explores the relationship between a form of Japanese poetry called haiku and traditional Japanese architecture by focusing on three qualities: the use of pause, simplicity, and the role of five senses.

Kireji, a spoken punctuation in haiku, produces a moment of contemplation. Likewise, in Japanese architecture, a sense of "in-between" space, known as ma, prompts a visual and physical pause.

Simplicity is mainly shared by two aspects of haiku and traditional Japanese architecture. First, haiku is composed of objective descriptions of objects without analysis. Similarly, the most important Japanese architecture can be conveyed by using elements without decoration. Second, haiku is an objective form of poetry that can create subjective readings. Likewise, the space in Japanese architecture is simple and lucid, which affords different understandings and experiences to exist simultaneously.

When one reads haiku, they employ their five senses to imagine the scenes and finish the "unfinished" poem in their minds. Experiencing traditional Japanese architecture is similar because all senses are activated to truly feel the space. Inside Japanese architecture, one not only sees the space, but can listen to, smell, and touch it.

1. Conceived for Arch 3234a Renaissance and Modern 1; executed in Arch 3293b Polychromatic Reconstruction of Architecture taught by David Gissen.

Along with buildings, architects might also design the medium in which those buildings are suspended. Considering ground instead of figure, medium design inverts some dominant cultural logics about problem-solving and offers additional aesthetic pleasures and political capacities.

FACULTY
Keller Easterling

Manpower, Worklife, and the Making of Human Resources
Gabrielle Printz

"Human Resources" is a kind of medium. It organizes working relations: imagined capacities that meter the demands of for-profit enterprise, state regulation, and the intimate needs of an individual life-as-livelihood. This paper looks at the cultivation of "Human Resources" as a project that unfolds in the 20th century towards the steady incorporation of life into work, and work into life. The judicious depiction of American work by the U.S. Department of Labor publications and programming in the 1960s and 1970s emphasized human dimensions of the nation's "manpower problems." In the view of Labor administrators and editors, work was a site of social provision and expenditure: where federally-funded programs could redeem the marginalized with job training and temporary work. These efforts featured in the Department's limited circulation magazine *Manpower* (1969–1975), later renamed *Worklife* (1976–1979), a rebranding that registers a conceptual shift from the defensive reserves of a civilian workforce to the lifestyles furnished by human resource development. Across a decade of issues, the publicatory enterprise set out to actively reshape the identity of the American worker to include Black women and men, mothers, the formerly incarcerated, migrants, disabled people, the "hardcore unemployed" and many others who had served as specific socio-economic targets for Department of Labor programs.

3284a   Architectural Writing

This course introduces students to how writers have addressed and described places and their relationships to such spaces, and through a series of assignments teaches students to learn to write clearly about place.

FACULTY
Cynthia Zarin

Calendar
Liwei Wang

Conflating the 365 days of the calendar year with solar events reveals some incompatibilities. A solar year is an astronomical phenomenon; it is the time it takes the sun to return to its same position, observed from the perspective of a fixed point on earth, through the cycle of seasons. The mean solar year lasts 365.2422 international system (SI) days and is measured from inflection points in the trajectory of the sun's changing angles—the solstices and equinoxes.

Our contemporary experience of the year was introduced in 1582 with the Gregorian calendar, which spaces leap years over 400-year cycles so that the average year is 365.2425 days long. It was introduced to stop the drift—an observable difference between calendar and reality—between the equinox's date and its actual phenomenon. By 1582, the drift had already created a discontinuity of ten days. The discrepancy proved to be extremely problematic for the Catholic Church in calculating the exact date of Easter, which in principle falls on the Sunday following the full moon on or after the vernal equinox. Because leap years correct the drift every four years, the solstices and equinoxes land between a range of two days. For example, the summer solstice is observed in the northern hemisphere on June 20th or 21st. The spotlight, which takes 365 days to complete one rotation on the island, can account for this difference because the totem marks the precise point of midnight between these two dates.[1]

1. The "spotlight" refers to the project *Calendar*, designed by Liwei Wang for Arch 1105a Archipelago, page 83.

History and Theory

Coursework

Fall 2019

The design of the built environment is considered in relation to patterns and practices of urban life and culture—a response to historical transformations of the political, economic, and technological forces that have always shaped cities.

FACULTY
Alan Plattus and Andrei Harwell

LAKHTA CENTER AND THE ESTABLISHMENT OF A NEW, MODERN CIVILIZATION
Colin Chudyk and Rachel Mulder

The original city plan for St. Petersburg offered a three pronged planning scheme where streets radiated north from the Peter and Paul fortress and south from the Admiralty, defining the form of the city beyond the borders of these monuments. In contrast, the Lakhta Center is an icy fortress that offers no scheme for the creation of a new city. It is a dead end, connecting only to a luxury yacht club.

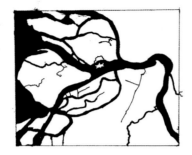

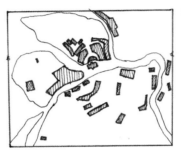
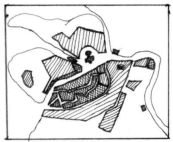

4213a   The City and Carbon Modernity

Humanity has moved through three energy paradigms, each producing different built environments and social organizations. At each transition the productive capacity of human society was transformed, engendering a social, spatial and architectural paradigm.

FACULTY
Elisa Iturbe

OVERCOMING OMA'S *MISSION GRAND AXE*
Deo Deiparine

Peeling back the applied layers of OMA's tabula rasa reveals the buildup of material waste it was built upon. The grid accelerates the economic logic of financial speculation and commodified real estate. A series of interventions aims to resist the vertical autonomy of the existing fabric and introduce horizontal connections. The horizontally linked buildings can now be tied to more communally oriented modes of productivity.

This seminar on urban research focuses on archives, fieldwork, photography, and filmmaking. Strengthening the designer's tool kit of social and historical methods—to bring storytelling to site research—students engage with work in varied disciplines.

FACULTY
Elihu Rubin

ST. RAPHAEL THRIFT SHOP
Xiaohui Wen

St. Raphael Auxiliary Thrift Shop at Chapel and Orchard was closed on December 20, 2020 to make room for a new parking facility. For decades it has served the need for affordable clothing in an underprivileged neighborhood. Like many heartbroken regulars who returned to say goodbye, I dropped by to chat with the lovely ladies, who have been volunteers here for years, and hear what they wanted to say.

4222a   History of Landscape Architecture:
Antiquity to 1700 in Western Europe

This course surveys the history of landscape in Western Europe from the Ancient Roman period to 17th-century Rome. Students examine the evolution of garden typologies, related architectural typologies, and water in gardens and fountains.

FACULTY
Bryan Fuermann

HORTUS CONCLUSUS
Maya Sorabjee

Geoffrey Bawa's Colombo residence was built by gradually combining four adjacent bungalows, resulting in a labyrinth of domestic spaces. Each hortus conclusus presents a different method of bringing landscape into the dwelling—from the roots of a tree that line a corridor to the leafy patios outside the bedrooms. Bawa's urban abode fragments the relationship between interior and exterior, creating a contained arrangement of landscape and architecture.

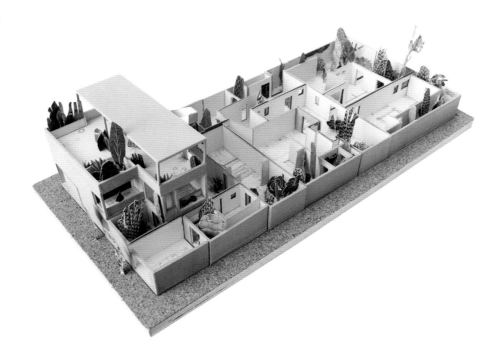

What if the U.S. Army Corps of Engineers had developed "soft infrastructures" for dealing with the flows of the Mississippi in New Orleans? Students explore such counterfactuals through a comparative perspective on the history of patents.

FACULTY
Anthony Acciavatti

THE TOILET SNORKEL
Limy Fabiana Rocha and
Brenna Thompson

The Toilet Snorkel, patented by William Holmes in 1981, arose from incessant fires in dense, high-rise apartments. Prolonging inhabitants' survival, the device could provide fresh oxygen via the air trap of a toilet. Its potential arises from the replicability of the bathroom and the essence of the toilet as a banal item of domestic life. As the snorkel proliferates in the city, piping for uses beyond waste management seeks mass expansion of plumbing infrastructure.

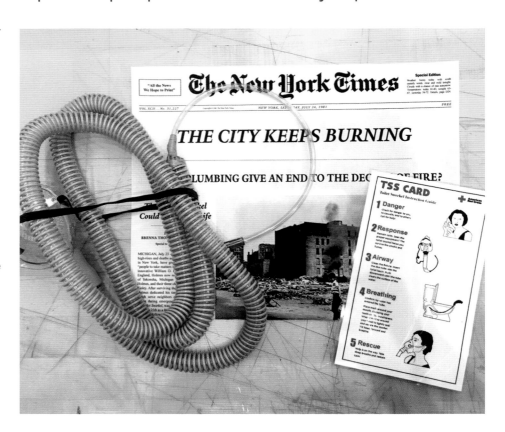

4242a Introduction to Planning and Development

Financial and political feasibility determine the design and character of the built environment. Students propose projects and then adjust them to the conflicting interests of a variety of public and private participants in the planning process.

FACULTY
Alexander Garvin

COMPREHENSIVE REZONING PLAN: HUNTER'S
POINT NORTH COALITION
Thomas Atlee, Christopher Cambio, Jackson Cole,
Julian Macrone

Our Comprehensive Rezoning Plan for Long Island City, Queens creates a vibrant, livable community that capitalizes on New York's greatest assets. It guarantees environmental health and resilience through waterfront open space, green infrastructure, and people-centric street design. Zoning provisions deliver affordable housing, sensible density, and a diverse building stock. It honors neighborhood history by preserving manufacturing uses and building a true live-work neighborhood.

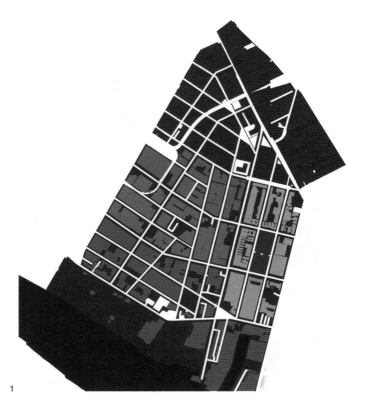

1. Purple: Zone M1-5/R9A, Yellow: Zone R6, Red: Zone C2, Salmon: Zone C4, Maroon: Zone C5

Established in the Fall Semester of 2019, Urban Studies is an interdisciplinary field grounded in the physical and social spaces of the city and the larger built environment. The Urban Studies major is situated within Yale's liberal arts framework and draws on the broader academic context and expertise of the Yale School of Architecture, including the areas of urban design and development, urban and architectural history, urban theory and representation, globalization and infrastructure, transportation and mobility, heritage and preservation, and community-based planning.

Retrospecta 43: Can you begin by speaking about the history of urban studies at Yale and the process behind the revitalization of the urban studies program?

Joyce Hsiang: The Department of City Planning ran from 1957–1968 and became a full department in 1961. It had a Master of City Planning and a Master of Urban Studies, added in 1964. This was headed by Christoper Tunnard and later Harry Wexler and it came to a very tumultuous and difficult end fifty years ago, coincident with massive societal discontent and unhappiness with administration and bureaucracies. It became this really contentious relationship between the administration and Kingman Brewster, and the city planning forum, which is what it had been called in conjunction with the local Black Workshop. So basically in 1970, Kingman Brewster began the process of shutting down the Department of City Planning.

Over the course of the last 20 years, there have been recurrent calls for an urban studies major. The major became a priority of Deborah's when she became Dean and the process of creating the major started in 2016, using the existing urbanism track in the school of architecture and strengthening it by changing the courses that were being offered and the prerequisites. The Urban Studies proposal was associated with the creation of Elihu Rubin's class, American Architecture and Urbanism, and the class Bimal Mendis teaches, Scales of Design.

R43: Given the controversial shutdown of the Department of City Planning in 1969, how has this complicated history of urban planning at Yale affected the way this new urban studies program has been formed?

JH: Maybe I've benefited from being ignorant—or naive, let's say—of some of those issues. I remember there was a vote in the spring last year—I remember thinking that after all of this work and effort, after this multi-year process of strengthening concentrations and creating new coursework, any Yale College faculty member could just vote against it and the major would die. And from what I understand, over the last years there have been failed initiatives to start the major. Yale College is extraordinarily supportive. All of the people in Yale College were really keen on creating this major. It was very much a university-wide sentiment that this was long overdue, and needed to happen.

R43: How has the new urban studies program tackled issues of diversity?

JH: In the urban studies major now 90% are either women, people of color, or both, which really reflects the diversity of the students in this first year. People who are interested in it are personally invested in these kinds of issues. I think that's very much the interdisciplinarity of this major, meaning that even though the School of Architecture hosts this major, it's necessary and expected that the students are taking classes across the university like anthropology and sociology, and addressing issues of decolonization and so on.

R43: What kind of work have you started to see coming out of the first year?

JH: In a normal year I would have seen the senior presentations, but there were such a rich range of senior theses this year. It was really nice to have a collective of students who were all examining different urban issues that ranged from looking at refugee camps and settlements to bike transportation infrastructure to the notion of tabula rasa. It's great to see what will come from the current juniors, who have also been doing equally exciting and rich work in the classes they've been taking.

R43: Could you offer a brief reflection on the first year of the new urban studies program?

JH: It's hard to reflect on this year, which has been so deeply changed by the disruptions of COVID. It's interesting for me because I realize that it's been fifty years since all the revolts of 1969–70 happened. And it's been one hundred and fifty years since women have been admitted to Yale. What has come to bear personally in the experience of teaching and talking and interacting with all the students has been this larger set of systemic failures and inequities that are now coinciding with these anniversaries at Yale. It's hard for me to reflect on anything specific to this one year, disassociated from these broader questions that we're confronted with.

Joyce Hsiang is the Director of Undergraduate Studies and an Assistant Professor. Along with her partner Bimal Mendis, she is the founding principal of Plan B Architecture and Urbanism, an interdisciplinary design and research practice based in New Haven, Connecticut.

Undergraduate Studies

Fall 2019

If we are said to live in an urban world, then what does a term like "urban" tell us about the nature of cities and the built environment? And if, as some scholars have argued, everything from the peaks of the Himalaya Mountains to the depths of the Pacific Ocean is urbanized, then what explanatory power does "urban" wield? Such queries suggest how to redefine binary relationships like urban and rural or natural and artificial, but also how an "urban world" challenges the scale and materiality of urban life. Urban, as it is casually used today, demands redefinition.

FACULTY
Anthony Acciavatti

PARTICIPANTS
Jojo Attal, Laura Clapp, Ariel Claxton, Ekaterina Danchenko, Kayley Estoesta, Kenia Hale, Lucas Holter, Lauren Kim, Grace Kyallo, Gema Martinez, Courtney Nunley, Lauryn Phinney, Rasmus Schlutter, Daud Shad, Ethan Treiman, Alex Whittaker

■ FACULTY REFLECTION
Members of the urban lab moved like sinusoidal waves between fieldwork in the great outdoors of New Haven and New Orleans and lab-based work at Rudolph Hall. Throughout this perpetual process of spatial analysis and synthesis, we traversed the margins of cities through drawing and collaging along with storytelling—all to coalesce into a series of graphic novels that explore the limicole layers of life in estuarial cities.
— Anthony Acciavatti, Daniel Rose (1951) Visiting Assistant Professor

NOLA: THE CHANGING RELATIONSHIP WITH WATER
Gema Martinez

This project documents New Orleans's complex relationship with water and underscores the city's efforts to implement green infrastructure to mitigate its effects.

GHOST HOMES
Lauryn Phinney

This graphic novel seeks to explore the structural remaking of New Orleans post-Katrina and what was lost in the process: the intimate and mundane routines of everyday life, rituals that are just as much an essential city-making process as any other.

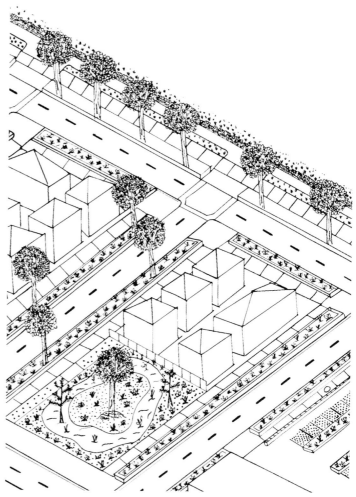

What constitutes relevant space? This studio explores the experiential relationship of the body to space through a series of increasingly complex architectural problems. The non-human bat makes a major contribution to the discussion by his non-visual assessment of space. Always measuring its changing configuration by the beeps he sends out and the echoes he receives back, he is like the ultimately engaged space lunatic aficionado, always locating himself with exactitude within the space, always swerving and never blundering, the space prompting him like a dancer in an elegant ballet. To be a bat trapped in Francesco Borromini's St. Ivo might be as close to ecstasy as it gets.

Undergraduate Studies

Fall 2019

FACULTY
Turner Brooks and Adam Hopfner

PARTICIPANTS
Hafsa Abdi, Angel Adeoye, Trevor Chan, Hana Meihan Davis, Cole Fandrich, Sebastian Galvan, Julia Hedges, Jane Jacobs, Ivy Li, Karin Nagano, Graceann Nicolosi, Ash Pales, Sophie Potter, Sam Rimm-Kaufman, Adam Thompson, Reanna Wauer

■ FACULTY REFLECTION
We started with the 'dominant' void project, a quest for making a space which paradoxically is more palpable and present and 'full' than whatever defines it. The 7th floor pits and an exterior court were filled with 'real scale' constructions that flickered in and out of their dominating spatial presence. The studio went on to design two community-based projects for human interaction: a nature trail 'head house' with related smaller constructions along the trails, and a 'little league' clubhouse and related facilities near Hillhouse High School in New Haven. That the studio in the end was a total mess of models seemed a good thing.
— Turner Brooks, William Henry Bishop Visiting Professor and Professor Adjunct

BEAVER POND GARDEN MAZE
Julia Hedges

A network of thin paths, small rooms, and gathering spaces are created through an arrangement of amoebic garden beds.

MOTHER AND CHILD: NATURE PAVILIONS
Hana Meihan Davis

Pictured is the central 'mother' hub: a space designed for learning and the contemplation of nature.

This semester marks the 53rd consecutive year in which first-year MArch 1 students have embarked on a Building Project. It is a program born from student unrest in the fervor of the 1960s to demand an active engagement in addressing societal needs through a physical construct. Students work in tems to design proposals for a residence. Once one team's scheme is selected, all students work to refine and develop the chosen design, and then engage in a summer of construction. To begin the design process, the class engages with a real client: a progressive nonprofit organization that provides both immediate shelter and long-term social services and housing services to those at risk of homelessness. The course works within the city of New Haven, a culturally and ethnically rich, yet economically impoverished, citizenry where one fourth of the population lives below the poverty line. To that end, students become leaders in gathering insights from the population with whom the course engages. Students learn of the vulnerabilities, and more importantly, the aspirations of those who have experienced homelessness.

FACULTY
Adam Hopfner (director), Martha Foss, Alexander Kruhly, Beka Sturges

---

■ **DIRECTOR'S REFLECTION**
The Building Project was restructured this year in order to foreground both the persons for whom we are building, and the place in which we are building. I speculate that the deep empathy the students brought to their analyses and designs nurtured their will to persevere in the face of the pandemic. The devotion of the class to thoughtfully develop a design despite the remote learning environment and the commitment of the School to physically manifest that design in the face of myriad obstacles are testament to a potentiality latent within the School.
    — Adam Hopfner, Critic

A   Lillian Agutu
Audrey Hughes
Jack Rusk
Janelle Schmidt
Wenzhu Shentu
Jun Shi
Hao Xu
Calvin Yang Yue

B   Brandon Brooks
Claire Hicks
Suhyun Jang
Abraham Mora-Valle
Yikai Qiao
Diana Smiljkovic
Christina Chi Zhang

C   Claudia Carle
Sam Golini
Chocho Hu
Yushan Jiang
Morgan Anna Kerber
Andrew Spiller
Alex Mingda Zhang

D   Katie Colford
Zishi Li
Meghna Mudaliar
Kevin Steffes
Joshua Tan
Yang Tian
Jessica Jie Zhou

E   Lindsay Duddy
Jessica Kim
Zhanna Kitbalyan
Caroline Kraska
Calvin Liang
Hao Tang
Tianyu Wang

F   Audrey Fischer
Sarah Kim
Hannah Mayer Baydoun
Paul Meuser
Gustav Neilsen
Jingyuan Qiu
Anjiang Xu

G   Adare Brown
Lauren Carmona
Sangji Han
Veronica Nicholson
Brian Orser
Taku Samejima
Tian Xu

H   Jingfei He
Perihan MacDonald
Dominiq Oti
Abby Sandler
Rachael Tsai
Timothy Wong
Yuan Iris You

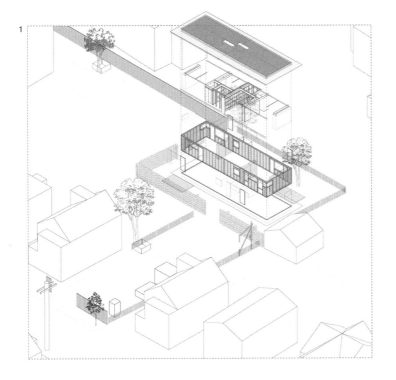

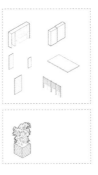

1. Exploded axonometric of construction assembly sequence for selected design proposal

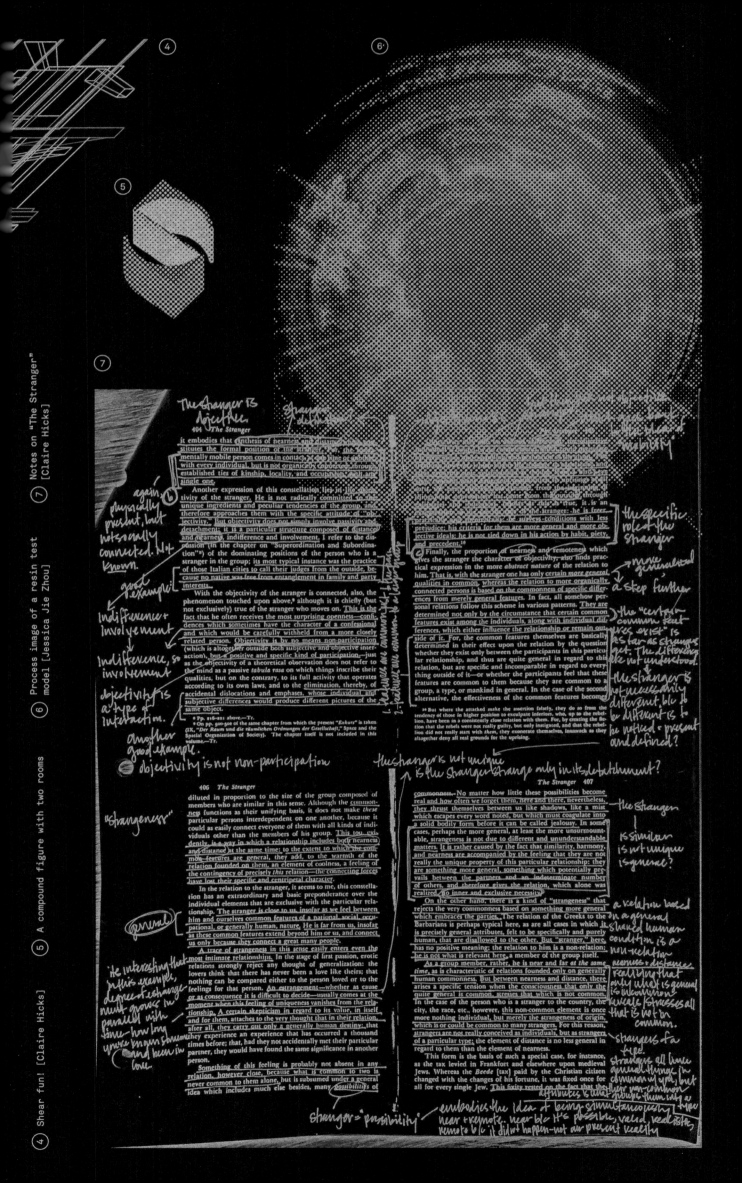

④ Shear fun! [Claire Hicks]
⑤ A compound figure with two rooms
⑥ Process image of a resin test model [Jessica Jie Zhou]
⑦ Notes on "The Stranger" [Claire Hicks]

104 The Stranger

it embodies that synthesis of nearness and distance which constitutes the formal position of the stranger. The mentally mobile person comes in contact, if we may use the figure, with every individual, but is not organically connected, through established ties of kinship, locality, and occupation, with any single one.

Another expression of this constellation lies in the objectivity of the stranger. He is not radically committed to the unique ingredients and peculiar tendencies of the group, and therefore approaches them with the specific attitude of "objectivity." But objectivity does not simply involve passivity and detachment; it is a particular structure composed of distance and nearness, indifference and involvement. I refer to the discussion (in the chapter on "Superordination and Subordination"*) of the dominating positions of the person who is a stranger in the group; its most typical instance was the practice of those Italian cities to call their judges from the outside, because no native was free from entanglement in family and party interests.

With the objectivity of the stranger is connected, also, the phenomenon touched upon above,* although it is chiefly (but not exclusively) true of the stranger who moves on. This is the fact that he often receives the most surprising openness—confidences which sometimes have the character of a confessional and which would be carefully withheld from a more closely related person. Objectivity is by no means non-participation (which is altogether outside both subjective and objective interaction), but a positive and specific kind of participation—just as the objectivity of a theoretical observation does not refer to the mind as a passive tabula rasa on which things inscribe their qualities, but on the contrary, to its full activity that operates according to its own laws, and to the elimination, thereby, of accidental dislocations and emphases, whose individual and subjective differences would produce different pictures of the same object.

* Pp. 216-221 above.—Tr.
* On pp. 500-501 of the same chapter from which the present "Exkurs" is taken (IX, "Der Raum und die räumlichen Ordnungen der Gesellschaft," Space and the Spatial Organization of Society). The chapter itself is not included in this volume.—Tr.

...from the stranger: he is freer, practically and theoretically; he surveys conditions with less prejudice; his criteria for them are more general and more objective ideals; he is not tied down in his action by habit, piety, and precedent.[10]

Finally, the proportion of nearness and remoteness which gives the stranger the character of objectivity, also finds practical expression in the more abstract nature of the relation to him. That is, with the stranger one has only certain more general qualities in common, whereas the relation to more organically connected persons is based on the commonness of specific differences from merely general features. In fact, all somehow personal relations follow this scheme in various patterns. They are determined not only by the circumstance that certain common features exist among the individuals, along with individual differences, which either influence the relationship or remain outside of it. For, the common features themselves are basically determined in their effect upon the relation by the question whether they exist only between the participants in this particular relationship, and thus are quite general in regard to this relation, but are specific and incomparable in regard to everything outside of it—or whether the participants feel that these features are common to them because they are common to a group, a type, or mankind in general. In the case of the second alternative, the effectiveness of the common features becomes

[10] But where the attacked make the assertion falsely, they do so from the tendency of those in higher position to exculpate inferiors, who, up to the rebellion, have been in a consistently close relation with them. For, by creating the fiction that the rebels were not really guilty, but only instigated, and that the rebellion did not really start with them, they exonerate themselves, inasmuch as they altogether deny all real grounds for the uprising.

106 The Stranger

diluted in proportion to the size of the group composed of members who are similar in this sense. Although the commonness functions as their unifying basis, it does not make these particular persons interdependent on one another, because it could as easily connect everyone of them with all kinds of individuals other than the members of his group. This too, evidently, is a way in which a relationship includes both nearness and distance at the same time; to the extent to which the common features are general, they add, to the warmth of the relation founded on them, an element of coolness, a feeling of the contingency of precisely this relation—the connecting forces have lost their specific and centripetal character.

In the relation to the stranger, it seems to me, this constellation has an extraordinary and basic preponderance over the individual elements that are exclusive with the particular relationship. The stranger is close to us, insofar as we feel between him and ourselves common features of a national, social, occupational, or generally human, nature. He is far from us, insofar as these common features extend beyond him or us, and connect us only because they connect a great many people.

A trace of strangeness in this sense easily enters even the most intimate relationships. In the stage of first passion, erotic relations strongly reject any thought of generalization: the lovers think that there has never been a love like theirs; that nothing can be compared either to the person loved or to the feelings for that person. An estrangement—whether as cause or as consequence it is difficult to decide—usually comes at the moment when this feeling of uniqueness vanishes from the relationship. A certain skepticism in regard to its value, in itself and for them, attaches to the very thought that in their relation, after all, they carry out only a generally human destiny; that they experience an experience that has occurred a thousand times before; that, had they not accidentally met their particular partner, they would have found the same significance in another person.

Something of this feeling is probably not absent in any relation, however close, because what is common to two is never common to them alone, but is subsumed under a general idea which includes much else besides, many possibilities of

commonness.—No matter how little these possibilities become real and how often we forget them, here and there, nevertheless, they thrust themselves between us like shadows, like a mist which escapes every word noted, but which must coagulate into a solid bodily form before it can be called jealousy. In some cases, perhaps the more general, at least the more unsurmountable, strangeness is not due to different and ununderstandable matters. It is rather caused by the fact that similarity, harmony, and nearness are accompanied by the feeling that they are not really the unique property of this particular relationship: they are something more general, something which potentially prevails between the partners and an indeterminate number of others, and therefore gives the relation, which alone was realized, no inner and exclusive necessity.

On the other hand, there is a kind of "strangeness" that rejects the very commonness based on something more general which embraces the parties. The relation of the Greeks to the Barbarians is perhaps typical here, as are all cases in which it is precisely general attributes, felt to be specifically and purely human, that are disallowed to the other. But "stranger," here, has no positive meaning; the relation to him is a non-relation; he is not what is relevant here, a member of the group itself.

As a group member, rather, he is near and far at the same time, as is characteristic of relations founded only on generally human commonness. But between nearness and distance, there arises a specific tension when the consciousness that only the quite general is common, stresses that which is not common. In the case of the person who is a stranger to the country, the city, the race, etc., however, this non-common element is once more nothing individual, but merely the strangeness of origin, which is or could be common to many strangers. For this reason, strangers are not really conceived as individuals, but as strangers of a particular type; the element of distance is no less general in regard to them than the element of nearness.

This form is the basis of such a special case, for instance, as the tax levied in Frankfort and elsewhere upon medieval Jews. Whereas the Beede [tax] paid by the Christian citizen changed with the changes of his fortune, it was fixed once for all for every single Jew. This fixity rested on the fact that the...

The Stranger 107

① Search for soft infrastructure in NYC wetlands [Ives Brown]

② More dogs/ less people [Rebecca Commissaris]

③ Along/ Across/ Over/ Under [Rebecca Commissaris]

④ Sparrow [Rebecca Commissaris]

⑤ [Shiqi Valerie Li]

⑥ A compound figure with two spaces and a structural support

"I think we need more dogs and less people"

A

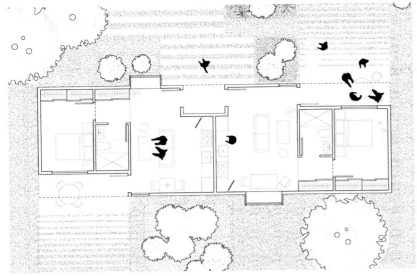

Our project is formed by exploring the transition from the public street to intimate interior spaces, and is designed to facilitate the transition from short-term homelessness to long-term domesticity.

B

Our proposal offers the residents latitude to shape certain characteristics of their internal environment so that each may begin to claim this house as their home.

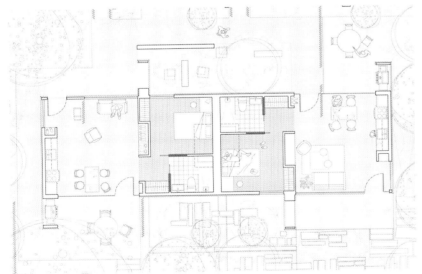

C

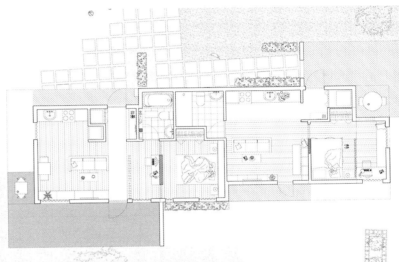

Our design provides refuge and opportunity for individuals who have once experienced homelessness by expressing a sense of property, enclosure, and safety.

D

Our project splits the site in sections, giving the lower unit the understory and the upper unit the canopy, allowing individual experiences of a single landscape.

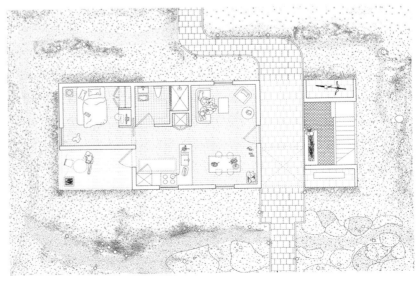

E

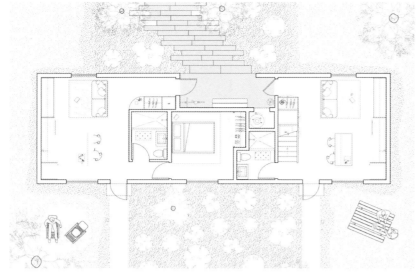

Our proposal creates a central core of interlocked and nested volumes to provide secure and intimate private spaces for each resident.

F

Drawing from principles of Gestalt therapy our proposal provides moments along an imagined sequence of daily rituals to reinforce an awareness of self within the home environment.

G

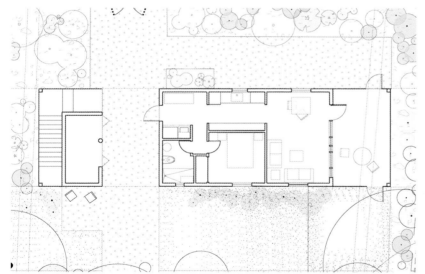

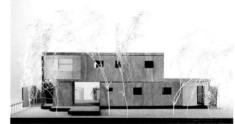

In our scheme the landscape holds the house and the house holds two homes. The design balances privacy with connection to the neighborhood and to nature.

H

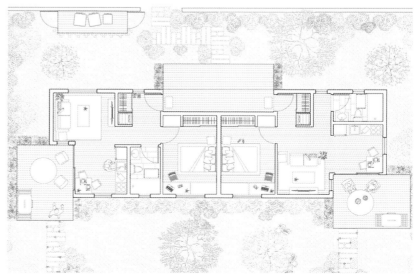

Our design strategy stemmed from a desire to generate a dynamic relationship between site conditions and the new building while negotiating the occupancy of two individuals under one roof.

This second semester studio in a sequence of four core studios explores space and building at the scale of human occupation and inhabitation. Dwelling is examined across multiple scales and conceptions including the body, site, form, space, program, time, culture, and the environment. This studio is designed as a series of three research-based experiments in which students are asked to take an informed position, using research as the basis for design experimentation, and to articulate a unique thesis: research, experimentation, and conceptualization. This studio puts an emphasis on exploring, developing, and testing various methods of representation, both in two and three dimensions. Drawing and model-making are not seen simply as prescribed deliverables to be completed at the end of each assignment, but rather as an integral part of the design process: students are required to see, to test, and to experiment by virtue of making.

JURY
Ramona Albert, Sarosh Anklesaria, Jose Araguez, Benjamin Aranda, Sunil Bald, Andy Bao, Norma Barbacci, Annie Barrett, Andrew Benner, Andy Bernheimer, Stella Betts, Julian Bonder, Brennan Buck, Marta Caldeira, Karolina Czeczek, Trattie Davies, Koray Duman, Karen Fairbanks, Leslie Gill, Ariane Lourie Harrison, Jerome Haferd, Brandt Knapp, David Leven, Barbara Littenberg, Nicholas McDermott, Shane Neufeld, Alan Organschi, Megan Panzano, Lyn Rice, Phil Ryan, Aniket Shahane, Sarah Strauss, Beka Sturges, Michael Szivos, Jonathan Toews, Marc Tsurumaki, Brittnay Uitting, Ife Vanable, Mersiha Veledar

FACULTY
Miriam Peterson (coordinator), Peter de Bretteville, Elisa Iturbe, Amy Lelyveld, Joeb Moore, Eeva-Liisa Pelkonen

■ COORDINATOR'S REFLECTION
The challenge of second-semester studio is pushing expansive thinking while cultivating critical disciplinary skills. This semester, students were asked to set their own design parameters—digging deep into history, the natural world, culture, and economics, to take an informed position about design. Through this process of research, experimentation, and conceptualization, students were confronted with what we can know and what we cannot. Now, our cities, our country, and the world are faced with the unknowable—it is uncomfortable territory. In these times is also potential for creativity, invention, and architectural provocation. It is time to ask challenging questions and put forth provocative design solutions.
— Miriam Peterson, Critic

Miriam Peterson
Adare Brown
Claudia Carle
Katie Colford
Gustav Nielsen
Dominiq Oti
Taku Samejima
Abby Sandler
Janelle Schmidt
Christina Chi Zhang

Peter de Bretteville
Brandon Brooks
Lindsay Duddy
Jingfei He
Claire Hicks
Suhyun Jang
Jun Shi
Tianyue Wang
Hao Xu
Jessica Jie Zhou

Elisa Iturbe
Chocho Hu
Yushan Jiang
Zishi Li
Calvin Liang
Paul Meuser
Meghna Mudaliar
Veronica Nicholson
Diana Smiljković
Joshua Tan
Hao Tang

Amy Lelyveld
Lillian Agutu
Lauren Carmona
Audrey Hughes
Jessica Kim
Sarah Kim
Caroline Kraska
Timothy Wong
Tian Xu
Calvin Yang Yue
Alex Mingda Zhang

Joeb Moore
Audrey Fischer
Hannah Mayer Baydoun
Zhanna Kitbalyan
Brian Orser
Jack Rusk
Andrew Spiller
Yang Tian
Anjiang Xu
Yuan Iris You

Eeva-Liisa Pelkonen
Sam Golini
Sangji Han
Morgan Anna Kerber
Perihan MacDonald
Abraham Mora-Valle
Wenzhu Shentu
Kevin Steffes
Rachael Tsai
Yikai Qiao
Jingyuan Qiu

Core Studio

Spring 2020

TO BE HEARD, TO BE SEEN
Christina Chi Zhang

This residential building devotes its body to protests. Its curved walls offer optimized surface area for posters and banners; its shell protects the residential units from the public; its balconies connect the private realm and the plaza, offering a choice to engage or retreat. It shouts the demands of underrepresented communities to be heard and seen.

GOWANUS PLAYS ITSELF
Gustav Nielsen

The project seeks to instigate a counter-culture to the existing film industry in Gowanus, Brooklyn. A proposed Studio Club hosts production facilities and short-term apartments for the precarious film crew. Apertures direct and obscure visual connections between apartments; in two large atrium spaces natural and artificial light mix, blurring boundaries of time and space.

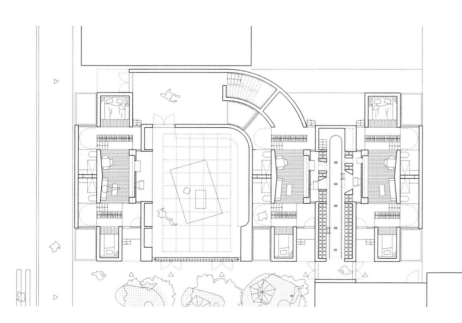 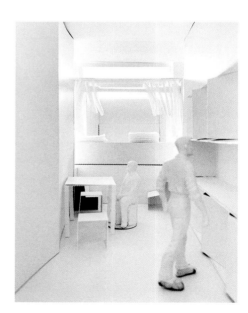

■ FACULTY REFLECTION
The students in my section showed great strength this semester—strength of character as they transitioned to working in a new way and perseverance, as they developed their research and design with maturity, exhibiting enormous faith in themselves and the importance of their work. We felt close to each other throughout, despite the distance between us. I have immense respect for all of them.
— Miriam Peterson, Critic

VENETIAN GOWANUS
Jessica Jie Zhou

Can negotiation be productive? Venetian Gowanus attempts to answer this, suggesting that through spontaneous and controlled interventions of surrounding elements, the "space in between" can be activated and become socially and ideologically generative, encouraging new programs, interactions, and spatial realms.

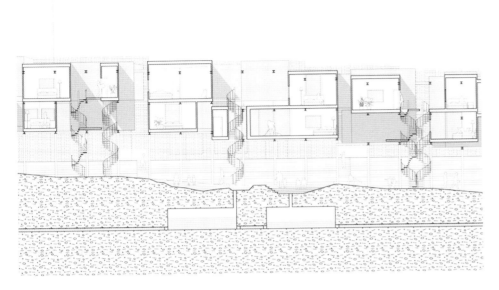

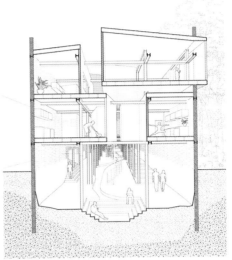

INTERSTITIAL DWELLING
Claire Hicks

This project considers dualities of dwelling—specifically the friction between private and public realms in a co-living environment. Tension is mediated through filtered light and directed views that frame and reflect specific parts of the neighborhood. These "portals" amplify friction between individual space and common space, disrupting expectations that the public invades one's privacy.

1
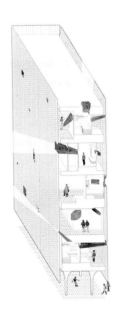

2

1. Transverse section highlighting the relationship between private and public areas
2. Direct views from eye level on 4th floor

∎ FACULTY REFLECTION

The second semester studio can be characterized as emerging from two notions of reflection. While the introductory exercises were to some extent historical and driven by precedents, the final project was about thought as the students formed a thesis based on their critical understanding of this two-part reflection as they shaped a project that addressed the context, social, cultural, physical and environmental, simultaneously developing ideas about dwelling and the domestic.
— Peter de Bretteville, Critic

GOWANUS TERRACES
Diana Smiljković

Gowanus Terraces finds inspiration in Chantal Mouffe's theory of agonism, especially concepts of fluctuation (between private and collective) and productive tension. The single unit is inhabited by two precarious workers, and fluctuates between shared border, absent border, and their unification. Using enfilade, ramps, and terracing, the space celebrates the mundane.

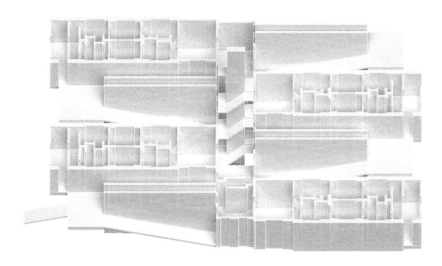
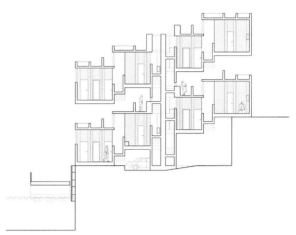

THREE NON-BINARY BODIES
Meghna Mudaliar

This minimum dwelling is presented with the presence of three non-binary bodies belonging to three different generations. Binary spaces created for binary bodies produce familiarity, whereas non-binary bodies demand ambiguity. If the body to some extent defines the space, then in order for ambiguity to be achieved the space must react to the presence of the body in unprecedented ways.

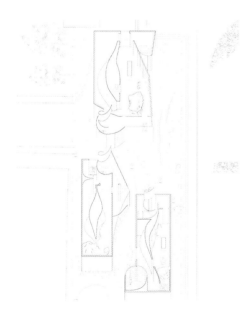

■ FACULTY REFLECTION
In the midst of a studio dedicated to domesticity, our ways of life were profoundly changed by the pandemic. There are few moments in which the status quo is so disturbed that change becomes possible. I hope this studio, which worked to question everything about how we live, has helped to prepare each student to be active as designers and critical thinkers in what may become a moment of transformation.
— Elisa Iturbe, Critic

PUBLIC LIFE
Lillian Agutu

Inspired by the NYC Housing Authority public housing projects that are located around the Gowanus neighborhood in Brooklyn, NY, a proposal for invitational spaces sees the building literally bridging the neighborhood to existing amenities at the head of the canal. The façade invites wildlife, light, and air, while the hallways invite residents to linger, extending their constricted public housing units.

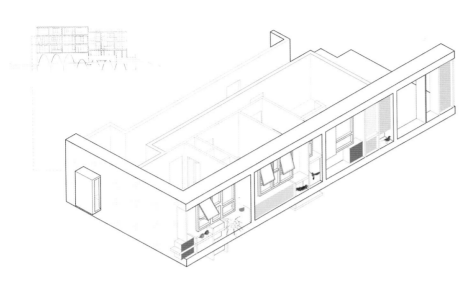

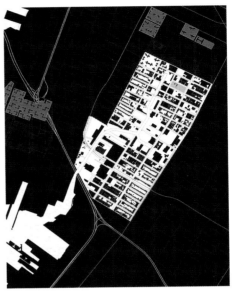

THE GUTS OF NEW YORK
Lauren Carmona

In an effort to break down the invisible borders between residential and industrial patterns in the Gowanus area, the placement of subterranean structures provides an interactive space where people are not only involved in the clean-up and improvement of the Gowanus Canal, but experience life underground, learning how to detach from the excesses of contemporary life.

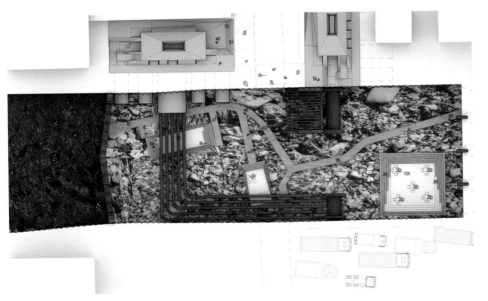

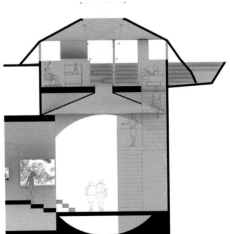

■ FACULTY REFLECTION
Enveloped by the brume of COVID-19, we can't not reflect. Days spent logging in and out, staring at "Hollywood Square(d)" screens of students and colleagues. Talking through form, building ideas in two dimensions—faces studying faces. The work is tenderized by the ground it's being planted in—absorbing the people and politics of the place. Aware of its taint and contradictions, it is tended to and rendered with hardboiled empathy.
— Amy Lelyveld, Critic

SOFT EDGES
Brian Orser

A tartan grid and system of intersections generate a soft, multi-layered edge between self and city, activated by vision and climate. This gradient of space facilitates a multiplicity of stances, views, and experiences of neighborhood. The proposal is two bars of mixed-rate housing which intersect with streets-in-the-air hosting public parks and community space.

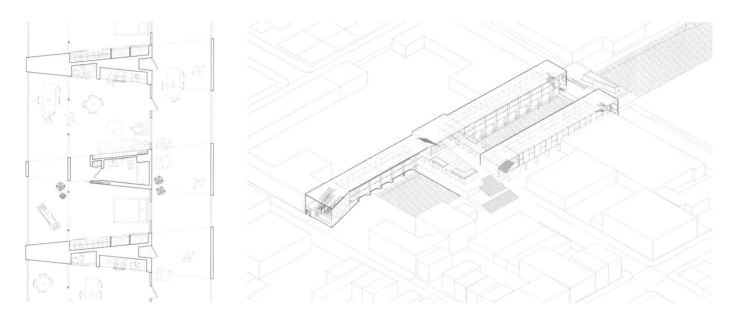

PEASANT FOREST
Yang Tian

Without promises of stability, Matsutake mushrooms live in a forest disturbed by humans. By reappropriating the historic and highly polluted Gowanus canal, the project makes new possibilities for housing and harvesting. Using small itinerant aquatic interventions, this project weaves formerly isolated and troublesome areas back into the city.

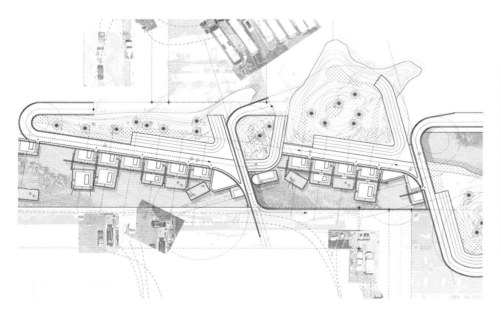

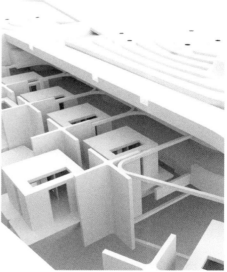

■ FACULTY REFLECTION
Lawrence Halprin's idea that "the environment exists for the purpose of movement" was the provocation for the studio. Thinking in place about the Gowanus Canal and the emergence of the COVID pandemic maelstrom, students have been acutely sensitive to transitions and lacunas between visible and invisible systems of the urban environment. Their projects sought to define theses and new forms of cohabitation between people (organisms) and a constantly changing environment.
— Joeb Moore, Critic

WATER PALACE
Sangji Han

The infrastructure that enables our modern way of living has always been hidden behind, under, or beyond the realm we see. Now, plumbing and pipes are exposed and are the driving force of the design process. *Water Palace* is environmentally interactive architecture, reacting to environmental changes and functioning as a closed ecosystem as needed.

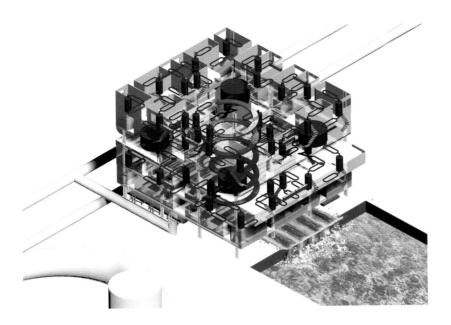

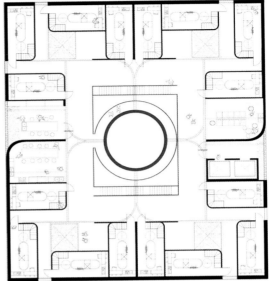

ECOLOGY AND ECONOMY
Rachael Tsai

Ecology and Economy is established in the Gowanus neighborhood as a self-sustaining, ecological collective generating vibrant public space, a business, and a collective way of living. The project addresses issues faced by a younger generation in terms of dwelling, working, and living, seeking to redefine how we can cohabitate and work within the same space.

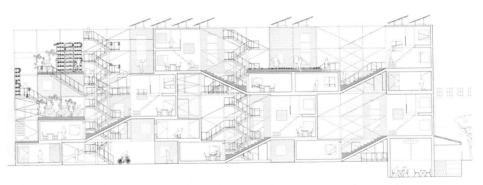

■ FACULTY REFLECTION
Our section spent the weeks of isolation reflecting, somewhat longingly, on how space enables and governs human interaction. We studied housing projects designed by B. V. Doshi and Jaap Bakema and considered recent experiments in "communing." Students built on these and other precedents when designing multi-unit housing projects with various cultural, ecological, economic, psychological, and social parameters in mind.
— Eeva-Liisa Pelkonen, Associate Professor

This fourth and final MArch 1 core studio expands on the fundamental architectural skills introduced in the previous three studios to examine the role of architecture and the architect at the scale of the city. Extending beyond the bounds of a building, this course examines a variety of forces—architectural, urban, social, economic, ecological, political, and other—that shape and order our built environment, emphasizing and cultivating a range of architectural themes and skills.

The Bronx struggles to address problems found city-wide: affordable housing, education for all, and environmental resiliency. Fordham Landing, a one-mile-long, 44-acre tract of land that clings to the western edge of the Bronx, is a site poised for revitalization. Sandwiched between the Harlem River to the west and Moses's Major Deegan Expressway to the east, the property also lies well below the grade of Fordham Heights, the neighborhood perched to its east. Like other sites scattered across the city, this sliver of urbanism lies isolated and alienated—a holdover of older ideas of renewal, awaiting newer ones.

JURY
Elizabeth Goldstein, Jae Shin, Trattie Davies, Ed Mitchell, Amid Tadj, Elihu Rubin, Suzanne Schildler, Margie Ruddick, Keller Easterling, Sarosh Anklesaria, Danielle Choi, Andrei Harwell, Marta Caldeira, Billy Fleming, Kaja Kuhl, Jesse LeCavalier, Julio Salcedo, Daisy Ames, Eve Baron, Joseph Heathcott, Brian Holland, Amin Tadj

FACULTY
Aniket Shahane (coordinator), Anthony Acciavatti, Alicia Imperiale, Bimal Mendis, Alan Plattus

■ COORDINATOR'S REFLECTION
One of the characteristics of an 'urban' project is its interdependency—its embrace of the entangled social, political, formal, and temporal conditions of the city. There have always been, and always will be, disruptions that upend our daily lives: a missed train, a novel virus, a hurricane, a war. Though in these situations we might be in need, we are also needed. As cities, citizens, students, and critics, we are deeply interdependent. We should act accordingly—with smarts, artistry and a fierce commitment to the people and ideas we feel are important. After all, we are architects, aren't we?
— Aniket Shahane, Critic

Aniket Shahane
Christopher Cambio
Rosa Congdon
Malcolm Rondell Galang
Louis Koushouris
Tyler Krebs
Hiuki Lam
Angela Lufkin
Rachel Mulder
Scott Simpson
Ben Thompson
Max Wirsing

Anthony Acciavatti
Jiachen Deng
Janet Dong
Ian Gu
Ashton Harrell
Sze Wai Justin Kong
Pabi Lee
Dreama Simeng Lin
Alex Olivier
Shikha Thakali
Peng Ye
Leyi Zhang

Alicia Imperiale
Ives Brown
Colin Chudyk
Liang Hu
Yidong Isabel Li
April Liu
Leanne Nagata
Naomi Ng
Heather Schneider
Christine Song
Shelby Wright
Kaiwen Zhao

Bimal Mendis
Natalie Broton
Isa Akerfeldt-Howard
Kate Fritz
Anjelica Gallegos
Jiaming Gu
Alicia Jones
Araceli Lopez
Louisa Nolte
Sarah Weiss
Yuhan Zhang
Sasha Zwiebel

Alan Plattus
Ife Adepegba
Martin Carrillo Bueno
Xuefeng Du
Paul Freudenburg
Yangwei Kevin Gao
Niema Jafari
Hyun Jae Jung
Mingxi Li
Qiyuan Liu
Nicole Ratajczak
Stella Xu
Sean Yang

CROSS BRONX SKYWAY
Tyler Krebs, Angela Lufkin, and Scott Simpson

Cross Bronx Skyway is an aerial cable transit system that seeks to liberate the Bronx from a conspiracy of geology, hydrology, and urban-renewal infrastructure. It proposes to link urban islands, connect to existing mass-transit, and bolster urban networks in an impactful way. An idiosyncratic flow of gondola typologies creates a new spectacle.

CADILLACS AS CATALYSTS: A STORY OF DISMANTLING
Rachel Mulder and Max Wirsing

A facility that processes 300 cars/day could decommission all of New York City's fossil-fuel vehicles in 15 years. With a timeline that considers rising floodplains at its Fordham Landing site, this dismantling plant also facilitates waterfront remediation and creates transportation connections via water and rail.

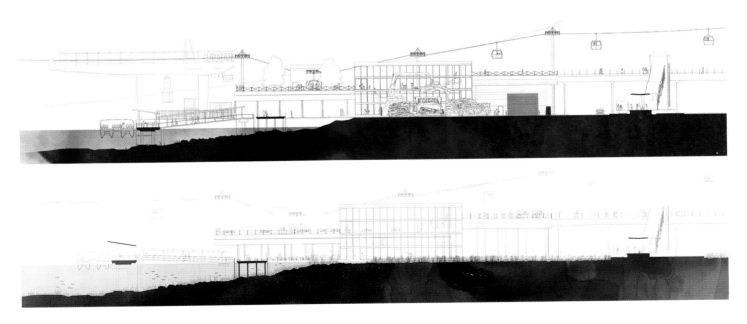

■ FACULTY REFLECTION
Through a series of exercises, our section attempted to frame the interdependencies that often define urbanism. In the end, not only did these students make a valiant effort to understand the relationships among systems of housing, commerce, transportation and public space, they did so by assuming the reality of another group's project in the design of their own. Put differently, they tried shouldering someone else's problems in defining their own.
— Aniket Shahane, Critic

Jiachen Deng, Alex Olivier, and Leyi Zhang

This project capitalizes on transforming two outmoded infrastructures: the Harlem River, transformed into a living estuary, and the Major Deegan Expressway, decommissioned to become a public space. By integrating the terraces and estuary, housing and intermodal hubs, the project serves as a model for how to live along the waterfront.

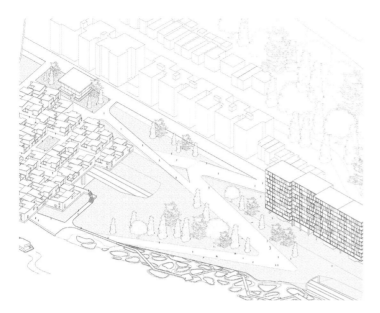

LIVING WITH THE PUBLIC: THE DENSIFICATION OF WEST BRONX
Janet Dong, Ian Gu, and Sze Wai Justin Kong

Intending to increase housing affordability and access to social amenities and infrastructures in the Bronx community, we propose an urban model combining the innovations made in São Paulo's SESC complexes with housing across underdeveloped sites. By incentivizing new public-private development projects, our proposal is able to offer a new public waterfront.

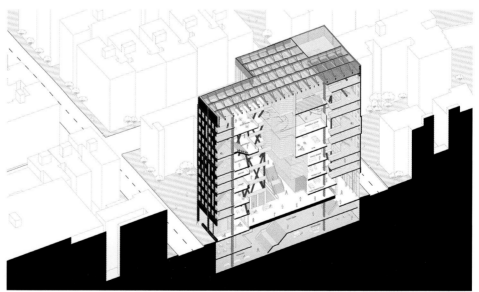

■ FACULTY REFLECTION

In *Shallow Water Urban Dictionary,* each project vividly imagined new ways to live within the dynamic estuaries that define the New York Metropolitan Region. From designing new forms of public space that are shaped daily by the rhythms of the tides to paring new live-work spaces with light manufacturing and recreation in the Bronx, these projects explore how contingent spatial transformation is on the art of description.
— Anthony Acciavatti, Daniel Rose (1951) Visiting Assistant Professor

DE-OPTIMIZING THE FLOW
Colin Chudyk and Leanne Nagata

Our project proposes a development by and for Fordham United Network group, which supports local initiatives and institutions in an effort to redistribute wealth, power, and agency back to the neighborhood. We propose to daylight the creek beneath Fordham Road, allowing for slow-filtration of storm runoff while providing infrastructure for community projects.

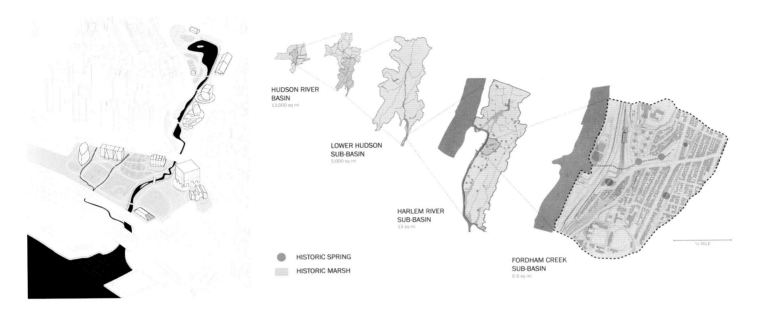

CYBERNATURAL: IMAGES, MACHINES, AND NONHUMAN AGENCY
Heather Schneider and Shelby Wright

Cybernatural reaffirms technology as a natural process, experimentally increasing the interaction between the material and technological worlds. Machine learning is used to produce a series of images, animal habitats, and native plant species. These images become a new ideal, interrupting notions of an ideal landscape inherited from 18th- and 19th-century landscape painting.

■ FACULTY REFLECTION

It was almost insurmountable to imagine the Harlem River waterfront before the road and rail tracks: it takes an act of imaging and imagining the imaginary. Using Cornelius Castoriadis's concept of the social imaginary and Amitav Ghosh's *The Great Derangement: Climate Change and the Unthinkable* as inspiration, the group wrote, drew, dreamt, modeled, and acted on these stories to move from fiction to an engagement with the real.
— Alicia Imperiale, Critic

BIRDS AND BABIES
Isa Akerfeldt-Howard and Sarah Weiss

We seek to prioritize public health and environmental justice in the Bronx by undermining the boundary between human and non-human health. Mobilizing the existing health infrastructure to better serve human constituents, as well as non-human ones, we have founded Fordham Community Land Trust—a non-profit organization dedicated to environmental wellness.

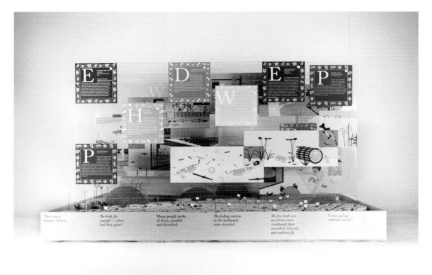

THE TENANT UNION OF AMERICA
Louisa Nolte and Sasha Zwiebel

We established the Tenant Union of America (TUA) to empower tenants in the Bronx by focusing on the needs of women. The TUA's mission is to increase long-term security by adaptive preservation of affordable housing, renovating and enhancing rent-stabilized apartments which are grounded in the community and interwoven into the existing city fabric.

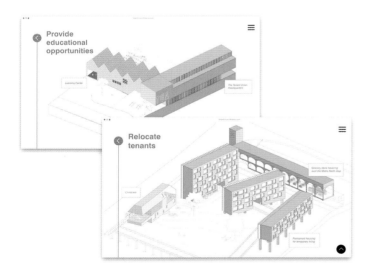

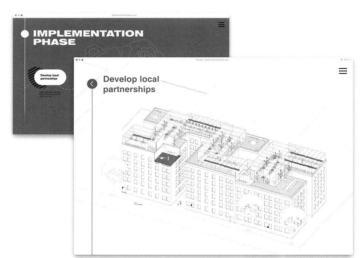

■ FACULTY REFLECTION
We began by considering catastrophe as an instrument of urbanization. Catastrophes are often the pivotal ingredients that initiate collective action. Whether it is the Great Depression and Roosevelt's New Deal or the Second World War and Metabolist movement in Japan, we see how catastrophes can instigate political action and public will. We began by asking: What is at stake for us today? And: What is the catastrophe that defines our context?
— Bimal Mendis, Assistant Professor Adjunct

9TH AVENUE BRIDGE PARK
Xuefeng Du, Yangwei Kevin Gao, and Niema Jafari

The Harlem River splits Manhattan and the Bronx, crossed by 14 bridges that ineffectively interconnect the two boroughs. The proposed pedestrian bridges become a transitional zone between water and land, allowing soft landscapes to merge into future development and advocating the river as a shared resource for neighboring communities.

FORDHAM LANDING AS THE EPICENTER OF THE GREEN NEW DEAL
Martin Carrillo Bueno, Paul Freudenberg, and Mingxi Li

A graphic narrative generates a catalogue of building strategies giving fertile ground for new micro circular economies within the Bronx. This economy proposes to rethink the role of gas stations, jails, storage facilities, and parking structures, converting them into trade schools that will feed into a new socially and environmentally conscious industry.

■ FACULTY REFLECTION

A critical, progressive agenda for architecture is alive and well in this studio, given an even greater urgency and energy by our recent challenges. So too is the studio's commitment to collaborative and non-hierarchical, not to say smoothly consensual, ways of working. Traces of cynicism that have often accompanied urban assignments at Yale have been driven out—or at least underground—by a poignant awareness of our community's fragility, and the contingency of our discipline.
— Alan Plattus, Professor

Auroville, a 'city-in-the-making' in South India, was founded in 1968 as a model city for the future where all aspects of city life could be radically rethought as an integral experiment. This studio investigates urban co-housing prototypes in a high-density context, with a focus on redefinition of private and shared spaces in the context of community living. Auroville is radical in its relationship to land as a non-ownable resource belonging to the 'commons.' Alongside new ideas of mobility, circular economy, and green infrastructure, non-ownership of land allows the development of collective living models that are restricted not by plot definitions but by land-use definitions. The site lies within a compact residential area designed to house 8,000 inhabitants and related services. Taking note of the growing imbalances in current urbanization, and visiting cohousing projects in Copenhagen, the studio applies integral thinking to address environmental, social, and economic impacts of development. The need of the hour is to design self-reliant urban communities—healthy environments where residents feel nurtured, happier, healthier, and more peaceful.

JURY
Gavin Hogben, Lisa Gray, Swarnabh Ghosh, Andrew Benner, Michael Marshall, Sunil Bald, Ratan Batliboi, Lily Chi, Deborah Gans, Ritu Mohanty, Riyaz Tayyibji

FACULTY
Anupama Kundoo and Sarosh Anklesaria

PARTICIPANTS
Camille Chabrol, Andrew Economos Miller, Katie Lau, Thomas Mahon, Alex Pineda, Baolin Shen, Arghavan Taheri, I-Ting Tsai, Justin Tsang, Anna Borou Yu

■ FACULTY REFLECTION
This studio investigates prototypes for high-density cohousing using the utopian city of Auroville as site and prompt. "Commoning" allows for transformative social paradigms promoting new forms of collective living, empowering local communities, and offering stewardship of resources. Student projects demonstrate a broad range of speculative architectures—a food commons with community kitchens; a cyclical, incremental, material collective; a synanthropic housing/food lab; and contested commons facilitated through mobile and temporal architectures.
— Anupama Kundoo, William B. and Charlotte Shepherd Davenport Visiting Professor of Architectural Design, and Sarosh Anklesaria, Critic

This studio traveled to Copenhagen, Denmark.

THE AUROVILLIAN
Justin Tsang

The Aurovillian has reinvented the conventional hotel model by capturing traces of experiments in co-hospitality at Auroville. Over the years, the city has attracted many visitors and researchers to explore and adventure, while at the same time creating thousands of jobs for the surrounding neighborhoods. The unique nature of Auroville allows for commoning and hospitality together, known as co-hospitality—a new typology that creates novel encounters and a constantly reconfiguring neighborhood.

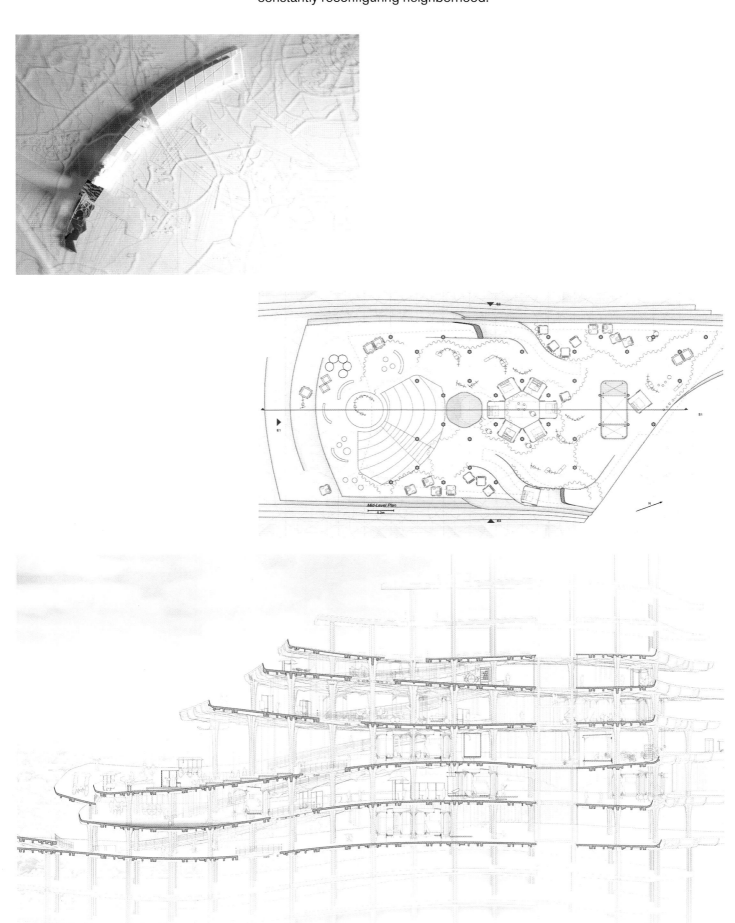

BEDS AND BEDS
Camille Chabrol, Thomas Mahon, and Alex Pineda

Our project rethinks the relationship between housing and food systems, across multiple scales of processing and production. Compact bedroom units allow for space to be given to a "Food Commons." Bedrooms form clusters, creating mid-scale social units. The clusters reach out to access a thickened "growing façade." In this way, the traditional housing "unit" is expanded to encapsulate a bedroom, a piece of the façade, and participation in the Food Commons.

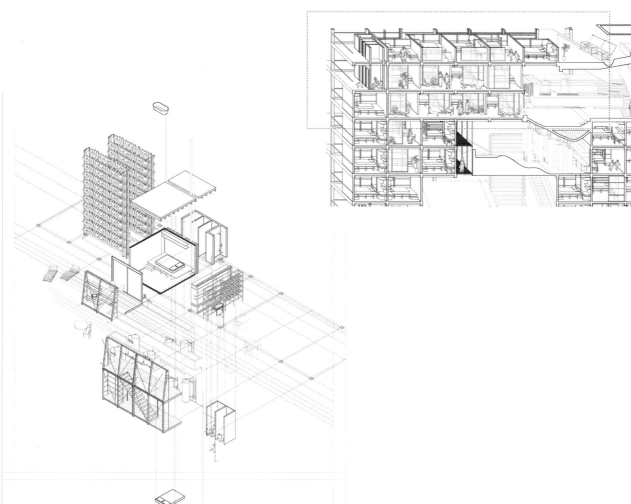

Why is it difficult to imagine new futures for many urban communities in the United States? This studio debates that question through the act of "social dreaming" and architectural speculation. Alternative architectural futures are designed against the backdrop of historic decisions made for an impoverished urban neighborhood thirty years ago. Students are asked to consider the latent social, political, and urban potentials of the site in West Oakland, California, while operating at an architectural scale. Students give form to a speculative space based on a close reading of history and cultural practices. This studio's cultivation of an imaginary, parallel future intends to radically shift current communal perceptions of possible presents. Students travel to South Africa to review recent architecture, art and urbanism projects in Johannesburg, documenting the presence of an Afro-Futurist imaginary in everyday life. Looking back, armed with what we know today, how might we even begin to dream—and see certain communities anew? Can dreaming today give us courage to be prophetic tomorrow, breaking away from paternalistic rhetoric and actions?

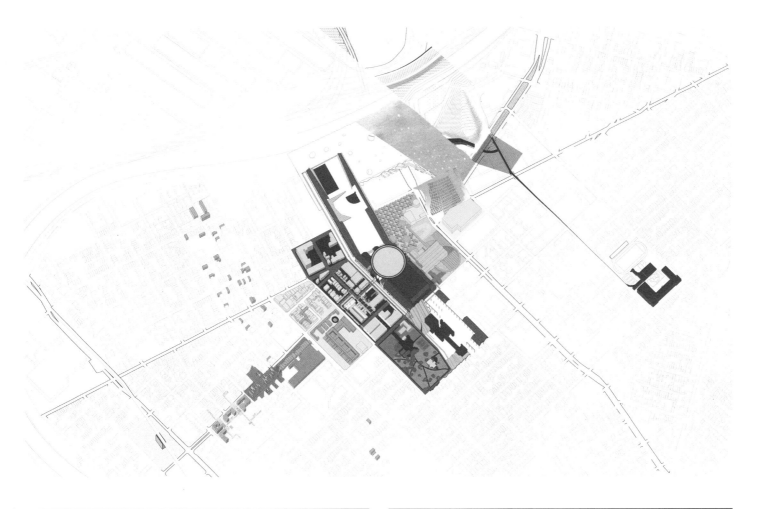

JURY
William Gilchrist, Thiresh Govender, Olalekan Jeyifous, Anupama Kundoo, Michael Marshall, Elihu Rubin, Ife Vanable, Amanda Williams, Mario Gooden

FACULTY
Walter Hood and Andrew Benner

PARTICIPANTS
Michael Gasper, Gabriel Gutierrez Huerta, Rishab Jain, Kelley Johnson, Andrew Kim, Matthew Liu, Manasi Punde, Rukshan Vathupola, Darryl Weimer, Paul Wu

■ FACULTY REFLECTION
When all appears well in our world, it is difficult to dream, speculate and imagine realities for others who are different and less fortunate. But in difficult times when all of our probable futures are called into question, the plausible and possible seem attainable not only for ourselves but for those others. As the semester unfolded, our students' speculations on alternate pasts, presents, and futures gained an eerie urgency.

— Walter Hood, Diana Balmori Visiting Professor of Landscape Architecture, and Andrew Benner, Critic

Advanced Design Studio

Spring 2020

This studio traveled to Johannesburg, South Africa.

This speculative urbanism project looks critically at the single family home, a typology designed for the now archaic nuclear family. As a reconsideration of how neighborhoods are developed, I study how 10,000 new homes built for 10,000 different types of families can reshape the city into a space where people of color and women with children don't have to fight for housing.

RE-IMAGING OAKLAND
Matthew Liu

Re-imaging Oakland occupies a campus on Mandela Parkway in West Oakland. Historically significant but under-utilized industrial warehouses and public amenities are transformed into community-based testing grounds for digital media development. The project re-imagines gaming recreation, the media industry and bodily representations on local and global scales. *Re-imaging Oakland* is a redefined community center with the mission of documenting and prioritizing the body in space.

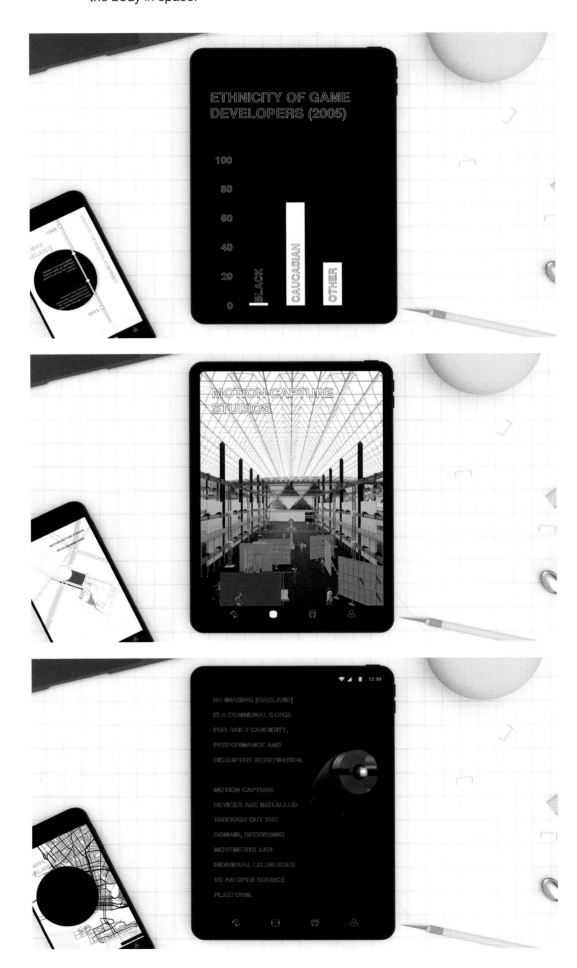

This studio confronts the challenge of a new paradigm emerging alongside a new American culture which can be termed "Americanity" or "Pacifican." Americans need to reconnect with their origins, to go back to the land and understand it as sacred. They face the urgency of reconnecting in order to begin a new narrative about the territory, to make building healthy cities possible, and rebalance life in a post-technological world. This paradigm shift must be accompanied by the re-balancing of feminine and indigenous communities in the cultural process. This studio approaches that challenge through a concrete project: the MAM Women's Museum for the Twenty-First Century, based in Santiago, Chile. The Women's Museum seeks to remember, recreate, and activate the sacred spaces of arche-typal women, to acknowledge the force of equilibrium and balance that is critical to the challenges humanity faces at the dawn of the 21st century. More than a technique for producing objects, architecture must become a technique for the construction of relationships in space.

JURY
José Araguez, Norma Barbacci, Ana Mariá Durán, Francine Houben, Aaron Tobey, Joel Sanders, Isaac Calisvaart, Solano Benítez, Rick Joy, Teresa Moller, Thomas Phifer, Adam Yarinsky

FACULTY
Cazú Zegers and Kyle Dugdale

PARTICIPANTS
Guillermo Acosta Navarrete, Katharine Blackman, Page Comeaux, Rebecca Commissaris, Clara Domange, Nathan Garcia, Will James, Rachel LeFevre, Zack Lenza, Kelsey Rico, David Scurry

■ FACULTY REFLECTION
Our studio in some way was visionary because of its focus on a "world out of balance," and how architecture can restore the balance by creating healthier cities, healthier environments, and healthier relationships. I'm really pleased with the answer to this question that the student proposals gave, each one of them opening new possibil-ities in an original way, giving powerful responses to the social and environmental crisis we are living today.
— Cazú Zegers, Eero Saarinen Visiting Professor of Architectural Design

This studio traveled to Santiago, Chile.

MUSEO ABIERTO
Page Comeaux

Museo Abierto takes into account the sociopolitical context of the site and the historical context of the museum typology. Taking cues from the classical museum, this proposal aligns a focus on education with the deconstruction of the museum's own institutional framework. By connecting to an existing network of *escuelas abiertas,* the museum becomes a space for an education that deconstructs the classroom into the territory of Chile.

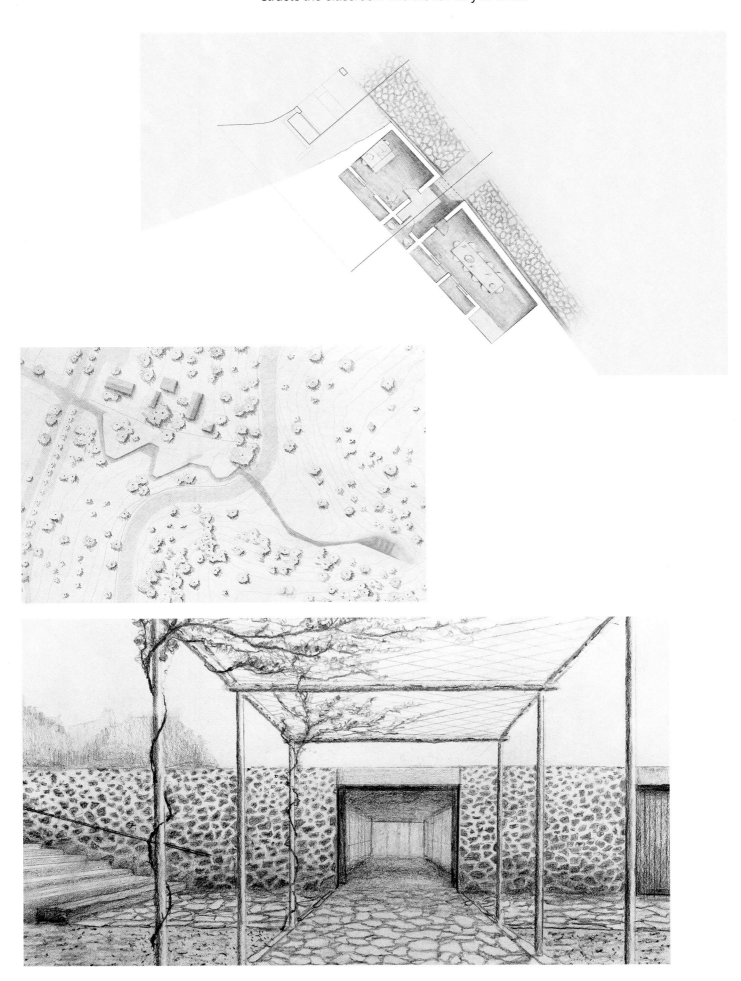

Water Architecture responds to the water crisis in the region of Santiago. It challenges the studio's call for an exclusive women's museum by resisting both the common association of women with nature (understood as objects of exploitation), and its binary inversion (wherein respect for nature represents the feminine). Instead, this project rehearses a more complex attitude to gender and to nature, presenting water both as a resource and as something with intrinsic value.

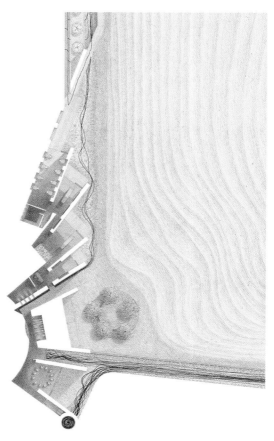

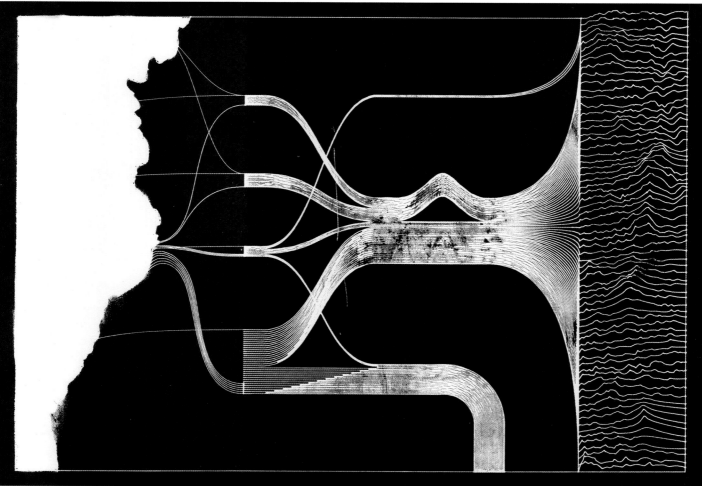

Advanced Design Studio

Somehow, in the midst of a commercialized contemporary culture, the library remains as a free space to sit, read, check out a book, and have access to WiFi and information—a place to learn, which often functions as a supplement to schools and universities. This studio begins with an examination of free civic space and the politics of these spaces. This study extends beyond the simple distinction between public and private to include a deeper awareness of embedded hierarchies, visibility, and formal and informal definitions of space. Where are these public spaces located? Who are they serving? How are these spaces designed to be welcoming and hospitable as a means to promote inclusion, equity, diversity, and accessibility? This studio aims to recognize that as architects, we are responsible for the politics inherent in the spaces that we create. How a building is organized, positioned, designed, and structured has the power to promote changes in culture, challenge norms and conventions, and to invite a more open democratic civic space.

Spring 2020

JURY
Turner Brooks, Thomas de Monchaux, Martin Finio, Leslie Gill, David Leven, Astrid Lipka, Miriam Peterson, Ada Tolla, Tatiana Bilbao, Ana Mariá Durán, Chris McVoy, Marc Tsurumaki

FACULTY
Stella Betts

PARTICIPANTS
James Bradley, Daniella Calma, Shuang Chen, Elaine ZiYi Cui, Yuhao Gordon Jiang, Max Ouellette-Howitz, Jonathan Palomo, Jenna Ritz, Limy Fabiana Rocha, Jen Shin, Brenna Thompson

■ FACULTY REFLECTION
Crisis and tragedy demand understanding, support, nimbleness, invention, creativity, and an open approach to life and work. This semester we looked at public space and equity through the lens of the public library. Unbeknownst to us, these issues would take center stage globally this spring. These issues are not new, they just have a brighter light shining on them at this moment, demanding us to take action more than ever.
  — Stella Betts, Louis I. Kahn Visiting Assistant
    Professor of Architectural Design

This studio traveled to Paris, France.

PENETRATION IN SPACE: STOREFRONT TO READING ROOM
Yuhao Gordon Jiang

A free library should provide easier access for everyone. The original storefronts on one side of the site are preserved as a secondary entrance to the library, offering direct accessibility to the library programs. Walls extend into the library and transform into furniture and staircases. The vertical relationship shifts and intertwines, creating spatial possibilities for different programs. This gesture brings the urban context into the library and diffuses its boundary.

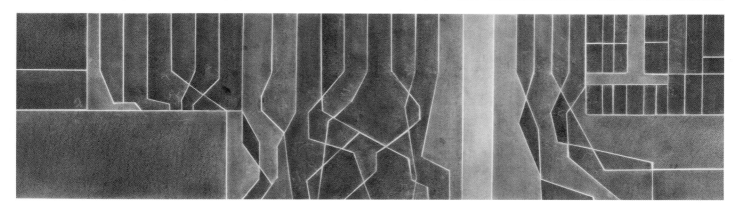

QUEENS TABLE
Jen Shin

Queens Table allows for all components of civic life to happen in one free space, nurturing a robust social infrastructure and providing the setting for deep participation in public life. It is at once monumental and ordinary. Its approachability allows the library to bestow nobility upon each patron as they pursue growth and personal development, intrinsically augmenting the unfolding democratic project that is the Queens Public Library.

1

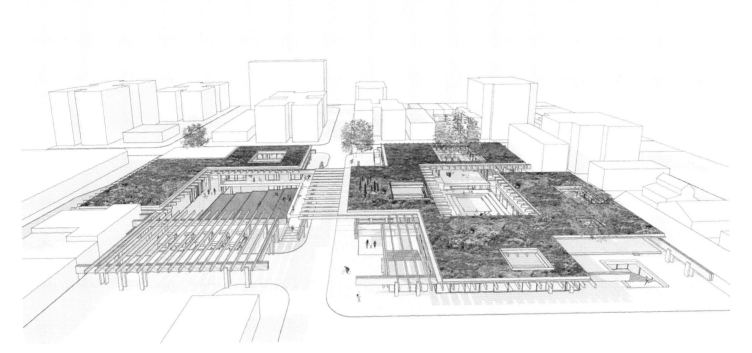

2

3

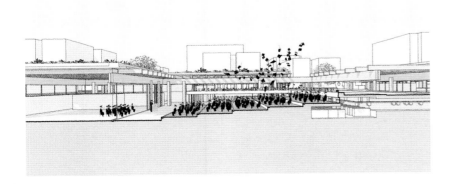

1. The horizontal roof democratizes public space with sensitivity to context.
2. The horizontal line persists while spaces shift in section.
3. Queens Public Library dignifies the work of building social cohesion.

This studio challenges students to rethink what urban life could be beyond the idea of property. Focusing on the relationship between the home and the settlement, students experiment with the possibility of commoning. The studio explores spatial principles of settling that can challenge the urban subdivision of private and public space; it also experiments with forms of land tenure in which confrontation and negotiation among communities are not subsumed within a totalizing urban framework, but are acknowledged as principles of coexistence. The studio travels to Rome, where it engages in extensive field-work on site, studying both city and countryside in their most salient historical episodes. After carefully investigating the political economy of commoning, each group of students selects a specific settlement within a Roman suburb, Ager Tusculanus, and proposes a strategy of gradual transformation based on the principle of the "dispersed home" and processes of commoning. This gradual transformation involves both the house and the settlement, spaces for production, and spaces for reproduction.

JURY
M. Surry Schlabs, Michael R. Cohen, Elisa Iturbe, Tatiana Bilbao, Stefan Gruber, Alicia Imperiale

FACULTY
Pier Vittorio Aureli and Emily Abruzzo

PARTICIPANTS
Sara Alajmi, Michelle Badr, Serena Ching, Ruchi Dattani, Changming Huang, Layla Ni, Luka Pajovic, David Schaengold, Xiaohui Wen, Kay Yang

■ FACULTY REFLECTION
The studio focused on the retrofitting and transformation of suburban settlements around Rome known as *toponimi*. At stake in the transformation of these settlements was the possibility of introducing forms of commoning as a way to live together beyond the legal and existential limit of private property. Each of the seven projects aims to facilitate and enhance the sharing of both production and reproduction.
— Pier Vittorio Aureli, Charles Gwathmey
    Professor in Practice

This studio traveled to Rome, Italy.

LABOR OF LOVE: A PROJECT FOR SAN CESAREO
Serena Ching and Kay Yang

This project finds its starting point as families share responsibilities and resources beyond the household. As social and spatial relationships expand, the incremental nature of the proposal reclaims backyards, streets, and new civic spaces within San Cesareo. Through renovation and self-build strategies, elements are incrementally introduced and dispersed, transforming the settlement into a landscape of commoning practices facilitated by a willingness to extend and remove boundaries of private property.

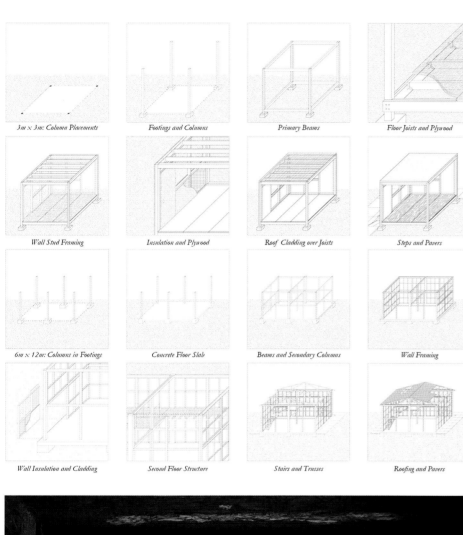

3m × 3m: Column Placements · Footings and Columns · Primary Beams · Floor Joists and Plywood

Wall Stud Framing · Insulation and Plywood · Roof Cladding over Joists · Steps and Pavers

6m × 12m: Columns in Footings · Concrete Floor Slab · Beams and Secondary Columns · Wall Framing

Wall Insulation and Cladding · Second Floor Structure · Stairs and Trusses · Roofing and Pavers

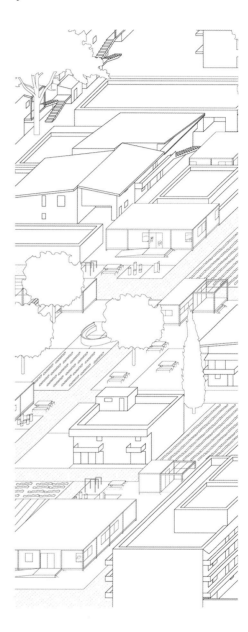

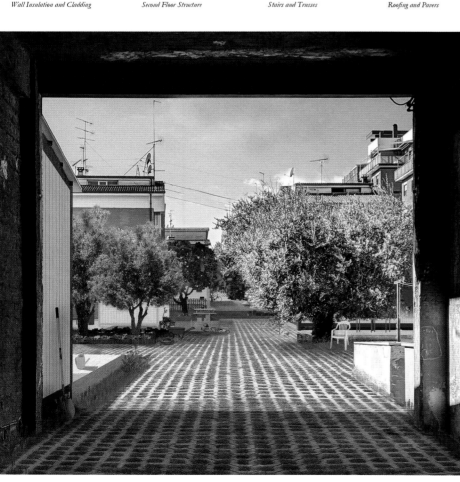

LADDERS, FIELDS
Changming Huang and Xiaohui Wen

Hidden among layers of *forre*, the settlement is covered with olive trees and orchards. We identified the rural fabric of land divided by fences into strips as "ladders," and propose to gradually overlay a system of "field conditions," a bottom-up approach established by local connections without an overarching geometry. The project is a reimagination of rural life and a speculation on how it can be achieved through three incremental phases.

This studio examines the concept of the commons as a tool to apply to new housing typologies. The commons can be defined as a shared resource that is sustained, supported, and improved upon by participants that contribute to its maintenance. Applied to housing, it creates an arena for collective living whose success is dependent on social contracts and the flexibility to evolve with shifting needs. Students investigate the viability of collective housing through a series of precedents. Examples, such as the modernist development of a shared kitchen in multifamily housing in Sweden in the 1950s, draw together both architectural innovation and the sociological phenomenon of releasing women from domestic duties, empowering them to join the workforce. The studio challenges students to design places made for change and adaptation as a tool to increase the longevity of a project. Using the research on commons, this studio proposes new ways of living. Student proposals expand the dictionary of housing typologies to integrate the unique and particular needs of people.

Advanced Design Studio

Spring 2020

JURY
Pier Vittorio Aureli, Sol Camacho, Stefan Gruber, Elisa Iturbe, Anna Puigjaner, M. Surry Schlabs, Eduardo Medeiro

FACULTY
Tatiana Bilbao and Andrei Harwell

PARTICIPANTS
Taiming Chen, Helen Farley, Gretchen Gao, Michael Glassman, Mari Kroin, Ho Jae Lee, Jackson Lindsay, Christine Pan, Deirdre Plaus, Gus Steyer, Alper Turan

■ FACULTY REFLECTION
We hoped the studio would not only explore the potentials of commoning as a design subject, but that it could also function as a commons, within which everyone could contribute and benefit from a shared endeavor. The studio far exceeded our expectations—the students immersed themselves, collaborating closely until midterm, allowing work to continue after COVID-19. The final work had a strong sense of shared identity and rich, complex ideas.
— Tatiana Bilbao, Norman R. Foster Visiting Professor, and Andrei Harwell, Critic

This studio traveled to Mexico City, Mexico.

The studio was a discussion and investigation of the commons in the context of the Santa Maria la Ribera neighborhood of Mexico City. The work included exercises in commoning, group research, and a network of interventions across the neighborhood. These explorations combined into a large studio site model and site drawing which became roadmaps of the projects and the life of the neighborhood.

The group site model of Santa Maria la Ribera took two months of planning and fabrication, and is comprised of 12 panels totaling 15' × 9'.

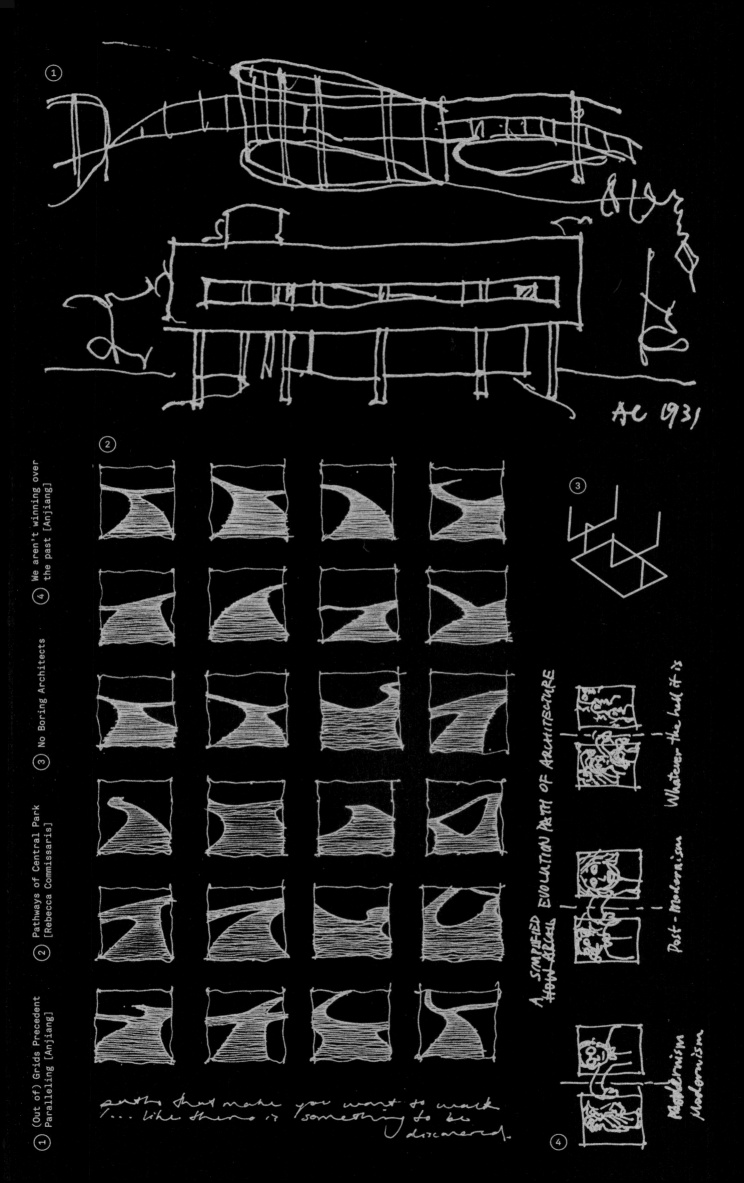

① (Out of) Grids Precedent Paralleling [Anjiang]

② Pathways of Central Park [Rebecca Commissaris]

③ No Boring Architects

④ We aren't winning over the past [Anjiang]

AC 1931

A SIMPLIFIED EVOLUTION PATH OF ARCHITECTURE
HOW ABOUT

Modernism   Post-Modernism   Whatever the hell it is

paths that make you want to walk ... like there is something to be discovered.

社員にとって重要な 価値の "多様化"

既存システムでは ニーズに対応し切れない

1. 取捨選択の □□□□□□□□□□ 限定的になっていくという □□

"民営化" と □□□□□

└→ 格□

最低限の コスト で □□□□□
└→ 小さくて 大
└→ デジタルテクノロ

① Japanese English Conflict Notes
   [Taku Samejima]

② home office in Brooklyn
   [Yuhao Gordon Jiang]

③ [Anjiang]

① ② ③

④ Image Analysis [Dominiq Oti]

⑤ Cross Section Study: Conjunto Dance Hall [Rebecca Commissaris]

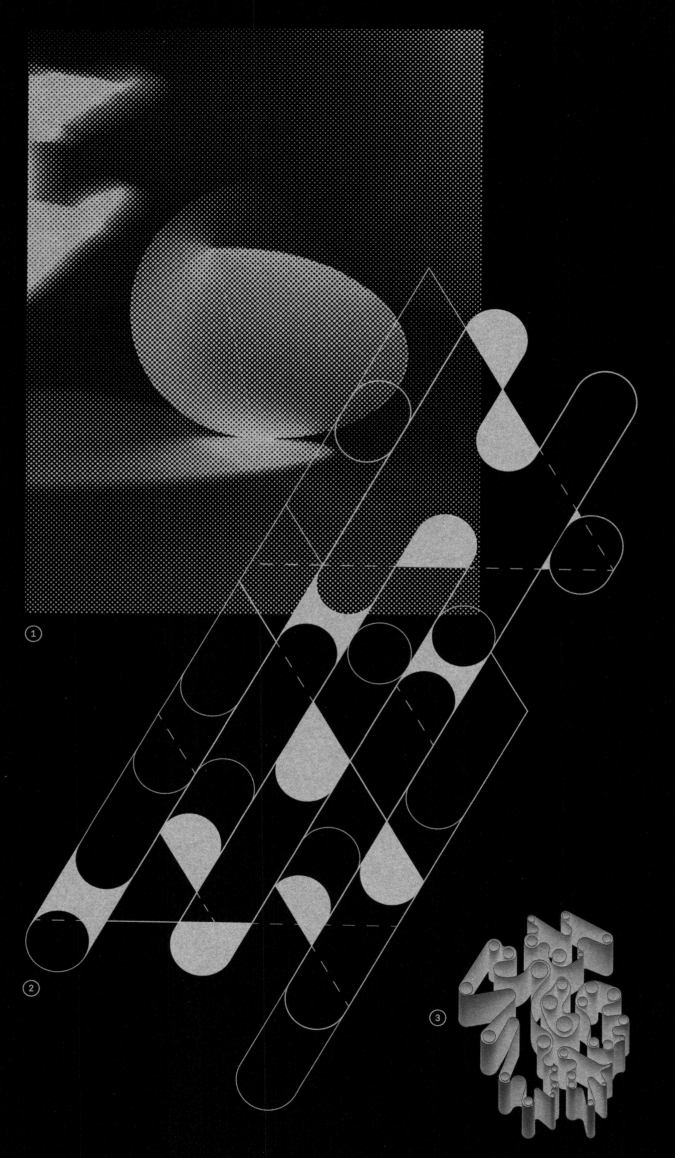

① [Calvin Yang Yue]

② Generative plan in three acts
(insert, compound and shear)

③ Plan Oblique, walls meander about
focal points stretching boundaries

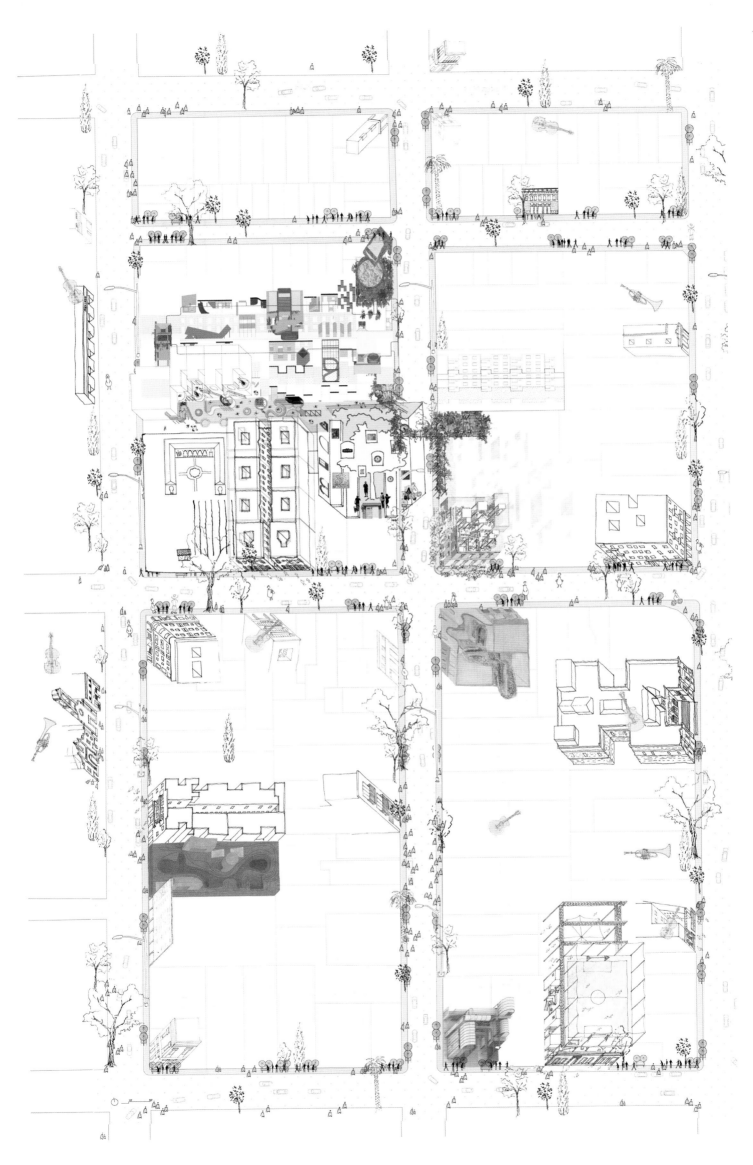

Advanced Design Studio

Spring 2020

Group research and exercises lead to interventions which create a network across the neighborhood.

Traditional opera houses have long been challenged for their inaccessibility to certain publics, notably the young, the poor, and the culturally diverse. This studio starts with the idea of bringing large and diverse performances to local communities by creating a demountable and adaptably scalable performance space that can be deployed in different public spaces and existing buildings for a few months at a time. Opera, with its elitist audiences and grand halls, is an art form in flux as public funding shrinks and HD broadcasts radically change the way many people experience live performances. A landmark piece of market research in the U.S. and Canada asked: "What is culture?" In the responses, opera houses, concert halls, and theaters were at the bottom of the list—below food, film, music, and local neighborhood events with a vibrant community. In this studio students propose flexible performance venues that are beautiful, exciting, and inspiring to all— sending signals of welcome and creativity.

JURY
Mary Lou Aleskie, José Aragüez, Sunil Bald, Donatien Grau, Jonathan Jones, Dana Karwas, Kyoung Sun Moon, Susanna Sirefman, Cazu Zegers

FACULTY
Francine Houben, Isaäc Kalisvaart, Ruth Mackenzie, George Knight

PARTICIPANTS
Cristina Anastase, Miguel Darcy de Oliveira Miranda, Adam Feldman, Eunice Lee, Samantha Monge Kaser, Jewel Pei, Leonardo Serrano Fuchs, Armaan Shah, Seth Thompson, Laélia Kim-Lan Vaulot, Liwei Wang

■ FACULTY REFLECTION
The brief required students to consider the ways in which revolutionary technologies transform artistic expression and performance. With the unanticipated reliance on remote learning and digital presentation at the end of the semester, the students themselves had to become storytellers, designers, narrators, animators, directors, actors, and musicians, with their five-minute final videos being their performance.
— George Knight, Critic

This studio traveled to Paris, France.

CULTURE
Liwei Wang

With inflatable architecture, the typical logic of construction no longer applies. What happens when the walls are plump and soft? How do you tap into a lineage of inflatables as facsimiles? For me, this was an opportunity to explore the language of danger. It would be irresponsible to design dangerous forms with concrete or metal. With inflatables, I can make an architecture of monsters and spikes.

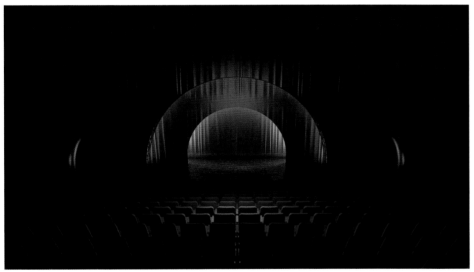

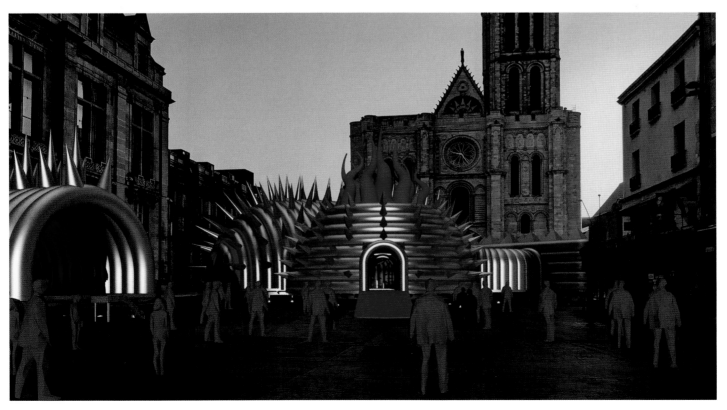

The Breathing Dome is an operable and temporary structure for opera and musical performances. Inspired by both Chinese and Italian opera house typologies, the opera house of the future offers a dramatic experience and a social platform. The operable kinetic tensile structure gives artists the freedom to experiment, and offers the local community an accessible experience with the choice of paying for a ticket or sitting down for a drink.

The City of New Haven is dedicated to building a new facility in the downtown area to house a Family Justice Center for victims of domestic violence. The urgency of the issue of family violence has inspired New Haven's city government to replace a temporary facility at Temple Street with a recognizable and accessible destination that is integral to the city. The typology of Family Justice Center is relatively new, housing in one place all venues of assistance for victims. A "one-stop-shop" reduces the confusion, stress, and difficulty of seeking help, which can often involve multiple long trips, missed work, and difficulty finding childcare. These difficulties have led to many victims giving up trying to find help, giving this project its urgent importance. Students tour the facilities in New Haven, and begin a sustained dialogue with program directors, Chief City Planner Aicha Woods, and others, including survivors of domestic violence who have participated in similar programs.

Advanced Design Studio

Spring 2020

JURY
John Nafziger, Alec Purves, Eeva-Liisa Pelkonen, Stella Betts, Aicha Woods, Alice Hawks, Marta Caldeira, Julie Johnson, Jasmit Rangr, Paola Serrecchia

FACULTY
Turner Brooks and Jonathan Toews

PARTICIPANTS
Shuchen Dong, Yue Geng, Shiqi Valerie Li, Ruike Liu, Smit Patel, Rhea Schmid, Qizhen Tang, Alexander Velaise, Daoru Wang, Hengyuan Yang

■ FACULTY REFLECTION
As a new urban prototype and presence, the Center for Family Justice choreographs bodies, often consumed by trauma, within space, and creates an extended 'liminal' zone from the street to the different services that this institution offers victims of domestic violence. Students' designs exhibited spaces of transition that clearly orchestrated destinations and private areas for the various consultations and treatments the program demanded.
— Turner Brooks, William Henry Bishop
    Visiting Professor and Professor Adjunct

This studio traveled to Amsterdam, Netherlands.

MEDIATOR
Hengyuan Yang

Trauma makes people feel either like somebody else or like nobody. In order to overcome trauma, one needs help to get back in touch with one's body and senses. The new building could be a mediator between the world and the body. A sequence of walls creates layers of space, interweaving courtyards, public spaces, and intimate service rooms, bringing light, air, intimacy, and veracity to every visitor.

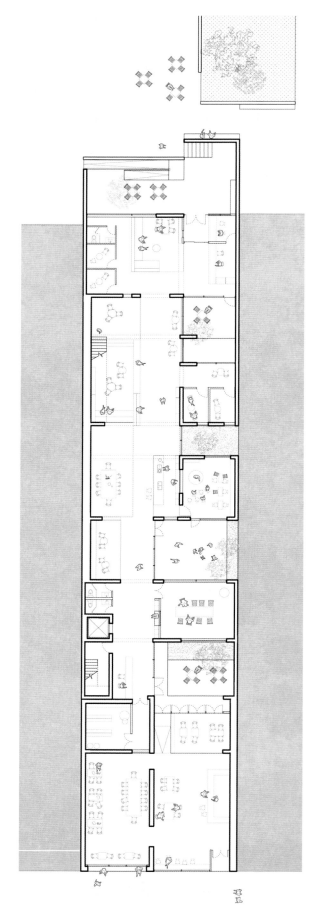

RE-FAMILIAR
Smit Patel

The project creates a safe haven for victims of domestic violence on their journey towards becoming "thrivers." To create this safe haven, the users should have a sense of ownership over the project, their own small-scale urban environment which would be a city with different partner services coming together. Architecture is a language to re-familiarise the body to the urban and the domestic with elements of surprise and moments of recognition.

This studio explores the relationship between cultural heritage and the richness of contemporary urban life through imagining the restoration and future possibilities for the Ladeira da Misericórdia, a steep street that connects the upper and lower areas of the historic center of Salvador da Bahia, Brazil. The site includes Baroque fabric, open areas, and deteriorated works of architect Lina Bo Bardi, who spent many years working in Salvador. Students propose new architectural interventions that engage the city's rich sociocultural context. The studio works with the complex historical layers accumulated at the site to both rehabilitate what exists and propose a new architectural intervention that integrates urban dwelling and programs for cultural expression. These architectural proposals explore the contemporary potential of Lina Bo Bardi's belief that art can give agency to the multicultural population that inhabits the historic center of Salvador. The concepts of historic preservation, conservation, and sustainability are foundational to these proposals.

JURY
Barry Bergdoll, Fred Bland, Mario Gooden, Esther da Costa Meyer, Miriam Peterson, Eeva-Liisa Pelkonen, Javier Robles, Rosalyne Shieh, Billie Tsien, Cazú Zegers, Carla Zollinger

FACULTY
Norma Barbacci and Sunil Bald

PARTICIPANTS
Emily Cass, Gioia Montana Connell, Deo Deiparine, Miriam Dreiblatt, Tianyu Guan, Phoebe Harris, Srinivas Narayan Karthikeyan, Maya Sorabjee, Megan Tan, Hongyu Wang, Daniel Whitcombe

■ FACULTY REFLECTION
The Ladeira da Misericórdia studio focused on the symbiotic acts of intervention and preservation to address the challenges of urban disconnection, social inequality, and environmental degradation. Guided by the intrinsic belief that the socio-cultural richness of place is a vital agent for the sustainable revitalization of historic urban centers, the students' bold proposals to the studio's challenges convincingly argued for a way forward through re-imagining what exists.
   — Norma Barbacci, Robert A.M. Stern Visiting Professor of Classical Architecture

This studio traveled to São Paulo, Brazil, and Salvador, Brazil.

ESTRADA DA COMIDA
Deo Deiparine

Food production, retail, and affordable housing in this food commons in Salvador, Brazil connects the upper institutional and lower commercial areas of the city, previously separated by the city's dramatic topography. The project exhumes the various strata of history accumulated on the site. Geological, biological, historical, and quotidian time sync up in this project to create a monumental system that supports new chapters in Salvador's Afro-Brazilian heritage.

1

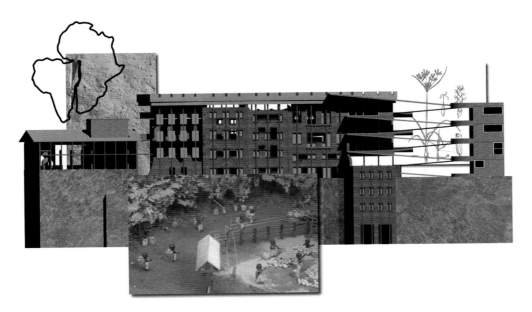

2

3

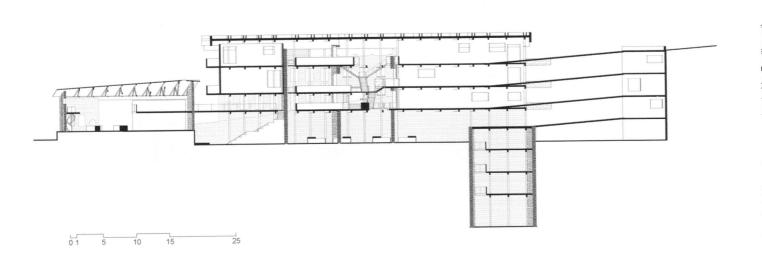

0 1   5   10   15   25

Advanced Design Studio

Spring 2020

1. Growing pads and retaining walls expose uniquely Afro-Brazilian soil.
2. Terraces for food growth neighbor areas for regrowth of Brazil's Atlantic Forest.
3. Anchor points throughout reflect the labor involved in Afro-Brazilian cuisine.

TERRA FIRMA
Maya Sorabjee

This proposal for the Ladeira da Misericórdia restores a row of crumbling colonial shells to create a space of communal domesticity. The intervention ties the site to the sustainable agroforestry efforts of *quilombos* and *terreiros* in the surrounding region, using rammed earth to create spaces for eating, cooking, making, and gathering. The ritual and alimentary aspects of the program are supported by a terraced landscape on the escarpment above.

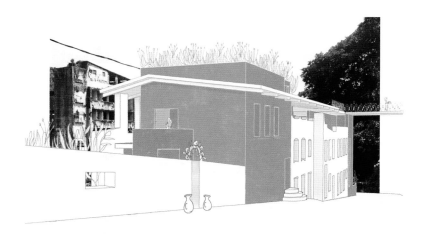

For architects, the book is a tool for clarifying, extending, and promoting ideas and projects. This seminar examines the book in architecture as an array of organizational techniques and as a mediator.

FACULTY
Luke Bulman

OF DUST: REFLECTIONS FROM A DAMAGED AFTERLIFE
Mary Carole Overholt

Sheltering in place is a global mandate—we have become more attuned to the microcosm of our interior worlds. This project considers dust, an ever-present yet oft-invisible material, at various scales—from the studio apartment to the cosmos. This book compiles artistic and literary representations of dust, exploring the death, disaster, and possibility present in this seemingly banal material.

1225b   Formal Analysis 2

What was the modern and what was the postmodern? The nature of that difference, for instance universalizing or contradicting, is explored with the intention of reconsidering the modern in a contemporary context.

FACULTY
Peter Eisenman

ANALYSIS: BARCELONA PAVILION
Ruike Liu and Jerome Tryon

Mies van der Rohe was interested in a balanced composition but rejected bilateral symmetry, favoring a grid-reflected symmetry and horizontal symmetry that resolves in the perspectival experience of the viewer. Furthermore, the walls and columns do not follow the rational grid system of the plinth, resulting in a tension between two architectures—one conceptual, one actual—and the space they imply.

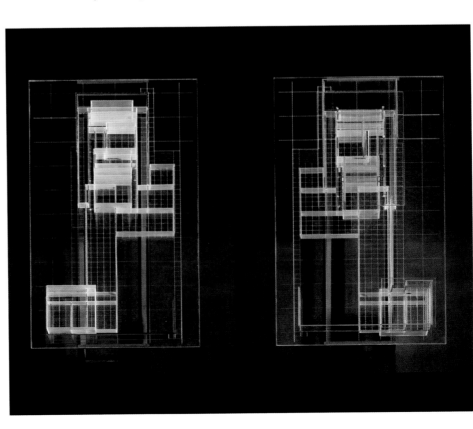

Design and Visualization

Coursework

Spring 2020

Architectural ruins index the total failure of individual buildings, technologies, economies, or, at times, entire civilizations. This course researches ruination and ruins—what produces them, what defines them, and how they impact society.

FACULTY
Mark Foster Gage

STREET AS RUIN
Helen Farley and Deirdre Plaus

The coronavirus pandemic has emptied streets in cities across the world, prompting discussion about how these spaces might change or be adapted for new use. Our project imagines alternative uses for the typologies of streets that characterize our settlements. This image looks at the way the zone of the suburban street might be re-appropriated as a ground for commoning resources.

1240a   Custom Crafted Components

This historically grounded, hands-on seminar requires individual aesthetic expression via the crafting of tangible, original, intimately scaled architectural elements. Exploration and experimentation with unusual sequences of analog and digital representation are encouraged.

FACULTY
Kevin Rotheroe

MALLEABLE: MONOLITHS
Sarah Weiss

These plaster "masonry units" were made with fabric. They are the products of cutting, pinning, stitching and gathering. They were poured and left to cure. These malleable monoliths make hard out of soft. They borrow from a long lineage of domestic technologies for fabric manipulation. They are sturdy building blocks made out of flimsy surfaces.

This course addresses the role of digital production and image making in art and architecture, in a world inundated by digital images. Students are asked to speculate on the image as an architectural medium.

FACULTY
Brennan Buck

AN IMAGINED LIFE OF AN IMAGE
Jack Hutton

This architectural drawing will never become a building, but it will become a world. A digital one, enjoyed by millions as the next hit battle royale video game's map. The aesthetic will inspire a generation of developers to create innovative gameplay under imposed constraints. However, eventually all the servers of the original game will shut down, and we will only revisit this world through memories, sharing our nostalgia through images.

1

2012b   Structures 2

This course continues to introduce students to the analysis and design of building structural systems, emphasizing geometric properties of structural shapes, resistances to stresses, and structural behavior including ductility, movement, and modes of failure.

FACULTY
Kyoung Sun Moon

FARAMITA
Chocho Hu

This spiritual center's vertical sequence gradually brings inner calmness and tranquility to visitors. The trusses on the top carry the load of the whole interior. The cables hang the interior walls, pathways, and stairs, giving an illusion of lightness as well as a sense of rising through their vertical lines. The cables strengthen the atmosphere of peace, helping different thresholds and programs to purify visitors' minds and lead them into "another world."

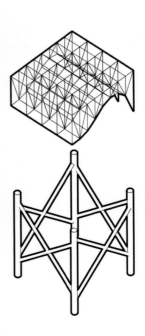

2

1. Source image: *Approach* by Liwei Wang (2015)
2. This project was designed for Arch 1012b Architectural Design 2. The structural systems were further developed in this course.

Design and Visualization

Coursework

Spring 2020

Students develop the technical systems of preliminary design proposals from earlier studio work, not only to achieve technical and performance goals but also to reinforce and re-inform the conceptual origins of the work.

FACULTY
Martin Finio (coordinator), Anibal Bellomio, Kristen Butts, Alastair Elliott, Erleen Hatfield, Robert Haughney, Kristin Hawkins, John D. Jacobson, Larry Jones, Jennifer Lan, Aaron Martin, Gina Narracci, Kari Nystrom, Laura Pirie, Victoria Ponce de Leon, Craig Razza, Pierce Reynoldson, Edward Stanley, Celia Toche, Adam Trojanowski

CUBE-CUBED
Isa Akerfeldt-Howard, Jiachen Deng, Janet Dong, Hyun Jae Jung

This proposal involves two juxtaposing systems: an outer volume within which an asymmetrical cube is suspended. With careful consideration of programmatic use types and loads, we created a mechanical system that compartmentalized the heating and cooling of the building. Additionally a screen-and-panel system attaches over the glazing to limit some of the solar gain inside the building.

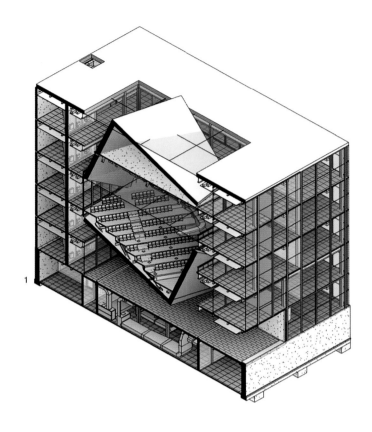

1

2223b   Structuring Architecture: Form and Space

Going beyond basic analysis of structural elements (columns, beams, trusses, arches, cables, slabs, and shells), this course examines how these components can be configured to create desired architectural forms and spaces.

FACULTY
Kyoung Sun Moon

STUDY ON MODERN STRUCTURAL CONFIGURATIONS AND THEIR POSSIBLE ALTERNATIVES
Qizhen Tang

These studies explore alternative structures for existing buildings, aiming to improve architectural and structural performance and quality. While both towers use a column grid and core, the annexes use different systems: mega trusses and space frames. The studies therefore explore replacement of the towers' column-core configuration with exterior structures such as diagrids or trussed tubes that might work as a more unified and integrated architectural and structural strategy for both towers and annexes.

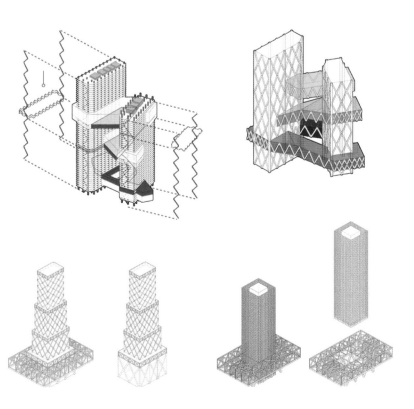

1. This project was based on studio work designed by Leanne Nagata.

The capabilities and limitations of architects' tools influence directly the spaces architects design. The potential of computational machines is revealed through design computation, the creative application of the processes underlying digital technology.

FACULTY
Michael Szivos

FACEARCH: FACIAL ARCHITECTURE GENERATOR
Janet Dong and Yidong Isabel Li

The intention is to create a facial architecture generator to explore the dynamic interactions between architecture and human. By using facial expressions as a new mouse for architects to produce and design architectural massing models in Rhino, we recognize this project's potential in different scenarios and with different user groups for a more interactive design process.

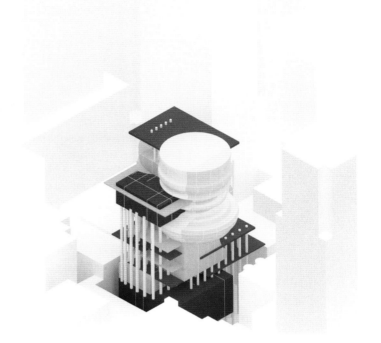

2229b   Regenerative Building: Horse Island

This seminar explores design and building techniques that seek to reduce environmental impacts across the building lifecycle, promoting metabolic, non-mechanistic approaches to the production of the built environment.

FACULTY
Alan Organschi

BEYOND THE BUILDING LIFECYCLE
Samuel David Bruce

An emergy analysis tracks solar input through raw material formation, extraction, and manufacturing into construction procedures, operational use, and the eventual cost of reusing, recycling, or handling waste. As a method of analysis, emergy sets up a way to scientifically standardize the stages of a building lifecycle and make comparisons between concepts otherwise extremely hard to qualify and quantify.

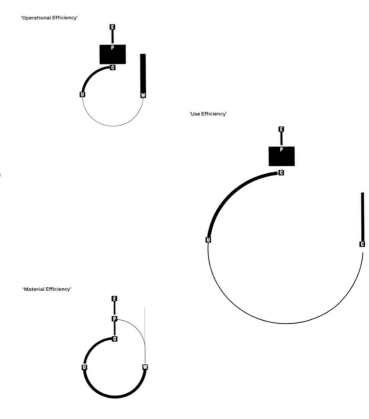

Technology and Practice

Coursework

Spring 2020

This course reimagines the value proposition of architecture practice, explores strategies used by better-compensated adjacent professions, and investigates methods and models by which architects can deliver—and be paid for—the value they bring to the building industry.

FACULTY
Phillip Bernstein and Brittany Olivari

Lanespace
Cristina Anastase and Liwei Wang

Lanespace is a startup that imagines a world where people can afford high quality homes. We were inspired by this business idea after seeing a friend go through the process of developing a laneway house. What is a laneway house? It is a secondary dwelling built at the rear of a lot near the lane. Laneway houses are under 1,000 sq. ft. and are usually intended for a single household. Living in a laneway house allows you to live in a detached unit at a fraction of the price of condos with similar square footage. In cities struggling with a tight, high-rent housing market, such as Vancouver, laneway houses are a convenient and affordable option. *Lanespace* has optimized a process that allows it to provide the fastest and simplest service to build high-quality laneway spaces.

In addition to developing laneway houses, *Lanespace* seeks to tap into existing city initiatives for universal childcare, artist studios, and independent living. Our firm's mission is leveraging laneway spaces to develop healthy neighbourhoods. We build *Lanespaces* that function as a range of facilities that can be used by the immediate community. Micro-daycares, artist studios, yoga studios and senior homes are a healthy way to densify neighbourhoods and create sustainable communities. In the age of COVID, Laneway houses are perfectly suited to be decentralized childcare facilities or senior homes.

2238b   The Mechanical Artifact

Machine learning threatens, or promises, to upend many industries. The goal of this seminar is to have students develop a sense of literacy around machine learning, its promises, pitfalls, and possibilities.

FACULTY
Dana Karwas

Dance through Architecture: Architecture through Dance
James Bradley

The AI-teration Method and the Role of AI in Architectural Design
Ekaterina Danchenko

Demystifying Gerrymandering through Machine Learning
Cindy Hwang

Dreamscape—Using AI to Create Speculative VR Environments
Rishab Jain

Transparency through the Eyes of AI
Jewel Pei

Live Letters: Strike a Pose, Get a Letter
Julia Schäfer

This seminar explores accidents, failures, and catastrophes, large and small, in buildings and—whether caused by bad luck, bad design, bad management, or miscalculation—how such incidents have impacted users, owners, and designers.

FACULTY
John D. Jacobson

Morandi Bridge Collapse
Rhea Schmid

The Morandi Bridge's tragic collapse (September 1967–August 2018; Genoa, Italy) was as straightforward a building disaster as they come. It was built, it failed, and there was incredible destruction and loss. This project unpacked the disaster's underlying complexities and inevitabilities through the following lenses: its historical context, both political and economic; its structural failures, both physical and organizational; and, the involvement of people, both as perpetrators and victims of negligence. The Morandi Bridge was a fracture critical bridge in more ways than one. It lacked redundancy in its reinforced concrete, cable-stayed design, and lacked redundancy within the governmental and private bodies tasked to inspect and maintain the bridge. When a civic structure of such importance collapses, the destruction isn't over when the dust clears. The Morandi Bridge was more than a bridge—it was an artery that sustained lives and fed whole communities around it and beyond. So, as aspiring architects, how do we understand and design for the magnitude of a building's reach? What is our relationship to maintenance? What is negligence a symptom of and can design address the source? The lessons gleaned from the bridge's tragic collapse reveal issues more insidious than a faulty cable that simply needed replacing.

3073b   Design Research 2: Retrofuturism

Students worked in small groups to develop proposals around the theme of retrofuturism, addressing unprecedented urban development, population growth and migration, and the resulting impacts on natural and social environments.

FACULTY
Joel Sanders

Nostalgia Rewired
Daniella Calma

Scaffolds
Shuang Chen

Local Intelligence
Rebecca Commissaris

Surveillance and Data Gathering
Elaine ZiYi Cui

Vernacular Chinese Proto-forms
Shuchen Dong

New Yurts in Inner Mongolia
Yue Geng

Acts of Service
Gabriel Gutierrez Huerta

Towards a New Water Future
Rishab Jain

Testbed for Autonomous Vehicles
Yuhao Gordon Jiang

Urbanscape and Water in Deccan Cities
Srinivas Narayan Karthikeyan

Not Found
Mari Kroin

Atmosphere Generator
Shiqi Valerie Li

Residential Houses during Pandemic
Ruike Liu

NAFTA: Shopping Mall Phenomena
Guillermo Acosta Navarrete

Re-assembling Aleppo
Luka Pajovic

Dirty South Metamodernism
David Scurry

Re-thinking Qilou-Arcaded Streets
Qizhen Tang

Ideological Monument Wars
Alper Turan

Preservation or Destruction
Daoru Wang

Sunken Cave Architecture
Hongyu Wang

New Ethnic Tourism Development Strategies
Hengyuan Yang

Technology and Practice

Coursework

Spring 2020

1. Morandi Bridge, Genoa, Italy, 1967

This course explores Western architectural theory, from 1750 to the present, through close readings of primary texts, ranging from theories of origin, type, and character, to more contemporary debates on historicism, technology, and environmentalism.

FACULTY
Marta Caldeira

Student Paper Topics
Lina Bo Bardi in Brazil
Camp Architecture
Homes for Single Mothers
Architecture and the Sea
Theories of Architecture and Nature
Post-industrial Society
The Silk Pavilion
Hip Hop Architecture
Cybernetics
Place-Making and Perception
Chinese Architecture
Case Study House #8
Outside of Architecture
Discipline in Architecture
Modernism and Montage
SUPERSTUDIO
Unbuilding [An]architecture
Carceral Architecture
Public Health
Architecture and a Damaged Planet
The Architectural Zeitgeist
The Modern Kitchen
Socially Constructed Hierarchies
The Global Archipelago
COVID-19 and the Environment
Uselessness
Grids
Frank Scott's Gardens
The Living Space
Soviet Socialist-Realist Architecture
Building Performance
The Architecture of Interiority
Infrastructure and Social Justice
Forms of the City
Virtual Spaces
Playgrounds
Architecture Boundaries
Place in Phenomenology
Formal Diagrams
Digital Design
British Natural Gardens
Combustion to Construction
Taste
Moriyama-san
Taylorism
Bonsai
Individuality
3rd Industrial Revolution
Mimetic Architecture
Paper Architecture
Identity and Belonging
Crisis Response

Specificity, Coexistence, Experience: Rethinking the Teleological Narrative
Joshua Tan

To understand the appropriation of land in the United States, one would need to uncover the history of spatial practices and cultural customs. This essay investigates the spatial conceptions of Indigenous and European Americans, critiquing current modes of land use and the teleological narrative of European American progress. By examining the origins of land practices, one finds that the Indigenous American conception of space prioritizes the specificity of place, coexistence with others, and a spiritual experience with the land. In contrast, the European American conception was more abstract and time-based, having its origins in the prophesied fulfilment of the Promised Land, eventually prioritizing progress and productivity.

Rather than understanding the conflict between the two in terms of its outcomes, and therefore assigning an evolutionary superiority to one of them, the paper argues that Indigenous American conceptions of space provide an alternative spatial practice that could be more equitable or meaningful. Ultimately, the paper argues that by investigating alternative practices in terms of their contexts, architects can be freed from the dogmatic tropes of the Western canon and use approaches from past civilizations to ground architectural theory. A whole history of spaces has yet to be written about the people who did something else.

Potential Energy: The Social and Spatial Dynamics of Distributed Energy Infrastructure
Jack Rusk

The infrastructure for the provision of energy has been constantly contested through time and, by this contestation, has both shaped and reflected social and spatial relationships. Central to this contestation has been the cyclic establishment of "energy commons" by wide social bases and their subsequent enclosure by the ruling elite. The emancipatory potential of an energy commons is grounded in its concern with the forces that shape and reproduce human life, with the "mode" of living, and not its political formulation. Tracing a history of energy transitions from water to coal to fossil energy, the article traces a history of failures. At the dawn of each transition, a liberatory model of energy distribution is put forward and is, in each case, quashed. Through this lens, the Green New Deal is seen as the project of a constituent power that uses the renewable energy transition to reinstate the prerogatives of violence and territory that always underpin state projects. The recurrent historical practice of distributed energy infrastructure—the care and maintenance of an energy commons—suggests another way is possible. This article catalogues their past defeats to motivate a contemporary defense of an energy infrastructure with an emancipatory social form.

Within an urban space increasingly governed by financial capital and its algorithms, abstraction is everywhere realized in the material and immaterial spaces of our daily existence.

History and Theory

FACULTY
Pier Vittorio Aureli

Frames of Palazzi: An Apparatus for a Civilized Life in Renaissance Italy
Timothy Wong

The domestic organization of the Renaissance palazzo exemplifies its cultural milieu of devising a civilized pattern of life. Departing from the singular room of the medieval home, the proliferation of rooms in the Renaissance initiated the practice of their subdivision and specialization. Emerging with these processes was the apparatus of the architectural frame. Bernard Cache defined the frame fundamentally through its function of separation, selection, and arrangement as a means to configure life within a structure of possibilities.[1]

The frame's organizational principles are embedded across different representations of the palazzo. At the scales of the building, the model, the drawing, and the handbook for conduct, the frame's degree of control coincides with its degree of abstraction. Stemming from the elite's desire for privacy, the distribution of space became the fundamental task of the architect. With spaces divided, rooms specialized, and locations arranged, the palazzo conceptualizes a totalizing system of frames. Ultimately, this undermined and reduced the elite's individualism to a regulated pattern of behavior and thought.

While the palazzo was an explicit manifestation of the framed life, its logic persists in our contemporary times. The frame becomes increasingly invisible and inescapable in our everyday lives. No longer individual subjects, we are abstracted into a pattern, reproducing the logic of the civilizing frame.

Coursework

3229b   Sustainability: A Critical View from the Urban History of Amazonia

The urban frontier in Amazonia is among the fastest growing in the world. This seminar asks, with a critical understanding of sustainability: How can burgeoning forest cities be retrofitted and designed?

Spring 2020

FACULTY
Ana María Durán

HARDENING THE MADEIRA
Alix Pauchet, Alex Pineda, and
Limy Fabiana Rocha

Centralized powers extensively modified landscapes in the Amazonian territory, largely through infrastructure. The hydropower scheme along Brazil's Madeira River, where repeated attempts to create a transcontinental financial corridor amplified by policies of extraction, hardens and fractures riparian landscapes. A sectional approach reveals how a series of dams interrupt water and sedimentary flows, flooding expanses of land, and disrupting social and ecological patterns.

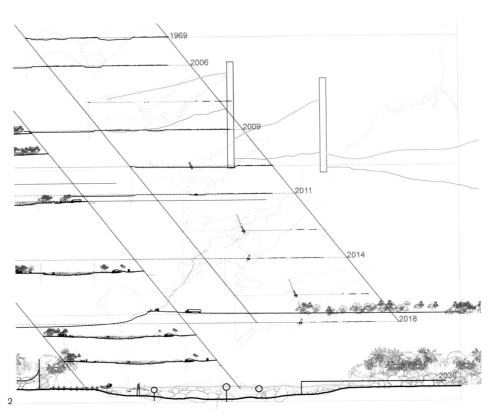

2

1. Bernard Cache, *Earth Moves: The Furnishing of Territories* (Cambridge: MIT Press, 1995), 22–30.
2. Sectional Timeline of the Madeira's Progressive Hardening

This course examines visual, verbal, and physical movement through post-1945 landscapes and cityscapes. Explorations of real and imaginary spaces in artists' works stage an inquiry into how these places are inhabited and experienced.

FACULTY
Fatima Naqvi

The Construction of Power in Space
Alicia Jones

Neutra's Nature and Indigenous Space
Anjelica Gallegos

In Search of Mirrors: Cinematic Journeys through Projections of Wilderness
Katie Lau

Alice between the Cities
Rachel LeFevre

La Terra
Mingxi Li

Soviet Mud: Nature and History in Aleksei German's Hard to be a God
Andew Economos Miller

Careful Architecture: Paris, Texas
Max Ouellette-Howitz

Abendland: Photographic Filmmaking and the Problem of Truth
Scott Simpson

What if Alice in the Cities *was in Polychrome?*
Sze Wai Justin Kong

Red Desert *and the Depiction of Industrial Landscapes*
Thomas Mahon

Spatial Horror as Depicted in The Shining *and the Winchester Mystery House*
Rukshan Vathupola

Spaces of Surveillance: From the Panopticon to The Lives of Others
Darryl Weimer

Authenticity and the Value of Images
Shelby Wright

3256b   Renaissance and Modern 2

This course discusses Modern Architecture from a critical perspective rather than from modernist persuasion and advocacy, not by attempting a survey but instead by singling out the fundamental issues architecture needed to confront as it transformed the modern world.

FACULTY
Peter Eisenman and Kurt Forster

Architecture, Art, and Construction: Disciplines Forged through Connection
Christopher Cambio

At the physical intersection of art and construction, a building results. Construction is inherently an art form, and art is inherently a process of construction. Their external connection results in a physical artifact. Architecture, however, exists not at the surface of this connection. The essence of architecture is rooted deep within the interpenetration of the philosophies of art, making, and building.

Sigfried Giedion's polemical work, *Building in France, Building in Iron, Building in Ferroconcrete,* provides a framework for a discussion of art, architecture, and construction as disciplines forged through both internal and external connections. Through an in-depth analysis and dissection of selected sections of the text, a provocative conversation on the interdependency of these disciplines arises. Architecture ultimately becomes defined through art and construction, both inherently experiential, and a complete physical artifact—a meticulous internal interweaving of ideology and an external outward expression of intricate tectonic connections.

This seminar discusses the most relevant concepts and categories elaborated by semiotics in order to provide analytical tools for "close readings" of verbal or visual texts, cultural objects, artifacts, events, and social situations.

FACULTY
Francesco Casetti

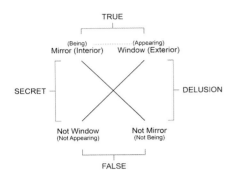

Greimas and the Domestic Interior: Toward a Theory of Action in Architecture
Gustav Nielsen and Diana Smiljković

In this paper we propose a reformulation of the language used for architectural analysis based on the *Narrative Grammar* and *Action Theory* of Lithuanian-French literary scientist and semiotician Algirdas J. Greimas. We consider *function* as a producer of *narrative action* which can be analyzed using a new *narrative vocabulary* for architecture. In examining a suite of historically distinct cases where functions of the home and the office overlap, we consider shifting narratives in architecture to be the driving argument for a new narrative approach to architectural analysis. We build upon Beatriz Colomina's analysis of the domestic interiors of Adolf Loos in her essay *Intimacy and Spectacle: The Interiors of Adolf Loos (1990)*, in the attempt to apply the narrative vocabulary of Greimas to the architectural analysis. Finally, we discuss the potentials of a Theory of Action in Architecture based on the new language for narrative analysis.

3272b Exhibitionism: Politics of Display

This seminar traces the typological evolution of art museums through an in-depth analysis of its key architectural elements, exploring how these mirror and perpetuate changing cultural attitudes about aesthetics, class, power, wealth, and gender.

FACULTY
Joel Sanders

*Post-pandemic YUAG
Lobby Wayfinding*
Audrey Hughes, Caroline Kraska,
Kate Meissner, Mianwei Wang

COVID-19 has augmented health hazards of public spaces, like the Yale University Art Gallery lobby. By comparing pre-pandemic observational data of lobby circulation with a post-pandemic student survey, we understand the areas under highest tension and propose alleviation through staff guidance, proper distancing, and increased sterilization. The arrival sequence can be strengthened and streamlined while ultimately maintaining the spatial experience of Kahn's gallery.

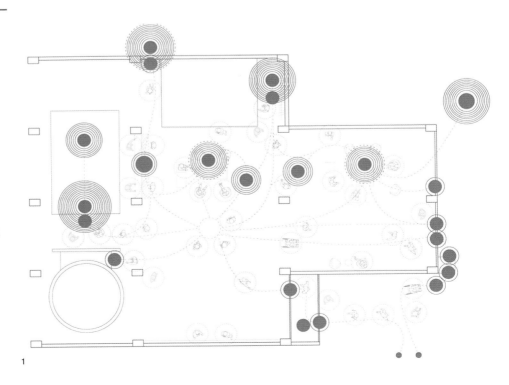

1

History and Theory

Coursework

Spring 2020

1. The dots indicate touch points of concern. Each solid ring = 2 people who expressed feeling "somewhat comfortable" or "less comfortable" with the touch point circled.

What was and what is postmodernism in architecture? This seminar treats postmodernism not as a style, but rather as a condition that arose out of the ahistorical, acontextual, materialistic modernism of the post-WWII era.

FACULTY
Robert A.M. Stern

STRADA NOVISSIMA
REBOOT

Anjelica Gallegos
"David Chipperfield"

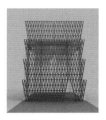

Clara Domange
"David Adjaye"

Dreama Simeng Lin
"Herzog & De Meuron"

Liang Hu
"Francis Kéré"

Michelle Qu
"Tod Williams & Billie Tsien"

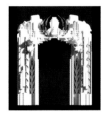

Max Wirsing
"Mark Foster Gage"

Qiyuan Liu
"Frank Gehry"

Scott Simpson
"Grafton"

Smit Patel
"FAT"

Stella Xu
"Rafael Moneo"

Sze Wai Justin Kong
"Demetri Porphyrios"

3292b   Architectural History / Theory of the Anthropocene

Anthropogenic climate change has presented architectural history/theory with a challenge. To produce a global, self-reflexive, and non-Eurocentric response demands a transnational collaboration questioning the autonomy of architecture.

FACULTY
Esther da Costa Meyer

Situating 'Blackness' within the Anthropocene
Ife Adepegba

Infrastructure, Landscape, and Place in the Bronx
Ives Brown

Imperialism and the Anthropocene
Ian Gu

Social Dreaming and the Anthropocene: On Analysis and Design for Social and Environmental Justice
Gabriel Gutierrez Huerta

Climate Injustice and Transitioning Ecosystems
Srinivas Narayan Karthikeyan

Architecture towards New Material Reality
Eunice Lee

Collective Consumption
Leanne Nagata

Car Trouble, Assembly Required
Rachel Mulder

Forms of Power: Overcoming Empire and Architectures of Carbon Existence
Leonardo Serrano Fuchs

The Subjecthood of Land: Community Land Trusts as Assemblages
Sarah Weiss

Managing Decline of the Harlem River
Leyi Zhang

For Arch 3283b After the Modern Movement: An Atlas of the Postmodern, 1945–1989 students conceptualize and design a facade in the manner of their chosen architect for a mock version of the *Strada Novissima*.

This seminar explores the history and practice of "polychromatic reconstruction" in architecture, in which architects, historians, and archaeologists reconstruct the lost, colorfully painted surfaces of ancient classical sculptures and buildings.

FACULTY
David Gissen

WET PAINT: A STUDY OF SUBWAY COLUMNS
Mari Kroin

The subway column paint chip is a nostalgic item for many New Yorkers. The chips reveal a wide spectrum of colors. Columns are never fully stripped of their previous layer of paint, creating a thick build-up. Edges grow less defined and debris collects between layers. Seven color phases from the 23rd street E,C station are investigated in this project.

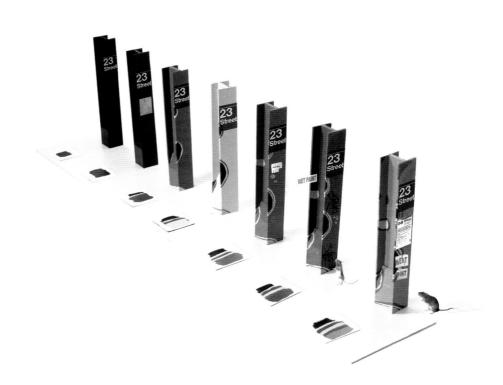

History and Theory

Coursework

Spring 2020

3300b   The Idea of an Avant-Garde in Architecture:
               Reading Manfredo Tafuri's *The Sphere and the Labyrinth*

This seminar undertakes a contemporary and critical reading of Tafuri's 1980 book, which offers an original genealogy—and not uncontroversial account—of the concept of the avant-garde in architecture from Piranesi to postmodernism.

FACULTY
Joan Ockman

Raoul Hausmann, the "Architect": Architecture Without Architects, the Adventures of the Avant-Gardes and the Politics of the Senses
Iris Giannakopoulou Karamouzi

Raoul Hausmann, founding member of the Berlin Dada group, is mostly known for his subversive photomontages and his political radicalism. Yet, in 1922, during the heyday of the European avant-garde movements, it would seem unanticipated, if not disconcerting, that the Dadasophist would some years later become fascinated with the traditional habitat of the island of Ibiza and its architecture, as well as with archeology, anthropology, ethnography, and documentary photography. From 1933 to 1936, Hausmann resided in Ibiza and produced a remarkable body of research including numerous photographs of landscapes, traditional houses, and people, as well as sketches, architectural drawings, and a collection of texts—some published and some unpublished. This essay investigates Hausmann's work during his exile in Ibiza and explores its historical, ideological, and intellectual status in relation to his prior avant-garde legacy. This material should be understood as a continuation of his avant-garde preoccupations and as a reclamation of the historical and political possibilities encoded in the very term avant-garde. By tracing the post-geographies of the Berlin Dada movement, this paper ultimately wishes to contribute to a better understanding of the kaleidoscopic histories that make up the early 20th-century avant-garde phenomenon.

Looking at Lewis Mumford, Robert Moses, Jane Jacobs, and Rem Koolhaas, this seminar addresses issues of civic representation and environmentalism, infrastructure development and urban renewal policy, and the role of architecture in the urban imaginary.

FACULTY
Joan Ockman

Processing Urban Density: North River Sanitation and Recreation
Miriam Dreiblatt

New York City's density engendered a rich culture in the 20th century, yet the byproducts of its growth put strain on urban infrastructure and natural resources. Water was integral to the city's expansion and predominant in its natural setting. The North River Water Pollution Control Plant and Riverbank State Park's development embodied the politics of density through the transformation of a health hazard into a social asset. The plant proposal originated during a period when Mumford posited the risk of urban growth to the surrounding region. Moses determined the plant's siting on the Henry Hudson River at the expense of northern Manhattan's African American and Hispanic inhabitants. In exchange for bequeathing views of New York's waterways to passing motorists, Moses offered parkland to affluent residents and little to West Harlem. North River's construction had uneven environmental impact—it benefitted the metropolis with healthful waste disposal and reduced river toxicity, yet it diminished air quality and land value for minority communities. After two decades of noxious fume exposure, local residents embraced Jacobsian organizing and gained a 28-acre park. Built on the plant's rooftop, Riverbank State Park provides waterfront recreation and river views while wastewater is treated below without odor.

4216a   Globalization Space: International Infrastructure and Extrastatecraft

This course researches global infrastructures as a medium of transnational polity. Lectures touch on networks of trade, communication, tourism, labor, air, rail, highway, oil, hydrology, finance, and activism.

FACULTY
Keller Easterling

Climate Migration
Michelle Badr, Angela Lin, and Alex Stiegler

The rise of climate change has informed new patterns of migration in which whole communities relocate to find relief from climate hardships such as drought, sea-level rise, or the loss of natural resources. While there is a legal framework in place for migrants seeking cross-border safety for socio-political reasons, climate refugees present an entirely different set of motivations and strategies for movement. As many states have yet to recognize climate as a cause for migration, individuals invoke alternative networks to relocate—often relying on relatives and contacts. The research compares three case studies of climate migration as related to communities of agricultural production in various parts of the world—the first analyzes long-term climate change such as droughts in Western Afghanistan, the second focuses on natural disasters like hurricane Dorian in the Bahamas, and the third highlights man-made climate effects in the Yangtze Valley, China. These case studies reveal patterns of movement in the wake of environmental degradation, how climate-affected individuals situate themselves in new communities, and the extent to which climate-refugees impact the new places and people they settle amongst. We ask: What are the socio-spatial ramifications of climate migration? How are these groups housed and how do they contribute to existing labor markets? The research reveals social and spatial shifts led by various climate-affected parties and their relative cultural and organizational interplays.

This seminar considers the changing patterns, functions, and images of port cities, particularly in the context of their regional and global networks of production, trade, culture, and power.

FACULTY
Alan Plattus

The Hanseatic League
Cristina Anastase

Modern Evidence of Portuguese
Trade Networks in the Belém
Neighborhood of Lisbon
Diane Boston

Analysis of the Urban Planning
and Design of Qingdao During
the German Occupation Period
Xuefeng Du

The Trade of Piracy
Ashton Harrell

Landscapes of Eradication
and Centralization in Hispaniola
Gabriel Gutierrez Huerta

New Orleans Ports:
Geology, Community, Industry
Kelley Johnson

Vancouver and the British Columbia
Timber Trade
Jackson Lindsay

The Port of Shanghai:
Past, Present and Future
April Liu

The Challenges of Urban
Development in the Greater Bay Area
Qiyuan Liu

The Urban Transformation
of the Port of Duisburg
Alex Olivier

Charleston and the Consumption
of Former Glory
David Scurry

Port of Piraeus: Terminal for
Merchants, Tourists and Refugees
Shikha Thakali

Colonization and the Port of
Manila: The Transportation of
Infrastructure and Ideals
Kay Yang

Port Influence on the Development
of Suzhou
Kaiwen Zhao

4221b   Introduction to Commercial Real Estate

Commercial real estate is income-producing property that is built, financed, and sold for investment. This course examines five basic types of commercial real estate from the standpoints of the developer, lender, and investor.

FACULTY
Kevin Gray

Investment Report on Madison Tower
Hiuki Lam

This report on Madison Tower presents the conclusions of different valuation metrics and potential investment returns. The purchase price of a 16-story, high-rise apartment building is calculated with three different metrics: direct cap method, yield cap method, and sales comparable method. The report's findings show that the yield cap method is the most reliable value estimation method. Considering the location of the building, the maintenance condition, the high projected return, and the prospective local market, Madison Tower is a recommended investment with a high rate of cash inflow over time.

This seminar examines the history of landscape architecture and country-house architecture in Britain from 1500 to 1900. Topics include Romanticism. Palladianism, the public park system, military landscaping, and early landscape modernism.

FACULTY
Bryan Fuermann

BRIDGES IN THE ENGLISH GARDEN
Kelsey Rico

Ranging from a few meters to over 200 meters, the bridges of English gardens are drawn to the same size, eliminating shifts in monumentality to highlight their individual character. Composed on the page geographically, the bridges are linked through the rivers they span. The interconnection of the bridges through their respective bodies of water eclipses the distinct boundaries of garden estates.

4233b   Ghost Towns

This seminar examines a spectrum of failed or almost-failed cities, using the ghost town and its rhythms of development and disinvestment to establish a conceptual framework for contemporary urban patterns and processes.

FACULTY
Elihu Rubin

BUILD YOUR OWN MYTH
Deo Deiparine, Leanne Nagata, Rebecca Potts, Max Wirsing, Kay Yang

In this interactive coloring book, you are invited to engage with the histories of the building that once housed the New Haven Clock Company. The afterlives of the space call attention to the way that heritage preservation often crafts a sanitized past to maximize profit in the present. This coloring book leans into this discomfort through the idiom of satire.

Exploring market forces, aesthetics, and technical factors that shaped Hudson Yards, the course asks whether it represents the end of megaprojects in this country or the start of a new paradigm in planning.

FACULTY
Michael Samuelian

HUDSON GARDENS ECOLOGICAL URBANISM
Jonathan Palomo

This proposal seeks to find the synergy that can catapult a project of this magnitude forward within the inter-phase between the built environment and natural elements. The intent is to capitalize on biophilic principles and environmental directives to evolve the urban fabric towards an integrated system and invite the community to work, live, learn, and play.

4244b   Cartographies of Climate Change

This seminar applies research, drawing, and spatial analysis to conceptualize and materialize climate change, urbanization, and inequality, and to more broadly consider the world as an architectural project.

FACULTY
Joyce Hsiang

NYLA AND THE CLOUD
Helen Farley

Nyla and the Cloud is a narrative *carte.* It tells the story of Nyla, a young girl enchanted with the world, and the cloud she finds. She travels across vast landscapes to return the cloud to the sky, learning about the cloud and discovering the beauty and harshness of the world along the way.

Urbanism and Landscape

Coursework

Spring 2020

This course examines the conditions and phenomena of urbanization at the scale of the entire world. Through processes of exploration and extraction, cultivation and consumption, movement and migration, tourism and territorialization, the world has become interconnected. According to ongoing debate by scientists, geologists, and environmentalists, the world appears to have crossed the threshold of a new geological epoch: the Anthropocene—in which humans are transforming the world at an unprecedented, irreversible scale. What are the centers of urbanization within this new epoch of human activity?

FACULTY
Joyce Hsiang

PARTICIPANTS
Jojo Attal, Gema Martinez Castillo, Laura Clapp, Ariel Claxton, Ekaterina Danchenko, Kayley Estoesta, Carina Hahn, Kenia Hale, Lucas Holter, Grace Kyallo, Lauryn Phinney, Daud Shad, Ally Song, Journey Streams, Alex Whittaker

■ FACULTY REFLECTION
This semester we continued our investigatory expedition from trash dumps to cryptocurrency mines, lost lakes to pirated bioresources, multinational supermarkets to foreign megaevent labor markets, smart cities to satellite constellations. The Unknown is all around us and often reflects a dynamic of exclusion based upon gender, race, or socioeconomics. As a subject and an approach, Unknown seeks to subvert the dominant geographies, physical forms, power dynamics, and infrastructures of marginalization, and socioeconomic inequity that have emerged through global urbanization. We endeavored to reveal, foreground, empower, build visibility and inclusion by giving physical form to the people and places of these Sites Unknown.
— Joyce Hsiang, Director of Undergraduate Studies and Assistant Professor

A FIELD GUIDE TO SMART CITIES: SONGDO CITY
Lucas Holter

This project develops an illustrated vocabulary for understanding and anticipating how smart cities develop through the lens of their global influences. The map and collage played an important part in the eventual field guide booklet.

DREAM CONSTRUCTION,
MISREGISTERED REALITIES
Lauryn Phinney

Seemingly disparate individuals converge in Qatar as it prepares for the 2022 World Cup. This project explores their shared aspirations yet unequal realities and the illusion of possibility that football promises.

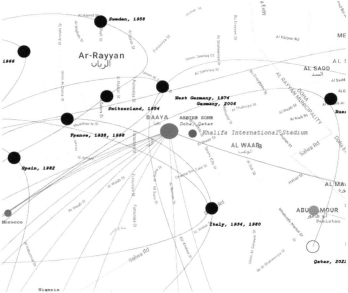

Senior Studio culminates the undergraduate design teaching sequence, focusing on the design of a major project based on urgent social and architectural themes. Students explore the architecture of nomadism as a contemporary American phenomenon. Although nomadism predates the settled patterns of agricultural and urbanized societies, it now survives only as fragmentary practices at the margins of hyper-normalizing global culture. Nomads live lightly and leave few traces.

FACULTY
Steven Harris and Gavin Hogben

PARTICIPANTS
Hafsa Abdi, Angel Adeoye, Trevor Chan, Hana Davis, Cole Fandrich, Sebastian Galvan, Julia Hedges, Jane Jacobs, Ivy Li, Karin Nagano, Graceann Nicolosi, Ash Pales, Sophie Potter, Sam Rimm-Kaufman, Adam Thompson, Reanna Wauer

■ FACULTY REFLECTION
This year's project explored the role of architects in working with profoundly nomadic cultures—a way-station for a circulating population of van-dwellers by the Salton Sea. The issues centered on how architectural perspectives might fit within a context where transience is the rule, capital is scant, and self-reliance is a primal force. The studio's schemes proposed dynamic improvisatory tactics with open-ended strategies, and focused on simple robust quotidian resources for amplifying the shade, water, power, and income sources that underpin nomad life.
— Steven Harris, Professor Adjunct, and
  Gavin Hogben, Critic

PALLET TOWN
Ivy Li

Pallet Town is a response to nomadic living at the Salton Sea, located in the Southern California desert. At *Pallet Town,* nomads can build a life for themselves out of inexpensive and widely available wooden pallets.

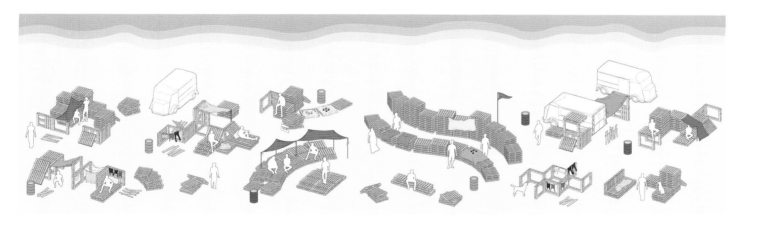

LIVING IN DATE-LAND
Karin Nagano

My proposition involves exploiting the relationship between the American nomad and their van a step further, enlisting the vehicle as a "working partner."

Taking the grid as a conceptual and formal datum, this seminar investigates areas of overlap between formal and informal organizational systems, and asks how digital tools and computational techniques may facilitate their study.

FACULTY
Dorian Booth

URINAL CAKE,
MYSTERY MEAT (2020)
Sarah Kim

A graphic pattern of tinned SPAM® is mapped onto a men's washroom. The serial repetition produces disorientation and a deadening uniformity that masks and belies the underlying gridded logic organizing the urinals, urinal cakes, and human figures within the scene.

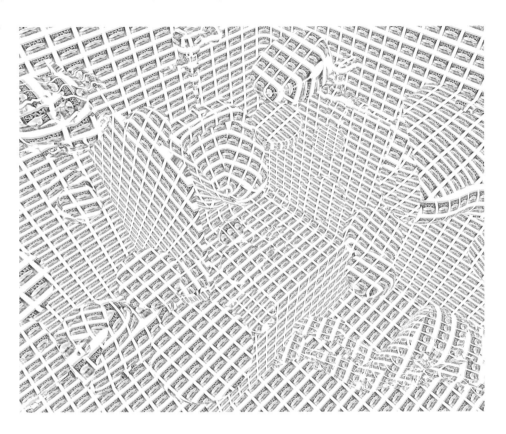

1019c   Visualization and Computation: Memory Palace

Students design virtual realities—questioning notions of authenticity, subjectivity, perception, and ontology within a world of their creation—to create a lattice of virtual rooms called the *Memory Palace.*

FACULTY
Beom Jun Kim

ENTROPY
Andrew Spiller

The world of *Blame!* by Tsutomu Nihei features a self-replicating city gone rampant, expanding into the solar system infinitely. *Entropy* invokes that city through procedural generation of a world combined with recreations of scenes from the manga. It also intends to encapsulate the atmosphere and its sublimity.

This course leverages immersive modes of representation—defined as "planetary images"—and critiques of representational technologies as cognitive agents of cultural organization, to reflect on human engagement with the built environment.

FACULTY
Daniele Profeta

ON TOUCHING
Meghna Mudaliar

On Touching is a series based on intimacies between bodies en-meshing and emanating as material worlds. Materiality is perceived through a monistic ontology, oriented toward transversal and relational alliances across species and forms, and dissolving notions of otherness into affective transmissions of dif-ference. Vital intersections pulse, combine, and distend within common environments, unfolding multiple subjectivities into worldings of collec-tive becoming.

Design and Visualization

Coursework

1291c   Rome: Continuity and Change (canceled)

FACULTY
Bimal Mendis, Joyce Hsiang,
George Knight, Elisa Iturbe

This on-site workshop examines historical continuity and change in Rome, investigating how some ele-ments and approaches were maintained over time and others abandoned.

Summer 2020

3000c   Deploying the Archive (canceled)

FACULTY
Iñaqui Carnicero

Working in the Norman Foster Foundation Archive in Spain, students interpret original documentation, analyze the processes behind design evolution, and deepen their architectural thinking.

4291c   The Urban Atlas (canceled)

FACULTY
Alan Plattus and Andrei Harwell

Students learn and practice methods of urban analysis, including graphic and modeling approaches, to understand the interface between building form and typology and larger patterns of urban use and movement in Gothenburg, Sweden.

ISBN 978-1-948765-90-9

$35.00

53500>